The World Bank and HI

The governance of HIV/AIDS has come to represent a multi-faceted and complex operation set and sustained by the World Bank. The governance of HIV/AIDS is a political project that seeks to embed liberal practice through individual, state, and community behaviour. At the heart of this practice is the drive to impose blueprint neoliberal market-based solutions on a *personal-global* issue.

This book unravels how the Bank's good governance agenda and commitment to participation, ownership and transparency manifests itself in practice through the Multi-Country AIDS Program (MAP), and crucially how it is pushing an agenda that sees a shift in both global health interventions and state configuration in sub-Saharan Africa. The book considers the mechanisms used by the Bank – and the problems therein – to engage the state, civil society and the individual in responding to the HIV/AIDS crisis, and how these mechanisms have been exported to other global projects such as the Global Fund and UNAIDS. Harman argues that not only has the Bank set the global agenda for HIV/AIDS, but underpinning this is a wider commitment to liberal governance through neoliberal incentive.

Making an important contribution to our understanding of global governance and international politics, this book will be of interest to students and scholars of politics, international political economy, international relations, development studies and civil society.

Sophie Harman is a Lecturer in International Politics at City University, London.

Routledge Advances in International Relations and Global Politics

The World Bank and HIV/AIDS

Setting a global agenda

Sophie Harman

Routledge
Taylor & Francis Group

LONDON AND NEW YORK

First published 2010
by Routledge
2 Park Square, Milton Park, Abingdon, Oxon OX14 4RN

Simultaneously published in the USA and Canada
by Routledge
711 Third Avenue, New York, NY 10017

Routledge is an imprint of the Taylor & Francis Group, an Informa business

First issued in paperback 2012

© 2010 Sophie Harman

Typeset in Times New Roman by Exeter Premedia services, India

British Library Cataloguing in Publication Data
A catalogue record for this book is available from the British Library

Library of Congress Cataloging in Publication Data
Harman, Sophie.
The World Bank and HIV/AIDS: setting a global agenda / Sophie Harman.
    p. cm. – (Routledge advances in international relations and global politics ; 85)
Includes bibliographical references and index.
1. World Bank–Africa, Southern.   2. AIDS (Disease)–Africa,
Southern–Prevention.   3. HIV Infections–Africa, Southern–Prevention.
I. Title.
    HG3881.5.W57H37 2010
    362.196'979200968--dc22
    2009050219

ISBN 13: 978-0-415-56290-4 (hbk)
ISBN 13: 978-0-415-50404-1 (pbk)
ISBN 13: 978-0-203-84994-0 (ebk)

Contents

Acknowledgements

Many people have helped me with this book. I would like to thank all the people who participated in my research, most of whom were kind enough to give me lots of their limited time and resources, and the ESRC for sponsoring my fieldwork.

This book has benefited hugely from the input and advice of Gemma Collantes-Celador, Rosaleen Duffy, Graham Harrison, Kelley Lee, Mick Moran, Inderjeet Parmar, Stuart Shields, Diane Stone, David Williams and Ralph Young. My crack team of readers, Cat Durose, Lucy Ferguson and Kieran Read, gave extremely helpful feedback on the first draft of the book; it reads much better for it. Lucy in particular kept re-reading chapters until the final draft; she is a great asset to the book and a fantastic friend. The feedback and advice of two anonymous reviewers was very useful in focusing the book around a central argument and the development of its core ideas. This book would not have been possible without Rorden Wilkinson and his belief in my academic ability. Had he not suggested I apply to do a PhD when I was an undergraduate at the University of Manchester, this book and my research into the World Bank and HIV/AIDS would not exist.

Thanks to my family and friends for providing much needed humour when I was researching and writing this book. Special thanks to Kieran Read for being brilliant; this book is for him and all the home-based carers at the frontline of HIV/AIDS.

Sections of Chapter 2 appear in A. Kay and O.D. Williams (eds) *Global Health Governance*, 2009, reproduced with permission of Palgrave MacMillan. Chapter 3 is developed from a paper 'Fighting HIV and AIDS: Reconfiguring the state?' published in *Review of African Political Economy* 36(121), 2009, reprinted here with permission of Taylor and Francis www.informaworld.com. Chapter 4 has in part been published within the *Journal of Health Management* 11(2), 2009, and is reprinted here with permission of Sage Publications. Sections of Chapter 5 have been previously appeared in 'The World Bank: Failing the Multi-Country HIV/AIDS Program: Failing HIV/AIDS' from *Global Governance: A Review of Multilateralism and International Organizations*, V. 13, #4. Copyright © 2007 by Lynne Rienner Publishers, Inc. Used with permission of the publisher. Part of the book's argument has been published in S. Harman and F. Lisk *Governance of HIV/AIDS: Making participation and accountability count* (Routledge, 2009), but has been significantly updated.

List of abbreviations

ABC	Abstain, Be faithful, use a Condom
ACT	AIDS Campaign Team Africa
AIDS	Acquired immune deficiency syndrome
AMREF	Africa Medical and Research Foundation
ART	Anti-retroviral therapy
CAC	Community AIDS Council
CAF	Community Action Fund
CBO	Community-based organisation
CCM	Country co-ordinating mechanism
CDC	Center for Disease Control
CDF	Comprehensive Development Framework
CHAI	Community HIV/AIDS initiative
CMAC	Community multi-sectoral AIDS committee
CSO	Civil society organisation
CSW	Commercial sex worker
DAC	District AIDS Council
DARE	Decentralised HIV/AIDS and reproductive health project
DFID	Department for International Development, UK
DPG	Development partners group
FAO	Food and Agriculture Organization
FBO	Faith-based organisation
Global Fund	Global Fund to fight HIV/AIDS, Tuberculosis and Malaria
GNP+	The Global Network of People Living with HIV/AIDS
GPA	Global Program on HIV/AIDS
GRID	Gay-related immunodeficiency syndrome
GTZ	Deutsche Gesellschaft fur Zusammenarbeit
HIPC	Heavily indebted poor country
HIV	Human Immunodeficiency Virus
IAVI	International AIDS Vaccine Initiative
ICC	Inter-Agency Co-ordination Committee
IDA	International Development Agency
IDU	Intravenous drug user
IFC	International Finance Corporation

ILO	International Labour Organisation
IMF	International Monetary Fund
INGO	International non-governmental organisation
JAPR	Joint Annual HIV/AIDS Programme Review
JSI	John Snow International
KANCO	Kenya AIDS NGOs Consortium
KENWA	Kenya Network of Women with AIDS
KNASP	Kenya National HIV/AIDS Strategic Plan
KHADREP	Kenya HIV/AIDS Disaster Response Project
K-VWORC	Kenya Voluntary Women's Rehabilitation Centre
LQA	Lot quality assurance
MAP	Multi-country AIDS Programme
MCG	Management co-ordination groups
NAC	National AIDS Council
NACC	National AIDS Control Council (Kenya)
NACONGO	National Council of NGOs
NACP	National AIDS Control Programme (Tanzania)
NASCOP	National STD and AIDS Control Programme (Kenya)
NGEN+	National Guidance & Empowerment Network of People Living with HIV/AIDS
NGO	Non-governmental organisation
NUSAF	Northern Uganda Social Action Fund
OVC	Orphans and vulnerable children
PEPFAR	President's Emergency Plan for HIV/AIDS Relief
PLWHA	People living with HIV/AIDS
PMTCT	Prevention of mother to child transmission
PRSP	Poverty Reduction Strategy Paper
RFA	Regional facilitating agent
SHDEPHA+	Service, Health and Development for People Living with HIV/AIDS
STI	Sexually Transmitted Infection
TACAIDS	Tanzania Commission for HIV/AIDS
TANEPHA	Tanzania National Network of People Living with HIV/AIDS
TASO	The AIDS Support Organisation
TMAP	Tanzania Multi-Sectoral AIDS Project
TWOA	Total War On HIV/AIDS
UAC	Uganda AIDS Commission
UNAIDS	Joint United Nations Programme on HIV/AIDS
UNDP	United Nations Development Programme
UNFPA	United Nations Population Fund
UNICEF	United Nations Children's Fund
UNIFEM	United Nations Fund for Women
UNGASS	United Nations General Assembly Special Session on HIV/AIDS
USAID	United States Agency for International Development
VCT	Voluntary counselling and testing

WAMATA	People in the fight against HIV/AIDS in Tanzania
WFP	World Food Programme
WHO	World Health Organization
WOFAK	Women Fighting HIV/AIDS in Kenya
ZAC	Zanzibar AIDS Commission
ZACP	Zanzibar AIDS Control Programme
ZMAP	Zanzibar Multi-Sectoral AIDS Project

1 The complexity of HIV/AIDS governance

The governance of HIV/AIDS has come to represent a multifaceted and complex operation that is not working. Instead of reversing the spread of HIV and AIDS, it is restructuring the political foundations of countries in sub-Saharan Africa through the pursuit of change in state, individual and societal behaviour through economic incentive. In some countries contributions to combating HIV/AIDS can constitute up to a third of the total of all foreign aid. States are introducing new mechanisms of governance to manage and distribute this aid. This often involves altering their perceptions of and relationships with the civil society actors they have often ignored or suppressed. Communities that have long self-organised to educate and care for the sick have received significant financial support and shifted to models of financially driven service delivery. The private sector has introduced HIV/AIDS components to various training manuals, health and safety, pension plans and non-discriminatory practice. This has also entailed a substantive shift towards the non-state service economy as the pandemic becomes big business. People are aware of HIV/AIDS: people are taking measures to address HIV/AIDS.

However, despite all of these changes and such a widespread upsurge in participation, levels of HIV/AIDS prevalence and new HIV infection rates remain relatively unchanged in sub-Saharan Africa. What we have now is an already complicated disease made more complex by the quantity and type of funding directed towards it. At the heart of this complexity that has come to constitute 'the global response' is the World Bank. The World Bank does not give as much money as other private and public donors, does not have the high co-ordination profile of the Joint United Nations Programme on HIV/AIDS (UNAIDS), or the funding profile role of the Global Fund to fight HIV/AIDS, Tuberculosis and Malaria (the Global Fund). Yet while it is widely ignored within the public health or politics literature for its role in HIV/AIDS, the Bank has carefully orchestrated the response to HIV/AIDS at every level of governance: the global, the state, the community and the individual. It has done so through a combination of timing, perceived expertise and knowledge, and a commitment to 'good' state-led and community-owned interventions. The type of 'good' governance applied by the Bank is a constraint for effective HIV/AIDS management. The problem is that what the Bank means by such leadership and ownership in HIV/AIDS reveals several contradictions to the World Bank's approach to development. This approach applied to such an extreme *personal–global* issue such as HIV/AIDS has led to several negative long-term outcomes in terms of both attempts to reverse the epidemic and the institutional fabric of poverty alleviation. This book unravels how and why the Bank has come to occupy this position, what it means for our understanding of the HIV/AIDS response, and crucially our understanding of the role and application of (good) governance reform in sub-Saharan Africa through HIV/AIDS interventions.

This book is about how the World Bank has set the global agenda on HIV/AIDS and what this agenda looks like. It argues that the Bank has established a strategy for combating the disease through a specific form of 'multi-sectoralism' that identifies the disease as a non-health-specific, development issue, involving the state, civil society, the individual and the international community. This approach is encapsulated and promoted throughout sub-Saharan Africa and the Caribbean by the Bank's flagship HIV/AIDS project, the Multi-Country AIDS Program (MAP). Underpinning this is the project of governance reform that promotes liberal good governance through neoliberal means. The book draws on critical governance debates to argue that HIV/AIDS is a medium used by the Bank to extend a specific brand of liberal governance reform beyond the state to local communities and individuals. It does so through (i) the promotion of a multi-sectoral approach that emphasises the role of multiple actors – the state, civil society, the private sector and non-health actors – in the implementation of HIV/AIDS projects; and (ii) through the introduction of new governance structures and systems which embed the MAP as the framework that states, civil society and international donors adhere to as the model of accepted HIV/AIDS practice. It is the institutional arrangements within the MAP and the problems of sovereignty, bureaucracy and competition that limit funds reaching local communities and people infected and affected by HIV/AIDS that highlights the contention between exporting a specific brand of liberal good governance through neoliberal economic incentive. In being the first significant multilateral commitment to HIV/AIDS and establishing processes of governance, the World Bank and the MAP have set and sustained the global agenda for HIV/AIDS. This agenda is problematic and thus raises the question: is a problematic agenda for HIV/AIDS better than none?

If the HIV/AIDS epidemic is so complex why isn't its governance?

The ability of the World Bank to set and sustain the global agenda for HIV/AIDS through the application of multi-sectoralism stems from the complexity or 'exceptionalism' of the disease. It is this complexity that explains the shift of HIV/AIDS away from health-based approaches to the framing of the disease as a development issue and gives the Bank justification for its involvement and extension of governance reform to the people infected and affected by it. It is thus important to explore what is meant by HIV/AIDS exceptionalism, and how the role of governance in regard to the state and the international community has been understood.

HIV/AIDS is understood as an exceptional global health problem because it necessitates monitoring and regulating the sex lives and habits of individuals and how these very personal habits are shaped by social, political and economic forces. Development and security concerns combined with migratory flows has made HIV/AIDS a global epidemic: one that threatens the world's population, and one that needs to be addressed through state and non-state co-operation at the global scale. The construction of HIV/AIDS along the development–security trajectory is a particularly pertinent factor in shaping responses to the global epidemic. Previous to this association, constructions of both the HIV virus and the full-blown AIDS epidemics in sub-Saharan Africa had been predominantly explained in relation to 'the behavioural approach' relating to high levels of multi-person relationships, polygamy and 'the sexual roving of men' (Boserup 1986: 37; Caldwell *et al.* 1992: 1172; Lawson 1999: 394). This approach has since been widely criticised for characterising all African males as 'hyper-sexualised' (Packard and Epstein 1991: 781; Poku 2002: 533; Stillwaggon 2003: 811 and 830). Although issues of polygamy and serial monogamy (Epstein 2007) remain influential factors for high rates of HIV transmission and underpin many interventions in sexual health, the over-arching paradigm in which HIV/AIDS policy operates is within development. The development approach is grounded within the cyclical relationship between HIV/AIDS and poverty. Poverty is both a driver of higher rates of HIV infection, affecting the lives of people living with HIV and AIDS. The epidemic itself deepens and exacerbates poverty (Ankrah 1989: 272; 1991: 970; Barnett and Whiteside 2002: 73; Poku 2001: 192; Whiteside 2002). It is this relationship with a two-way poverty cycle that illustrates the exceptionalism of HIV/AIDS as a health issue, as it is both driven by and drives poverty, and is rooted within human behaviour affected by the socioeconomic context in which people live.

Compounding this relationship to poverty are the economic drivers specific to developing countries in sub-Saharan Africa with high rates of HIV/AIDS prevalence. Neoliberal structural adjustment policies of the 1980s have had a long-term impact on the retraction of state services, specifically within healthcare, where many public hospitals and health centres closed or were chronically understaffed (Cheru 2002: 300; Peet 2003: 141; Poku 2002: 531; Whiteside 2002: 191–192). Shifts in employment trends away from agriculture to service industry and management jobs have seen migratory flows away from the rural community towards city-based centres of economic activity and opportunity. This leads to people moving away from their local communities and families to new and unfamiliar social contexts. These trends have been matched by regional and international migration as educated members of the workforce move to states with better paid jobs (Brockerhoff and Biddlecom 1999; Lawson 1990), resulting in the 'brain-drain', affecting countries with high HIV/AIDS prevalence as medical professionals move abroad to seek better pay.

The impact of a decline in public healthcare, migratory flows and high rates of HIV infection have been most acutely felt by women. HIV/AIDS has increasingly become feminised with women being physiologically more susceptible to HIV infection, socially more susceptible in regards to their ability to negotiate safe sex or refuse sex and their desire for motherhood, and economically in regard to their relative inability to secure financial independence from men. They are stigmatised for living with HIV/AIDS. Women face an increased burden of care for the sick without financial reward. Women care for orphans and vulnerable children, as well as sick relatives or members of their community. Combined with the lack of women's access to land rights, this may limit their long-term employment opportunities (Ankrah 1991: 971; Becker 1990: 1605; de Bruyn 1992: 249; Lawson 1999: 393; Maman *et al.* 2000: 476; Poku 2001: 197; Ulin 1992: 64). Each of these factors embeds dominant social roles of women into that of mother, carer and dependant and restricts their access to education or financial capital.

To make matters even more complicated, HIV/AIDS is no longer just a complex health and development issue; it is now also framed as a security concern. Two factors are cited as evidence that AIDS is a global security threat: (i) Security Council Resolution 1308 and (ii) United Nations General Assembly Special Session on HIV/AIDS (UNGASS) 2001. The first ever health issue raised by the Security Council, Resolution 1308, expressed concern as to the impact of HIV/AIDS upon international peacekeepers (SCRes 1308, 200). The security element of the 2001 UNGASS declaration refers to points 77 and 78 within the section on HIV/AIDS in conflict and disaster-affected regions. These points highlight the need for states to develop national strategies that address the spread of HIV among the armed services and for the inclusion of HIV/AIDS awareness training in guidelines for peacekeepers and other defence personnel (UNGASS 2001: 41). Hence the emphasis upon security and the disease has very much been situated within the context of state responsibility and international peacekeeping.

Conflict has long been seen as a vector for the spread of the disease (McInnes 2007), with international peacekeepers being seen as a potential source of infection and a high prevalence rates within militaries. This in turn impacts upon the state and the use of force as one of its primary sources of power (Singer 2002). However, HIV/AIDS transcends traditional notions of national and international dimensions of security in its relation to human security and biopolitics. Securitising HIV/AIDS raises questions of how the threat is being constituted or what is being securitised: the disease, HIV or AIDS, the body, the state, peacekeepers or the terrain. This is crucial to the two interpretations of the impact of securitising the pandemic upon health outcomes (Maclean 2008). The first sees securitisation as an effective way of increasing international awareness and thus helping to sustain much-needed funds for combating the disease. The second sees securitisation as diverting attention away from the rights of ordinary, non-military citizens, and has increased the role of institutions such as the United Nations (UN), and the World Bank, within the biopolitical economy of power (Elbe 2008). According to Elbe, the securitisation of the pandemic has potential dangers for racism, as the biopolitical character of populations becomes a matter of 'high' politics (Elbe 2005). All of this is bounded up with the notion of HIV and infectious diseases being posed as a biosecurity threat (McInnes 2007) that is both national and global.

Never one to be left out in matters pertaining to development and new forms of human security, the World Bank has got in on the security action. Often cited, ex-World Bank President James Wolfensohn (1995–2005) gave a speech to the Security Council in regard to Resolution 1308 in which he declared AIDS 'a major development crisis, and more than that, a security crisis' (Wolfensohn 2000). Framed along this all-encompassing development–security trajectory, these factors make addressing the problem of HIV/AIDS all the more difficult. Simply put, compared to other infectious diseases such as malaria, there are no bed nets for HIV/AIDS. There are condoms and clean needles but whether an individual has access to them, wants to use one, can use one, can make their partner use one, knows how to use one or is able to afford one is embedded in a complex interplay of rationality, gender relations, poverty, education, religion, culture, stigma and discrimination. Hence, the orthodoxy has been established that in order to solve a problem like HIV/AIDS you need to address issues of poverty and culture. This has been done by framing it as a 'development' issue, providing a comprehensive response to the epidemic that removes HIV/AIDS from the domain of public health and frames it as a rights-based development issue.

The complexity of the epidemic and the need to respond to it effectively within this approach requires the participation of all aspects of society: the local communities where the epidemic is most acute; the district and national governments where there is a need for leadership and direction in breaking stigma and co-ordinating the response; the private sector to mainstream non-discriminatory practices and increase awareness; the health sector in providing treatment, care and prevention, as well as surveillance of the epidemic; global donors to fund these activities; and co-ordinating agencies to maintain an element of order and evaluation to a multiplicity of interventions. Responding to HIV/AIDS thus becomes a free-for-all of activity that seeks to target the very foundations in which state–civil society relations in countries with high HIV/AIDS prevalence in sub-Saharan Africa are based. The war on HIV/AIDS can only be won by every person and institution taking some form of responsibility for the epidemic, hence sections of society that were previously anathema to collaboration have come together to form awkward alliances. What we have thus is a 'multi-sectoral' response to HIV/AIDS that involves every level of state and society to address the complex, multifaceted nature of the problem. The purpose of multi-sectoralism is to shift the response to HIV/AIDS away from solely health-based interventions, to include all aspects of society and the state. HIV/AIDS is thus not merely a health issue, but a multi-sectoral one that requires multiple actors to become involved in decision-making and implementation. The driving force behind such alliances and multi-sectoral interventions stem from international institutions, specifically the World Bank.

This form of multi-sectoral intervention has led to the emergence of a large volume of actors involved in the HIV/AIDS response and an increase in research attempting to characterise its governance. This research can be loosely characterised as that which seeks to understand (i) the role of the state; and (ii) that of civil society and global interventions.

The role of the state

The role of the state within HIV/AIDS governance predominantly relates to the capacity of governments to address the socioeconomic factors associated with the epidemic. Capacity in this instance has mainly referred to the money and political commitments needed to ensure widespread healthcare provision. The ability of states to address these issues has been undermined by a number of factors. State infrastructure is weak where a high death rate of state workers or civil servants exists (Barnett and Whiteside 2002; Chirambo 2007; deWaal 2003). Death in this instance reduces government consistency and experience, and leads to understaffing. Moreover, death of elected officials undermines democratic practice and the realisation of long-term strategic plans in combating the epidemic (Chirambo 2007). Countries with high HIV/AIDS prevalence rates are often poor 'fractured societies' (Poku and Sandkjaer 2007) with weak state infrastructure and lacking in the financial resources to provide healthcare for all. High death rates of people of working age, affect a country's labour productivity and position within global knowledge economies. This particularly impacts upon small business and micro-enterprise as a tool of poverty reduction, which bear the cost of this high prevalence rate (Poku and Sandkjaer 2007). Productivity is reduced as absenteeism through sickness increases, people die, recruitment and training costs increase, and investors are often unwilling to commit funds to countries where HIV/AIDS compromise returns (Barnett and Whiteside 2002: 242). Thus, global corporations lack incentives to invest in countries with high prevalence levels, job opportunities within the global economy are reduced and the cycle of poverty continues. This is compounded by the 'brain drain' of highly skilled workers as discussed above.

Both despite and because of these factors, academic emphasis on the role of government and the state in leading the response to HIV/AIDS remains (Poku 2001; Barnett and Whiteside 2002). Analyses of HIV/AIDS governance have consistently returned to the role of the state, and, moreover, what governments should be doing (Strand 2007). The role of the government is crucial as only it can put HIV/AIDS at the centre of the national agenda, create favourable conditions for other actors to play their role, and protect the poor and vulnerable (Poku 2001: 199). Lack of government ownership and response to their individual country's crisis sets a model for citizens, who believe that if the government is not taking the epidemic seriously then neither should they; doubts are subsequently reinforced, and stigma and misunderstanding continue (Caldwell *et al.* 1992: 1179). This emphasis has been met by a series of incentives by international organisations such as the UN and World Bank to place states, or more correctly governments, at the centre of the HIV/AIDS response. When understanding the role of the state in this context, responsibility is firmly placed in the hands of governments.

The silence and denial of governments surrounding the HIV/AIDS epidemic is of significant concern and should not be underestimated. Perhaps the most extreme case of this has been the denial that HIV causes AIDS by Thabo Mbeki's government in South Africa (for more on this see Youde 2007). However, as this book shall argue, focusing solely on government silence has several important consequences. First, it constructs states as 'good' or 'bad', depending on a government's previous ability to take a leadership role. This type of labelling is irrespective of shifts in government process or attitude in respect to HIV/AIDS. For example, Uganda has long been heralded a success story for the role of President Yoweri Museveni in taking a strong role in acknowledging the problem, especially in comparison to neighbouring states. However, this labelling has become increasingly outdated as neighbouring states such as Tanzania come into line with global leadership directives. Despite demonstrating responsibility and leadership in this regard, research into the role of states in combating the epidemic revert back to notions of 'good' and 'bad' states. Second, this approach shifts the focus away from the global, intergovernmental dimension of governance and responsibility where much of decision-making takes place and the origins of government decision-making lie. Third, it gives licence for donors and international organisations to restructure aspects of the government that are labelled as anti-AIDS, or in some way HIV denialists by the wider HIV/AIDS community. Those governments that are labelled good states receive more funding and international support the more they concur to these shifts in structure. Space for independent decision-making on the part of the government is narrowed so as to restrict independent innovation on the part of the state at the expense of being labelled in HIV/AIDS denial.

Civil society and global interventions

Problems and issues associated with the state have in part led to the upsurge of activity within civil society and donor-led strategies created by the Bank to involve these actors within the global HIV/AIDS response. As such, there has been increased recognition in regard to the rise of civil society organisations (CSOs) within the HIV/AIDS response and private service delivery (Poku 2002; Sanders and Sambo 1991; Whiteside 2002). Crucial to this has been the 'belated' (Rau 2007) recognition of non-governmental organisations (NGOs) by international institutions. Understandings of the role of civil society within HIV/AIDS have begun to reveal the complex interplay between community groups, NGOs and, importantly, international institutions. There is an emerging field towards conceptualising the 'global' governance of HIV/AIDS and the role of international institutions such as the Global Fund and the World Health Organization (WHO) (Harman and Lisk 2009; Lisk 2009; Seckinelgin 2008) but this is thus far underdeveloped or understood within the framework of civil society. In order to understand the way in which the response to HIV/AIDS is governed and the role of the Bank within this it is important to unravel what we know about HIV/AIDS, civil society and the international and, crucially, the concept of multi-sectorality.

The emphasis placed upon CSOs and their role in service provision has led to a rise in the range and number of actors addressing the response to HIV/ AIDS who in many cases are unaccountable to the people they affect (Whiteside 2002: 192). Conversely, in other respects civil society has come to represent a democratising function on the African state in its ability to directly represent communities affected by HIV/AIDS within government (Hayes 2009). Through institutions such as the Global Fund, civil society actors from across the world have been able to access global structures of decision-making. The place of CSOs on the board of the Global Fund under the rubric of multi-sectoral governance is a significant move towards more participatory governance. For some this role has the potential to fulfil a democratic deficit within international institutions and provide a more deliberative response to global health priorities (Brown 2009, 2010). The laws governing the board of the Fund and the founding principles of the Fund articulate the need for multi-sectoral partnership between governments, civil society, the private sector and the communities affected by the epidemic as a means of promoting consensus and deliberation. However, as Brown (2009, 2010) suggests, despite this articulation of multi-sectorality, voting caucuses and the dominance of key governments often narrow debate and exclude members of civil society. Hence the lack of safeguards within the Fund leads to the inevitable: those with the most money and strategic power are able to dominate deliberation and decision-making to the exclusion of civil society actors.

For some the function of civil society within HIV/AIDS governance is a little more complex. Hakan Seckinelgin's (2005: 351) research in Botswana, Rwanda, Uganda and Zambia suggests that CSOs have come to occupy a central position within the HIV/AIDS response. Seckinelgin's (2008) conception of the role of civil society is situated within his wider understanding of HIV/AIDS governance as a process of policy convergence developed by international organisations. CSOs exist and operate within a specific international governance system articulated by policy-makers such as international organisations, bilateral donors, and in some respects international non-governmental organisations (INGOs) (Seckinelgin 2005: 352; 2008). This international system articulates and constitutes a particular domain of governance whereby CSO activity is structured by a particular language and technology that promote a specific 'knowledge transfer' of ways of thinking (Seckinelgin 2005: 352). This 'knowledge transfer' is conducted under the rubric of 'capacity building' within standard donor–recipient relations. As a result, CSOs become constructed as resource categories producing particular forms of governance through service delivery (Seckinelgin 2005: 359). CSOs become incorporated into the wider governance system through their ability to demonstrate appropriate 'organizational characteristics' of legitimating norms and relationships that maintain the status quo of the pertaining governance system (Seckinelgin 2005: 359; 2008). The intertwining of CSOs within a particular system of governance undermines their agency to effect real change in the response to HIV/AIDS as international policy and procedure embed CSOs in a space external to the needs and perspectives of communities. CSOs acquire a specific form of agency through participating in particular ways and reflecting language of HIV/AIDS governance (Seckinelgin 2008). The response to HIV/AIDS rests upon a short-term perspective, when a long-term approach is required by the communities affected (Seckinelgin 2005: 364–365). The explanatory value attributed to why CSOs and international organisations enter such engagement is based upon the organisational characteristics of CSOs and their construction of language and technology in line with the dominant governance system (Seckinelgin 2005: 358–360). CSOs therefore have to frame their issues in light of donor requests that in turn structure the actions of such organisations, maintaining their overall influence upon specific governance regimes. The outcome of such expression results in a knowledge transfer of a governance regime upon CSOs that enter into contract with decision-makers. This knowledge transfer has the outcome of undermining the capacity of CSOs as agents of change, maintaining decision-making power in the hand of the elite, and reaffirming the stagnant short-term-only approach to HIV/AIDS (Seckinelgin 2005: 361–362). Crucially, for Seckinelgin the internationalisation of the HIV/AIDS governance structure has led to an anomaly between perceived and lived experience, and a disconnection between the way people experience the disease and policy practice (Seckinelgin 2008). This book will show that this disconnect occurs through the institutional arrangements of projects such as MAP, the disaggregated structures of decision-making and implementation, and the use of one approach as the overarching model of 'best practice' in which communities must adhere to in order to receive much-needed funds.

The structures arising from the global HIV/AIDS pandemic have led to large sums of money flowing from donors to recipients throughout the world. The amount of money committed to HIV/AIDS and the multiple actors involved in responding to the epidemic under the rubric of multi-sectorality present a characterisation of HIV/AIDS governance as that of 'the AIDS biz'. Elizabeth Pisani (2008) in her frank and refreshing book dismisses the AIDS complexity or exceptionality argument as overcomplicating interventions and creating a bloated AIDS business made up of 'sacred cows' of truth that cannot be questioned or criticised for fear of being seen as a sympathiser of the epidemic. While the downplaying of the socioeconomic characteristics of the African epidemic is somewhat problematic, Pisani's *The Wisdom of Whores* is one of the few books on HIV/AIDS that either mentions or discusses sex and sexual relationships in any real detail. It is also unafraid of confronting the 'sacred' structures of HIV/AIDS governance at the global level instead of the traditional path of blaming the state. Opinion on the AIDS biz is a growing concern among policy-makers and researchers. This is reflected in trends towards wider co-ordination and transparency to prevent multiple funding and 'double-dipping' yet is often ignored at the expense of keeping the money coming in. It has led to minor adjustments to the global response to include HIV/AIDS within existing development frameworks as opposed to creating additional frameworks, but the over-arching approach remains multi-sectoral in its expression, and having created it, the AIDS industry involving every sector of state and society shows minimal signs of decline. No-one wants to be seen to dismiss or divert money for HIV/AIDS for fear of not being seen to be doing something about it.

As much of the literature on civil society suggests, knowledge on the role of civil society within HIV/AIDS pertains to the role of international institutions such as the World Bank. This interaction between civil society and international interventions has come to offer a sophisticated understanding of structures of power not only within HIV/AIDS governance, but more importantly wider processes of global governance in regards to the inclusive and participatory processes established within the Global Fund and the norms and language used to disassociate the global realm of policy with lived experience. However, the focus remains very much on *either* the state or civil society and the international, with little critical assessment of the interlocutory relationship between these aspects of HIV/AIDS governance, and the blurring of distinctions and boundaries between them. This is a significant oversight, as interactions between the international and civil society occur within the state and are co-ordinated and managed by government structures. Likewise, it is the state that is characterised by its relationship with civil society and the international. It is how these structures of power interact that offers the most revealing portrait of HIV/AIDS governance and thus provide the framework of analysis for this book. The prevailing perception of HIV/AIDS governance is that the World Bank has only a minimal side role in explaining, understanding and agenda-setting within the HIV/AIDS response. This in part explains the over-arching failure to situate the state, civil society and global agenda-setting in relation to each other, as at the core of this interplay is the World Bank.

AIDS, health and the World Bank

Consideration of the World Bank's involvement with HIV/AIDS initially leads to research on the negative implications and outcomes of structural adjustment reform on health systems within developing countries. There is relatively little known about the MAP, or its impact and relationship with wider processes of state-led HIV/AIDS intervention in sub-Saharan Africa. This is a specific part of the Bank's agenda in that by working through state structures it permeates an unassuming role as the benevolent donor. The relationship between decline in health provision, structural adjustment and debt has occupied the majority of analyses of the Bank in global health. Structural adjustment policies are predominantly a form of conditional-based lending, in which states receiving funds from the Bank for a particular project or a loan from the International Monetary Fund (IMF) must adhere to specific policy recommendations towards privatisation of state services and commitment to macroeconomic reform. Key to which is the reduction of state intervention, the rule of the market economism and conditionality (Buse 1994: 98). These policies have led to the reduction of healthcare provision through a decline in hospital expenditure and staffing, the introduction of service user fees to be paid by the individual, and responsibility located away from the state and on to the individual (Ugalde and Jackson 1995: 537). As such, these policies encouraged policy-makers in developing countries to place the onus of healthcare provision on individuals and households, and to ignore wider concerns of the community and local health needs (Loewenson 1995: 55–56). The impact of these policies was most acutely felt within developing countries. Research suggests that such a decline in public healthcare provision has led to states becoming ill-equipped to address their HIV/AIDS epidemics, as they are unable to care for the sick or educate their populations regarding methods of prevention and treatment due to cuts in public education (Cheru 2002; Poku 2002; Whiteside 2002).

This research is important for understanding the Bank. However, it ends before the Bank's real forays into HIV/AIDS begin and mainly engages with wider shifts in the global political economy to which the Bank was central to but was not the only actor. Crucially, it does not say anything about the Bank in Africa post-2000 and the MAP or how any of the global response to HIV/AIDS relates to wider processes of the Bank's development strategy. Cathal Doyle and Preeti Patel (2008) have presented one of the few papers to consider the role of the MAP. However, they principally examine the legitimacy and problems in evaluating the effectiveness of CSO involvement within HIV/AIDS, and their prominence arising from their ability to enhance democracy and comparative advantage in delivering health interventions (Doyle and Patel 2008: 1929 and 1937). The discussion on the positive and negative aspects of legitimacy reflects much existing work on trends between CSOs and international organisations, without really focusing on the MAP itself as an arena of contested political activity or engaging with the Bank's role in HIV/AIDS governance in any critical manner. This builds on a wider problem of research into and the practice of HIV/AIDS governance, in which the Bank is either (i) ignored; (ii) spoken about in regard to structural adjustment; or (iii) acknowledged as a subsidiary actor that is part of the global HIV/AIDS response as a co-sponsor of UNAIDS and its seat on the board of the Global Fund. This is problematic, as the MAP provides the core foundation upon which the global HIV/AIDS response is built, and thus its approach, mechanisms and outcomes need to be carefully unravelled. To do so, it is best to start with a breakdown of what the MAP is before looking to how we can make sense of it.

The MAP

The Bank established its US$1billion MAP commitment to fighting HIV/AIDS in early 2000. The purpose of the MAP was to make funds available for any country in sub-Saharan Africa with a high HIV/AIDS prevalence rate and to engender a widespread 'multi-sectoral' response to the epidemic that involved every aspect of state and society. The central ethos behind the MAP was to recognise the pre-existing work being conducted in the community by providing financial support for existing projects and seed money for new forms of community-driven development to grow. All of this funding and community activity would be managed by the state, with community groups feeding back their ideas and issues with the project to local government agencies. The community would work with the state by regularly liaising with district officials and a specific body set up at the centre of government that would have the mandate to co-ordinate the national HIV/AIDS response. As such, funds were made available to those states that would accept and commit to the following conditions: the presence of a national strategic plan to fight HIV/AIDS; a national co-ordinating body; a commitment to directing 40–60 per cent of funds to CSOs and agreement by the government to use multiple implementation agencies, especially national NGOs and community groups (World Bank 2007). Key to the MAP's intervention was the role of governments and the state, and to reflect this role the Bank implemented National AIDS Councils (NACs) in the highest political office of each of the 34 countries that have received MAP funding.[1] These authorities were to co-ordinate the national response, select CSOs appropriate for funding, and implement the Bank's project (World Bank 2007a). The way the MAP worked was to channel the majority of funds to community groups through the following channels: World Bank (IDA); Ministry of Finance; National AIDS Council; national NGOs/faith-based groups; District/Community AIDS Council; community groups; individual.

Funds would flow top-down from the Bank, through the government, to the community, and ideas and issues with the HIV/AIDS response would flow bottom-up from the community to the regional and national government, and then back to first the Bank's in-country HIV/AIDS representative, and then the Bank's AIDS Campaign Team Africa (ACT Africa) in Washington. The MAP was divided into MAP-1 and MAP-2 interventions, with MAP-1 countries receiving funds in 2000, and MAP-2 regarding either the continuation of a country's MAP-1 project or the establishment of a new MAP project. For example, Kenya and Uganda were both MAP-1 projects established in 2001, whereas Tanzania was a MAP-2 project established in 2004. The MAP not only integrated the successful model of Brazil's response to HIV/AIDS, but incorporated wider trends in the Bank's approach to health, development and good governance. The MAP supported the sector-wide approach (SWAps) the Bank had developed in regard to healthcare since the late 1990s, emphasising a holistic form of health governance that promoted state ownership, civil society participation, and mechanisms of accountability and transparency (Cassels 1996). As such, the project was concomitant to the wider institutional good governance reform of the Bank and the implementation of the Bank's comprehensive development framework and poverty reduction strategy paper approach to addressing poverty and development. It is this relationship between the MAP and the wider institutional arrangements of the Bank for carrying out development that is key to understanding its role in HIV/AIDS, the type of agenda it has established and how it has set the global HIV/AIDS agenda.

Africa, (good) governance reform and HIV/AIDS

Thus far this chapter has introduced understandings of the complexity of the HIV/AIDS epidemic, specifically within sub-Saharan Africa, and how such complexity has been met with a specific form of HIV/AIDS governance that focuses on either the state or civil society and the international. It has argued that at the heart of this governance is the World Bank and its multi-sectoral MAP project. It has explained the substantive elements of the MAP project. In order to understand the MAP, what it represents in terms of the Bank's power, and the complex interplay between the state, civil society and the international, it is vital to situate the project within wider conceptual discussion of the Bank and governance in sub-Saharan Africa. As such, this book draws upon the critical governance debate in regards to conceptions of governance states, good governance and the over-arching liberal presence. Situating the MAP within this debate offers an alternative and original approach to HIV/AIDS governance that sees governance as a political realm concerned with more than the practice of governing and its constituent elements. The politics of HIV/AIDS needs to be understood by treating actors within a clear policy or context as a holistic device rather than constitutive elements of government policy or civil society activity. The World Bank's MAP offers a way of doing so. However, as this book will demonstrate, the World Bank has used the MAP to set the global HIV/AIDS agenda. Thus the politics of HIV/AIDS tells us as much about the Bank as it does the governance of the pandemic.

The World Bank's intervention into HIV/AIDS programmes can best be understood within the wider context of its governance reform strategies and historical evolution as an adaptable financial institution. Research on the Bank's governance reform of the mid-1990s suggests that interventions under the rubric of 'the fight against AIDS' do not exist in isolation of the reform agendas promoted by international organisations in sub-Saharan African states, and moreover not only fit with the Bank's wider use of government ownership as a means of state reform, but extends this specific type of reform to local communities themselves.

Since 1990, international financial institutions such as the World Bank have come to see the state as a central vehicle in which to promote market-based reforms. This shift in thinking has been attributed to developments in economic thinking (Bortolotti and Perotti 2007), wider Bank commitments to governance reform (Tuozzo 2004) and the logic that economic reform can only occur through social development (Griffin 2006: 574). The Bank's approach to governance reform of 1994 based upon capital and efficiency in public sector management, rule of law, accountability and transparency impacted on states in various ways (Harrison 2004a; Tuozzo 2004; World Bank 1994). As Williams (1999: 80) describes it, the Bank became engaged in 'detailed and intrusive activities' in countries in the pursuit of establishing market-based systems.

Shifts in World Bank–borrower state relations can best be understood within Harrison's conception of governance regimes. Harrison characterises the Bank's shift from 'Washington Consensus'-typified first-generation reform wherein the Bank would enter into conditional structural planning with states based on neo-liberal forms of neoclassical economics to an era of post-conditionality. Post-conditionality refers to what Harrison typifies as a form of second-generation reform, in which the Bank no longer imposes the stringent conditionalities for macro-programmes, but is now able to extend its influence through states. States that exhibit favourable social, economic and political reform or 'good' development are more likely to receive financial support from the Bank and wider recognition by the international community. These 'governance states' do so by attaining a specific form of 'showcase status' as models of best practice for other states to emulate. This showcase status is based upon favourable growth rates, stability and 'new beginning'-styled transition (Harrison 2004a: 41). For Harrison, governance reform refers to the public sector's ability to enhance economic growth (Harrison 2004a: 241). Within this, finance ministries have a specific role within the state and have risen to prominence in the government. Hence, it is governance states that have become the central vehicles in which to embed market-based governance reform within sub-Saharan Africa (Harrison 2004b: 82–90).

The Bank uses the showcase status of states to 'cherry-pick' between states with 'good' and 'bad' governance in sub-Saharan Africa, i.e. those states that carry out specific market-based reform and those that do not. States are divided into 'good' and 'bad' adjusters (Harrison 2004b: 76). Conditionality is presented within the context of state ownership and 'development' as a means of legitimising reforms. Hence states are encouraged to 'own' their reform, with conditionality being based on consensual 'participatory' decision-making. Civil Society has the function of embedding and legitimising this new form of governance and sovereignty and engaging in agendas set by donors (Harrison 2004b: 97–107 and 131; 2005: 244). Sovereignty is reconfigured through the 'sovereign frontier' in which it is constructed by the interplay of actors under the rubric of World Bank-led second-generation reform owned by the state (Harrison 2004b: 26). The limitations to the Bank fully implementing such reform are restricted by the ahistorical and apolitical nature of the Bank's conception of the state. Similar to conditionalities designed in Washington and exported to sub-Saharan Africa, this type of second-generation reform does not allow for any specific nuances within a country's social, cultural, economic or political fabric. Hence, despite using the state and civil society to embed reform, the outcome of governance reform produces short-term, quick-fix market solutions to historically embedded problems (Harrison 2004a: 255).

Research provides substantial evidence demonstrating the type of governance regimes depicted by Harrison. Bortolotti and Perotti suggest that through such reform the state encompassed a form of 'residual ownership' wherein it adopted responsibility or 'ownership' of national programmes and priorities but became 'progressively removed' from direct involvement in the economy (Bortolotti and Perotti 2007: 61–64). According to Tuozzo, in Argentina this approach affected the model of state–society relations, reducing social rights and democracy in the push for more market-oriented social policy (Tuozzo 2004: 103–104). The state in terms of the government and civil service was reduced in the delivery of services, with the Bank promoting the executive and the Ministry of Finance and nongovernmental forms of service delivery (Tuozzo 2004: 106 and 110). In Mexico, the World Bank's involvement in governance reform suggests that the state's agenda was ideationally identical to that of the Bank's second-generation reform agenda of governance, state ownership and civil society partnerships, encapsulated by the Comprehensive Development Framework and World Development Reports of the 1990s. The successful realisation of such reform however was limited by 'domestic political squabbles' where the managers of reform, i.e. politicians, failed to fully implement the Bank's governance agenda (Charnock 2006: 84–91). Similar to Harrison's depiction of short-term, ahistorical approaches to reform undermining long-term impact, the Bank's disregard for the political structures and culture within Mexico and overemphasis upon rational actors undermines its ability to enact reform in practice. Charnock argues that, as such, the Bank has had to confront the role of the state in implementing market-based reforms, to such an extent that it is the 'state managers' that implement such reforms and embed them within society (Charnock 2006: 91–92).

The findings of Harrison are pertinent to any understanding of HIV/AIDS governance, and in particular the prioritisation of the state at the forefront of the global agenda. Harrison's depiction of governance states and distinctions between good and bad reformers echoes the literature on HIV/AIDS and the state. Whereas one is based on economic reform and the other a leadership role or lack of silence, the two are inter-related in how states respond to HIV/AIDS. As this book will show, those states that adopt participatory and ownership practices emphasised by the MAP attain greater recognition and legitimacy from the international community than those states which do not. The Bank does not have to implement a stringent form of conditionality, but as Chapter 3 will show, by emphasising state ownership, the Bank is able to extend its influence on national HIV/AIDS priorities through structures of post-conditionality. It is thus important to unravel the role of neoliberal market reform within HIV/AIDS, as well as the implications of the blueprint nature of the project in sustaining the long-term benefits of limiting the HIV virus and reversing the trend of Africa's pandemic. As this book will demonstrate, HIV/AIDS is used as a vehicle in which the Bank can enact its specific liberal market-based governance reform throughout countries in sub-Saharan Africa, and use its HIV/AIDS interventions as a model for best practice throughout countries with high HIV/AIDS prevalence around the world. This book will show that concepts such as 'good' and 'bad' reformers, governance states and residual ownership are at the core of HIV/AIDS governance, as constructed and organised by the Bank. However, in the case of HIV/AIDS, these factors are not limited to the state, but are used to affect individual behaviour change, and there is a clear role for civil society organisations within this. Thus to an extent notions of post-conditionality and governance states are limited in fully understanding Bank reform in sub-Saharan Africa in that they principally focus on the role of the state, with little reference to the role of civil society or the individual.

Harrison does acknowledge the role of civil society as a part of the participation function of the Bank's wider governance reform but goes into very little detail as to its relationship to governance, the state and reform. As this book will show, this is problematic, as civil society is used as a specific device by the Bank to enact change within the government and embed specific practices. Moreover, as evidence from HIV/AIDS interventions demonstrate, the way in which civil society is empowered through funding mechanisms such as the MAP confronts the very structures of the state, and points to one of the over-arching contradictions of the Bank's approach to governance reform: the need to keep state and civil society separate while using civil society as a check on government. Despite an awareness of issues of participation, transparency and ownership as principles in which the Bank organises governance, the focus of Harrison *et al.* is very much on the state as opposed to wider social forces and actors. This is where Williams' work on good governance is particularly useful.

Good governance has become the operating principle of the Bank's activity since the early 1990s. For Williams (2008), global governance is the liberal project of social transformation operated through the programmes of the World Bank. Different from Harrison, it is liberalism as opposed to *neo*liberalism that underpins Bank activity. This distinction is important, as for Williams, neoliberalism operates as a form of neoclassical economic transformation, whereas liberalism encompasses multiple forms of social transformation that goes beyond the state and economy to also include civil society and the individual (Williams 2008). This is a crucial shift for the Bank, as it demonstrates a recognition that economic reform based upon market-driven neoliberalism depends upon the wider development of 'appropriate' institutions within state and society, hence there needs to be a shift away from the narrow confines of *neo*liberalism to the all-encompassing tenets of liberalism (Williams 2008: 69 and 87). Similar to Foucault's conception of governmentality, under the rubric of good governance, the Bank's concern is not to govern but social transformation through specific social relations (Williams 2008: 106). The state must be independent from civil society, the economy and the individual, but must also have a regulatory role (Williams 2008: 30).

In tracing the emergence of the good governance agenda and its central tenets within the World Bank from the 'crisis of governance' emerging from the 1989 report *Sub-Saharan Africa: from crisis to growth,* Williams shows how this agenda has come to reflect liberal positions in regard to the state, economy, civil society and the individual. Using the case study of Ghana, Williams then demonstrates how this agenda has been operationalised in practice. There are parallels to Harrison's work, in how the relationship between the Bank and the government Ghana operates, emphasis upon civil service reform, budget adherence, improved co-ordination and decentralisation (Williams 2008: 97 and 102), as well as the ahistorical approach the Bank takes to reform within specific countries where cultural and political complexity are ignored (Williams 2008: 121). As Chapters 3 and 4 of this book will show these factors are high priorities within the MAP.

Of significance is the role of civil society as fundamental to the participation element of the good governance agenda. Civil society has a crucial role within good governance in which the 'right' kind of civil society (or 'good' reformer as Harrison's conception would put it) that functions in the public interest and is non-political or not seeking public office is prioritised by the Bank. The Bank organises projects in a specific way to engender the inclusion of specific groups, and promotes their understanding of market economies and liberal values (Williams 2008: 88 and 113). The inclusion of civil society makes social transformation a more far-reaching project, as individuals become bound to a specific type of reform based on liberalism. Individuals as the central element of liberalism are seen as malleable by the Bank in their ability to adopt the 'right' kind of skills and social relations. The identification of their habits provides resources for transformation (Williams 2008: 114). This notion of individualism is particularly important for the governance of HIV/AIDS, as a crucial element of the Bank's work pertains to behaviour change communication in sexual practice and choice.

In encapsulating the central principles of good governance, the MAP can be interpreted as a clear example of the practical application of liberalism. Based upon Williams and Harrison's arguments, through HIV/AIDS the World Bank has the potential to widen its governance reform under the rubric of good governance by affecting state, community and individual behaviour. Indeed the central tenets of the MAP – participation, ownership, transparency and accountability – could be seen to function as a blueprint for operational good governance. Good governance is key here, as in emphasising transparency and participation, not only has the Bank been able to influence state-based decision-making within health policy, but has also embedded this liberal form of intervention within the national civil society, local community and the individual. This book will address how reform is applied through the MAP by looking at the state in regard to national and local government in East Africa in Chapter 3, and the community and individual in Chapter 4.

There are however several areas of contestation within this particular form of governance that are not fully explored within Harrison and Williams' accounts of the Bank and become evident when attempting to apply these arguments to the complexity of HIV/AIDS governance. The first substantive gap in existing conceptualisations of the Bank and governance is that despite acknowledging the role of civil society, and the need to go beyond the state, evidence to develop such arguments remains state- or Bank-centric. There is little research from the civil society actors or communities these policies affect. Research tends to take an over-arching 'development' focus that can, at times, obscure the nuances in the contradictions of the liberal approach to governing. The perspective and ideas, or how governance configures in a particular local setting, are assumed or ignored. This is particularly pertinent when considering the role of the individual and the abstraction of 'development' or in this case 'AIDS governance' as distinguished by Seckinelgin from that of HIV/AIDS experienced. If a crucial function of liberalism in practice is to affect the role of individual behaviour and skill development, it is important to not fall in the trap of the Bank and assume a particular form of relations between individuals living in countries in sub-Saharan Africa and the Bank. More importantly, to see how liberalism affects individuals and individual behaviour, one must look at factors that affect the individual. Development or governance reform of the state is abstract to the practical everyday lives of people: health concerns and HIV/AIDS have a direct impact on bodies, families and communities that is seen and experienced by the individual. The individual has a substantive focus within Williams' research, yet this site of political power is not *fully* conceptualised in conjunction with the state, civil society, the community or the international as there is little empirical evidence from which to base these interactions upon.

There is little understanding of the interlinkages between the state, civil society and the individual. Although these are seen as constitutive elements of the same liberal project, they are not understood in relation to one another – that is, in a co-constitutive manner. Though Williams highlights the central paradox of the state as maintaining its role of regulation and non-involvement with civil society, there is little evidence of how these two aspects of governance inter-relate. Moreover, civil society is seen as a cohesive entity with little distinction between national and international NGOs and community groups, or individuals. These distinctions are important as they assist the Bank in its operation of a specific liberal agenda. The organisation of specific projects and categories within the Bank is particular to how power is expressed and articulated and how reconfiguration of state and society is happening within the local, national and international contexts. The international and sub-Saharan Africa is important within this. The region of sub-Saharan Africa is often constituted as an area that is *acted upon* by the international, with relatively little understanding of how it in turn affects the international. Williams provides evidence of how other international donors and organisations have adopted the principles of good governance as a means of carrying out development; however, there is little exemplification of how these policies have been implemented beyond the context of sub-Saharan Africa as a region.

The purpose of this book is to develop critical understandings of the Bank's governance through the World Bank's flagship HIV/AIDS project the MAP. The book develops our understanding of the Bank and governance in the following ways. First, it uses extensive empirical research on the MAP in Kenya, Tanzania and Uganda to analyse the operation of governance in regard to the state, the community and the global. It unravels the practical contradictions and problems associated with the intertwining of these three spheres of political power from the perspective of not just the Bank and the state, but of various elements of civil society and the individual. Second, it elucidates how this governance agenda is no longer limited to countries within sub-Saharan Africa but shows how through global HIV/AIDS interventions, this agenda has begun to permeate through social structures throughout the world. Third, the book does not take institutional change within the Bank in the mid-1990s and its Washington headquarters as the main genesis for the development of the good governance paradigm within the context of HIV/AIDS, but rather traces policy-making within the Bank to Latin America and as such explores the inter-relationship of governance between the regions. Fourth, in looking at an issue as complex and personal as HIV/AIDS the book contributes to understanding of how the Bank's governance affects individual behaviour and opinion. Fifth, the book develops understandings of the practice of governance by unravelling specific institutional arrangements and relationships between the Bank, state and civil society that disaggregate decision-making structures so as to promote clear political governance outcomes. The book goes beyond Harrison's depiction of the African state to apply his conception of post-conditionality to that of civil society as a social function that embeds market practices and reform within local communities. Sixth, in exploring these different inter-relations within critical understandings of governance, the book aims to politicise conceptions of HIV/AIDS governance and highlight the role of the World Bank within this.

As such, the book argues that the World Bank has set the global HIV/AIDS agenda. It has done so through a specific form of good governance reform in which the state, civil society, local communities and intergovernmental organisations have embedded practices of neoliberal market-based strategies to combat the epidemic. This reform has been operationalised through the MAP across sub-Saharan Africa and the Bank's specific brand of multi-sectoralism. The governance of HIV/AIDS is not just about the practice of governing, but is a political project that seeks to embed liberal practice through individual, state and community behaviour. At the heart of this practice is the drive to impose blueprint neoliberal market-based solutions on a very complex, *personal–global* issue.

Research

The book develops these arguments by looking at the context of the MAP in three countries: Kenya, Tanzania and Uganda. The case study countries were selected for the following reasons. First, each of the countries had their own individual MAP project – the Kenya HIV/AIDS Disaster Response Project (KHADREP); the Tanzania Multi Sectoral AIDS Project (TMAP); and the Uganda HIV/AIDS Control Project (UACP). Each of these projects is at a different stage in their development, and despite being based on similar models, they had individual governance and political implications. The slight differences in their start dates offer nuances in the application and shifting priorities of Bank–CSO relations from MAP-1 to MAP-2. Each of the countries has similar HIV/AIDS prevalence rates of between 6 per cent and 8 per cent and comparable poverty indicators. Second, the history of the Bank's relationship with each of the countries and the wider development community differs, adding a further dynamic to the Bank's relationship with these countries: from Uganda the 'good' reformer; Kenya the 'corrupt' reformer; to Tanzania the ex-Socialist 'potential' reformer. The different labels and paths to development present an interesting context in which to explore the same model of HIV/AIDS intervention.

The findings of this book are based upon 6 months of fieldwork in Kenya, Tanzania and Uganda, New York and Washington DC in the USA, and Geneva in Switzerland from 2005–6, and an additional trip to Tanzania in 2009. Over the course of this fieldwork I conducted 166 interviews, prepared and issued 50 questionnaires and participated in community group and partnership meetings as a means of participant observation. The findings from the semi-structured interviews provided the main basis of the research. Interviews were carried out with key people in a range of CSOs – national NGOs, INGOs, community-based organisations (CBOs) and faith-based organisations (FBOs), multilateral and bilateral donors, UN agencies, local and national government agencies within Kenya, Tanzania and Uganda, and World Bank staff members. Interviewees were selected with regard to the following criteria. First, their relevance to the MAP – whether they were part of the structure, such as the AIDS Councils, or concerned with implementation and capacity building, such as UNAIDS. Second, whether they were in receipt of MAP funds such as the national NGOs and CBOs. Third, the level of their involvement and influence within the response to HIV/AIDS. Fourth, community empowerment groups that worked outside any particular framework or project. The purpose was to get a broad range of opinion on MAP-related and non-MAP-related participants to look at the practical workings of the project, alternatives to the MAP, and how such alternatives related to the MAP. The timing of the interviews was structured in such a way as to put the findings of the research in East Africa to the architects of the project in Washington.

Participant observation was conducted in regard to the national Annual General Meetings of NGOs, the Joint Annual HIV/AIDS Programme Review (JAPR) in Kenya and community visits by home-based carers in rural communities, hospitals and slums. Participant observation was selected as a research method as a way of assessing what was meant by 'dialogue' as a key form of World Bank implementation and how it was expressed at every stage of the MAP. Questionnaires were mainly issued to District AIDS officials, who because of a combination of time restrictions, access and geographical spread were not interviewed in the field. Fifty open-ended, semi-structured questionnaires were distributed to local HIV/AIDS representative authorities in Kenya and Tanzania but not Uganda as a selection of District HIV/AIDS Officers had been interviewed there. Questionnaires were also issued to other participants who could not find the time for a face-to-face or telephone interview. Requests for anonymity have been upheld where required. Permission to use people's names and statements was established prior to their participation. In three instances research participants were unwilling to provide their full names and are thus referred to by their first name and organisation only. The majority of research participants were happy to have their names used, and were often keen for their view, experience or opinion to be heard. Sensitivity has been shown to the content of the research and every care has been taken to not misconstrue or decontextualise responses.

Key concepts

The governance of HIV/AIDS is replete with acronyms and issue-specific concepts. Many of these are unavoidable when discussing specific issues within this book. The most common are in reference to the National AIDS Councils – the NACs; the District AIDS Councils – the DACs; and the Regional Facilitating Agents – the RFAs. These three concepts refer to the government structures established by the World Bank as a pre-condition of MAP funding. They implement the MAP for the Bank, co-ordinate the response to the epidemic at the national or local level, and provide a leadership function in establishing national priorities and strategic plans. The book does not use the acronym PLWHA when referring to people living with HIV and AIDS; instead, it uses people with HIV/AIDS.

The concept of civil society is applied as an associational concept to INGOs, national NGOs and local community groups. As Chapter 4 demonstrates, the difference between these groups is that national NGOs operate across the country whereas community groups work in a specific, smaller local community, and INGOs operate in multiple countries, with their host states normally, but not exclusively, in Europe or North America. The use of the private sector within the book does not fit in with this conception of civil society. The private sector refers to private and public companies, businesses and for-profit enterprise. Both the private sector and civil society fit into the notion of multi-sectoralism. To re-cap, multi-sectoralism is an all-encompassing term that refers to the involve-ment of international organisations, the state, civil society, the private sector and the individual in responding to specific development issues. In the case of HIV/AIDS, it principally refers to the need to involve non-health actors in addressing the epidemic.

Structure of the book

The book develops its argument in the following way. Chapter 2, Pathways to multi-sectoralism and HIV/AIDS, outlines the evolution of the MAP, multi-sectoralism and the Bank's role in global health. In doing so, it charts the institutional devel-opment of the Bank from its inception as a means of highlighting how the Bank has managed the state, specifically within the context of Africa, and responded and adapted to external pressure in the form of civil society, member states and emerging development concerns. This is an important function for understanding multi-sectorality and HIV/AIDS within the evolution of governance within the Bank. The purpose of the chapter is to explain (i) why the Bank became involved in global health, and specifically HIV/AIDS; (ii) where the MAP came from; (iii) how the Bank has adapted and adopted specific agendas and knowledge; and (iv) how the Bank has established the liberal antecedents for the global HIV/AIDS response. The chapter situates the book's argument within the wider context of the Bank's mandate to work with states, the central mechanisms and cumulative nature of policy-making in sub-Saharan Africa, and how the role of non-state actors has evolved and been reconfigured by the Bank. Crucially, the chapter argues that multi-sectoralism did not arise from wider processes within the HIV/AIDS community, but is a clear reflection of the Bank's approach to health, sub-Saharan Africa and the business of carrying out development.

Chapter 3, Owning HIV/AIDS: the state, focuses on the application of the MAP at the state level. As such, it considers the role of Ministries of Finance, the president, the National AIDS Councils, and the Ministry of Health within the MAP and the HIV/AIDS response at the national level. It explores the good governance principles of ownership, participation and what they mean in practice, and how they relate to institutional rivalry and the problem of co-ordination, implementation and ownership. The chapter develops the book's key argument by showing how the Bank has extended its liberal brand of governance reform beyond the absorption of ideas within the state to the formation and implementation of a state agency, and the problematic role of economic, neoliberal incentive in facilitating such reform.

The role of civil society and the individual within the MAP are the subject of Chapter 4, Constructing multi-sectoralism: the community. Chapter 4 unravels the consequences and impact of multi-sectoralism in practice, how governance reform is being constituted at the local level and how this affects individuals. The chapter shows how the MAP has constructed a specific form of multi-sectoral civil society that is firmly located within communities and the individual and driven by economic incentive. The result of this has been an upsurge in activity that is principally interested in service delivery, and a lack of feedback and input into structures of decision-making or accountable governance within the local and national government, or the wider international donor community. It extends the arguments developed in Chapters 2 and 3 to suggest that on application it is the problem of using neoliberal forms of economic incentive to create liberal outcomes that undermines the MAP, and the extension of the Bank's good governance agenda.

Chapter 5, Setting a global agenda, charts how through the MAP and multi-sectoralism the Bank has been able to set the global HIV/AIDS agenda. It does so by outlining how and why the interventions of specific multilateral donors such as the Global Fund, bilateral donors, UN agencies such as UNAIDS, and foundations such as the Bill and Melinda Gates Foundation have aligned with the Bank. The chapter shows how the Bank has used a combination of timing, position, partnership, and the construction and promotion of a specific form of knowledge and innovation to embed its role as the 'benevolent leader' of HIV/AIDS governance. It argues that despite the MAP ending in sub-Saharan Africa and the Bank withdrawing from HIV/AIDS interventions, its model of multi-sectoralism and framework of governance reform has become incorporated into global practice, and hence its agenda for combating the disease will continue to be sustained.

Chapter 6, World Bank, Governance and the politics of criticising HIV/AIDS, draws together the book's central argument in conclusion. The chapter outlines the main components of the Bank's multi-sectoral agenda for HIV/AIDS, what it looks like and the implications it has for the state, civil society and the individual in sub-Saharan Africa. It argues that post-conditionality has been extended by the Bank through its HIV/AIDS interventions to structures of local and global decision-making. This form of post-conditionality is underpinned by a contention over the pursuit of liberal outcomes through neoliberal economic incentive. It is this contention that has precipitated problems within the response to HIV/AIDS at every level of governance. The chapter then goes on to explore the ramifications of criticising the response to HIV/AIDS, and how it is important to see the World Bank and its influence on combating the disease.

2 Pathways to multi-sectorality and HIV/AIDS

To see how the World Bank has set the global agenda and what this agenda looks like, it is important to trace the antecedents of multi-sectoralism and the World Bank's involvement in HIV/AIDS. Multi-sectoralism has its origins in processes of civil society engagement within the Bank. These processes stem from how the World Bank has developed as an institution that is adaptable to change in response to internal and external pressure, while promoting the same market-oriented approach to carrying out development. Its role in global health, HIV/AIDS and multiple issues affecting countries in sub-Saharan Africa are grounded in the Bank becoming the lender of first resort in its role as lender of last resort where it funds development issues that no other organisation will. State-led governance reform is not a new phenomenon within the Bank but something that has been instilled within the institution since its inception. This is crucial to understanding the Bank, the MAP and HIV/AIDS governance, as the Bank is able to promote multi-sectoral partnerships and state responsibility while maintaining its role as a non-political actor as enshrined in its founding principles. It is these founding principles and their interpretation within the comprehensive development agenda and projects such as the MAP that continue to underpin the Bank's governance reform agenda and the use of economic incentive as a means of promoting liberal reform. The Bank's ability to adapt and establish itself as a leader in development knowledge not only explains the origins of the MAP in relation to its ability to adapt but explains how the Bank established itself as a leader in global health governance. Central to which is how HIV/AIDS policy has adapted within the institutional context of the Bank: from models of best practice emanating from Brazil, to specific individuals framing the agenda in accordance with the central principles of good governance reform. This chapter outlines the origins and institutional factors that underpin the Bank's multi-sectoral agenda towards HIV/ AIDS, and demonstrates how governance reform and global health interventions are not new for the Bank but a logical progression of institutional development from the Bank's inception that constrains methods of combating HIV/AIDS that do not have an economic incentive or liberal outcome.

The chapter unravels in the following manner. First, it demonstrates how the Bank's inception and subsequent development has instilled within its institutional structure an ability to adapt to external influence and the demands of member states and the international system. Second, the chapter explores the consolidation of the Bank's role in specific reference to sub-Saharan Africa, conditional lending, health and external relationships from the 1950s to the early 1980s under the presidency of McNamara. This period is the central precursor to the emergence of good governance, multi-sectoralism and the Bank's involvement in global health governance. Third, the emerging prominence of civil society organisations between the 1980s and early 1990s as influential actors both inside and outside the Bank is addressed in reference to trends in participation, the Bank's response and how these factors interlink with the wider programmes and structures of the Bank, and specifically adjustments in the Bank's health policies. Fourth, the chapter builds upon each of these factors to set out in detail the Bank's role in HIV/AIDS and the emergence of the MAP, specifically in reference to the role of individuals, timing and how the response to the disease in Brazil affected the framework of the project in sub-Saharan Africa.

Inception and adaptability

The founding principles of the World Bank say much about the form of HIV/AIDS governance and the relationships with states and civil society actors the Bank promotes. Agreed upon as part of the Bretton Woods agreement 1–2 July 1944, the principle purpose of the Bank was to work together with the International Monetary Fund (IMF) in the rebuilding of Europe (Gardner 1956: 74). The plans outlined for the Bank and Fund were underpinned by the institutions' main architects John Maynard Keynes and Harry Dexter White and their commitment to state-building economics, enshrined in three conditions: 'progress toward solving deeper political and economic difficulties; provision of liquidity to give confidence to members to abandon restrictive policies; creation of mechanism of adjustment to restore balance of payments equilibrium' (Gardner 1956: 80).[1] The institutions were to complement one another with the IMF maintaining currency stability through macro-economic stabilisation recommendations on the one hand and the Bank underwriting the private capital necessary for reconstruction on the other. The Bank was to have US$10 billion worth of capital stock that was a combination of local currency and member states' gold. This capital was to be supplied to the UN and states that required assistance with reconstruction and economic recovery (Gardner 1956: 75). The Bank would be seen as not part of the UN but as a specialised agency within the organisation's overall structure. The Bank had the power and ability to set interest rates and award grants to countries, and was 'intended to be run on "sound" banking principles' as a lender of last resort (Blough 1968: 153). The president, executive directors and general staff were seen as having influence over the Bank 'in interpreting and applying policy and the opportunity and responsibility to exercise leadership in seeking to change it' (Blough 1968: 157); however, the lending countries were still able 'to exercise a special veto over most lending transactions of the Bank' (Knorr 1948: 31). Crucially, as enshrined in Article IV of the Articles of Agreement, the Bank would be presented as a non-political organisation that would not be involved with or influenced by member state policies (Knorr 1948: 33).[2] Thus from the outset of its inception the Bank was mandated to work with the state on reform of welfare systems that would not specify but would include provision of healthcare, had a financial dependency upon member states and was affiliated to, yet crucially, independent of the UN. These three factors have been central to the Bank's form of state reform governance, and how it has used the balance between member state interests and relative autonomy from the institutional statis of the UN to articulate and sustain separate development agendas that would come to influence the work of UN agencies.

During its initial stages, the Bank faced several key problems that subsequently altered its purpose and work. The first was the lack of willingness of private investors and certain member states to provide loans to particular countries (Knorr 1948). The willingness of member states confronted the non-political nature of the organisation as states began to cherry-pick those countries it would lend to in line with their bilateral foreign policy objectives. These objectives stemmed from a reticence of the allied countries to lend Germany money for reconstruction purposes, and the perceived communist threat of the USSR. Central to this was the role of the US government and its emerging dominance over the Bank. Although enshrined as non-political in the Articles of Agreement, the influence of the US government ensured Bank lending would examine political factors when considering loan disbursement: the Bank would be based in Washington; the institution would not be autonomous from the interests of member states; loans would be based upon certain conditionalities.[3] This undermined the Bank's ability to obtain the resources it badly needed to reconstruct Europe effectively.

The second problem for the Bank at this time was its failure to strongly recognise the gap in institutional infrastructure across Europe. As one observer put it, a 'more farsighted policy was often … ruled out as impractical because the institutional framework was lacking which was an essential condition for effective collaboration' (Fisher 1947: 179). Loans did not comprehensively rebuild the infrastructure of countries. In sum, the institutions were seen as unable to meet the problems of the post-war world (Kindelberger 1951: 32). Third, contrary to the intended flexible nature of the Bank, desired formal commitments were seen to be stronger and more useful to the post-war world. Strong agreements fostered trust between countries and represented long-term commitments to solving long-term infrastructure problems. Thus, the international economic system was seen as dependent upon a clear constitution and working constitutional conventions (Fisher 1947: 183). However, this issue is deeply linked with perception of reality at the time, as the same perspective recognises a clear pooling of sovereignty between states in the Bretton Woods system. Fourth, controversy through 'a wide range of adverse comment' surrounded Bank staff salaries and allowances existed during a period in which the Bank was seen as relatively inactive (Kindelberger 1951: 32). This compounded the lack of trust felt by borrowing countries. Fifth, a delay in operational procedures as a result of the Articles of Agreement becoming effective in December 1945 meant that once it began lending the Bank did not have a large amount of borrowers as those recipient states had looked elsewhere

(Beyen 1948: 537). Thus, the Bank's initial period was marked by relative non-action. In overlooking the substantive structural reform and need for direction and knowledge leadership in the post-war world that would become the core of its future governance agenda, the Bank established itself as a non-player in global politics. It was only when the Bank learnt from these early mistakes and non-activity that it became the significant development actor it is today. At the time, however, the consequences and implications of these failures were compounded by the introduction of the 1947 European Reconstruction Plan, or the 'Marshall Plan'.

The Marshall Plan and the banker's bank

The purpose, scope and influence of the Marshall Plan led the Bank to change the focus of its initial mandate and provided the foundations for wider institutional reform that has come to underpin the Bank's governance agenda for HIV/AIDS. It was during this period that Africa came to occupy a central position within the Bank, and a holistic approach to conditional lending that prioritised state reform came to the fore. The Marshall Plan encapsulated and implemented the central objectives and influence of the US post-Second World War: to ensure European dependency on US aid thus buttressing against Soviet influence and establishing the US as the dominant world power (Hogan 1987: 52 and 147). The ideology behind the Marshall Plan to rebuild Europe was a synthesis of the existing US domestic New Deal and New Era interventions and foreign policy (Hogan 1987: 18). US Secretary of State George C. Marshall (1947–9) and his associates designed the Marshall Plan with the overall aim of replacing European separate sovereignties and redistributive politics with a unified order similar to that of US federalism (Hogan 1987: 293). The plan would present a framework for integration while protecting private enterprise and public order (Hogan 1987: 428). Despite sharing the same emphasis on reconstruction lending, stable currencies and the elimination of trade barriers as the Bank and Fund, the Marshall Plan sped up negotiations and the deployment of funds. Furthermore, the combination of the two demonstrated the USA's ability to dominate bilateral and multilateral diplomacy. The plan would provide aid for Europe's short-term needs whereas the Bank would finance the long-term objectives (Hogan 1987: 51). In the immediate aftermath of the Marshall Plan's introduction, Britain recognised the Bank's role in Europe's long-term reconstruction as a complement to the Marshall Plan's short-term aid relief (Hogan 1987: 51). The Bank thus acquired a minor role in assisting the US multilateral objectives of integrating the world economy and reducing restrictive trade policies (Hogan 1987: 17). Ultimately, however, the Marshall Plan subordinated the Bank and IMF further to US power, which overshadowed the post-war reconstruction role that underpinned the institutions' creation. Despite the Bank's second president, John McCloy (1947–9), and 16 of the Bank's member states being involved in the drafting of the plan, countries demonstrated a preference for Marshall Plan aid rather than Bank aid as it was cheaper (Beyen 1948: 541; Knorr 1948: 35).

The Marshall Plan fundamentally challenged the central purpose, need and existence of the World Bank. The Bank, however, responded to this challenge by altering its management structure, identifying new client countries, and developing a sound reputation within international banking markets so as to maintain independence from member states. Kindelberger (1951) has marked how fundamental to this response was the Bank's shift from 'Washington' policy to 'New York-Wall Street' management in its first 4 years as a working institution. This shift marked the first significant reorganisation of the Bank based on business and banking principles. An 'elaborate system' ensured all loans would be project based and carefully monitored. The Bank became 'a creative, adaptive institution which is performing useful and interesting work' through devising the tools necessary to suit international economic development (Kindelberger 1951: 43). Crucial to the Bank's ability to establish such a position during this period was the Bank's then president Eugene Black's (1946–62) ability to secure a good credit rating in the US markets while avoiding any dollar dominance of the Bank through the working basis of 18 per cent of own-currency subscriptions for member states (World Bank 2007b). Central to Black's presidency was the establishment of the International Finance Corporation (IFC) in 1956 and the International Development Agency (IDA) in 1960. The IFC was established to give the Bank 'flexibility to private entrepreneurship in economic development' whereas the IDA was set up to secure 'development credits' of 50-year interest-free loans with no government guarantee requirement (Blough 1968: 155). The purpose of the IDA was to provide 'soft loans' to very poor countries, specifically in sub-Saharan Africa. The strength of the agency grew further to its inception with President George Woods (1963–8) transferring large portions of the Bank's net income to the IDA as a signal of the Bank's commitment to its role as a development institution. Beyond technical assistance programmes, this era marked the Bank's introduction to the knowledge economy with the publication of various economic studies. The combination of these studies and technical assistance enabled the Bank to mark itself out as an expert, which facilitated wider involvement in the coordination of development activity through closer consultation to the extent that '(t)he Bank's greatest contribution probably has been to make economic development lending respectable' (Blough 1968: 177–178 and 181).

The establishment of the IDA and IFC reflected a second crucial response of the Bank to the impact of the Marshall Plan: it began to focus its attention on decolonisation and the development of countries beyond Europe. At the centre of this were states in sub-Saharan Africa. The Bank's approach and assistance to such states during this time underpins how it addresses the problem of HIV/AIDS and the structure of the MAP. The Bank recognised the fragility of such states and the role it could play in assisting with state reconstruction and economic development (Mikesell 1972: 71). This period marked the beginnings of the Bank's involvement in sub-Saharan Africa where 'development' came to replace the notion of 'civilisation' (Harrison 2004: 12–13). On 9 October 1952 the Bank announced its first mission to East Africa (World Bank 2005: 82). The Bank's role during this period was compounded by the decline in US aid in line with the advent of the Korean War. US attention switched to rearmament under fear of communist aggression and subsequently decreased its bilateral lending (Hogan 1987: 380). The Bank was thus subject to less lending competition. However, central to this period was the fact that the Bank managed to survive in its early years at a time when the institution could have been disbanded. It did so by adopting change based on banking principles and the primacy of the market, and the need to develop and promote a specific set of skills and knowledge towards newly independent states in Africa. The Bank held firm to its founding principles, but was not afraid to adapt to new emerging issues of relevance to its mandate under the loose description of development. In the early stages of the Bank's development then, we can see the emergence of Africa at the forefront of the Bank's lending portfolio, an ability to adapt and establish the development agenda, with the Bank's over-arching commitment to state-led market-based interventions throughout.

What this tells us about the World Bank and HIV/AIDS

The inception and early years of the Bank reveal several institutional traits that provide the foundation for its future involvement in HIV/AIDS. First, at the outset of its operation, the Bank demonstrated its prominence and influence as an international institution. The Bank demonstrates awareness of, and manipulates events and changes in, the international system to its own advantage. When the Bank's existence is threatened it maintains its relevance by identifying emerging issues that can be applied to its overall mandate, and uses its association with such issues to demonstrate its institutional knowledge and comparative advantage within international development. The Bank's current role in HIV/AIDS and the creation of the MAP reflects its association with emerging development issues as a means to maintain its perceptibly high level of development knowledge. Second, the Bank's main partners are states managed through set conditionality principles. As a specialist agency, the Bank operates within the UN's wider machinery but retains its autonomy. Third, the role of the Bank's president is central to the direction of the institution, and maintaining its ability to adapt and interpret member state directives and change effectively. Fourth, the political concerns of member states are central factors in determining Bank activity. Whereas the Bank's role in health was yet to emerge in the early stages of its development, the antecedents of change, knowledge and state-leadership underpinning its global agenda were set.

The 'pro-poor' Bank

The founding principles and expanded mandate of the Bank were developed by the Bank's president, ex-US Secretary of Defence (1961–8) Robert McNamara (1968–81). This period of the Bank's development marked the consolidation of the Bank's dominant role in sub-Saharan Africa; the beginnings of its involvement in global health; and the collapse of Bretton Woods and the introduction of structural adjustment. For Williams, it was the institutional and project-specific problems associated with this era of structural adjustment from which the good governance agenda grew (Williams 2008).

Bretton Woods collapse, Africa and structural adjustment

McNamara established the Bank's role in Africa as 'a leading player on the continent' by gaining support from the international bureaucracy and member states to triple previous Bank lending to Africa (Mallaby 2004: 89). The lending programmes were marked out in 5-year plans with the second being 40 per cent higher than the first. Lending commitments during McNamara's presidency increased from US$1 billion in 1968 to $13 billion in 1981 (World Bank 2007b). The era marked the introduction of a 'pro poor' Bank that moved away from investment banking to a detailed analysis of development issues such as nutrition, literacy, income distribution, employment and notably for its relationship with sexual health and family planning. The 'pro-poor' Bank was seen to comprehensively address the issues facing people living within what were then seen as 'third world countries' (Goldman 2005: 68; Woods 2006: 45). This approach embedded the demarcation between military security and economic development and the Bank's self-conception as an intermediary between the rich and poor countries (World Bank 2007b). With nutrition and family planning at the forefront of holistic development, health came on to the Bank's agenda.

At the outset of his presidency, McNamara expanded the Bank's international bureaucracy with the appointment of 4,000 extra staff. This expansion led to further restructuring within the Bank, with vice-presidents becoming responsible for lending approval and further decentralisation to in-country offices (World Bank 2007b). Decentralisation was a key part of McNamara's agenda with the increase in Bank field offices from two to 15 in sub-Saharan Africa alone and renewed emphasis upon government partnerships (Mallaby 2004: 89). Crucial to such changes was McNamara's relationship with the Bank's most influential member state: it is no coincidence that expansion of lending and reinvigorated concentration on development occurred as US President John F. Kennedy (1961–3) characterised the 1960s as 'the crucial decade of development' (Mikesell 1972: 76). During this period, not only was US aid substantially increased to the World Bank, but the US administration established itself as the central co-ordinator of development assistance within international financial institutions such as the Bank and Fund (Mikesell 1972: 77).

Central to the Bank and the Fund's development during this period was the collapse of the post-war economic system enshrined in Bretton Woods. The causes of Bretton Woods' collapse are situated within the discrepancies surrounding funding disequilibria arising from balance of payments. Conflict over an effective balance of payments system prevented any resolution to the problem in the aftermath of the Second World War. Thus, as European economies began to recover from the economic devastation of the war and resume full convertibility of currencies, the US gold reserves fell below overseas liabilities and its large balance of payments surplus and began to fall into deficit from the late 1950s onwards, ultimately leading to the US current account falling into deficit, precipitating a need to devalue the dollar. The USA, however, was reluctant to devalue the dollar. By 1968 the dollar had become inconvertible to gold, and this was formally recognised in 1971

(Ruggie 1982: 407). Compounded with the pressure placed upon fixed exchange rates by the growth of international capital, and with no means of addressing such stresses on the post-war financial system, the Bretton Woods system proved inadequate and subsequently collapsed in 1973 (Ruggie 1982: 398). This collapse led to a shift in international leverage towards conditionality, and the 'burden of domestic adjustment measures, therefore, fell disproportionately on the developing countries' (Ruggie 1982: 408). The Bank and Fund as institutions based upon the Bretton Woods system thus had to shift focus accordingly. In light of the changes in the international economic system in the aftermath of the collapse of Bretton Woods, McNamara established a taskforce – the Pearson Commission – to consider the future role of the Bank with the sole purpose of convincing the US Treasury of its commitment to the Bank. This taskforce set the foundations for the introduction of structural adjustment lending.

Structural adjustment arose out of a combination of the collapse of Bretton Woods and the need to respond to the Oil Crisis of 1973. In the decade preceding 1983, oil prices had risen from US$3.22 per barrel to US$34 per barrel. The majority of the Bank's client countries during this period were importing oil, creating a drain on their accounts and a move, in Africa's case, from a small surplus in balance of trade to a US$6 billion deficit (Harrison 2004: 39). At this stage, the Bank could no longer ignore the issues and concerns faced by its client countries. Structural adjustment was a deeper entrenchment of the conditionality principle established within the Bank's creation. The purpose of structural adjustment was rapid disbursement of funds combined with enforcement of conditionality (Mosley *et al.* 1991: 309). Structural adjustment lending deployed economic conditionalities as a means to change state economic policies with an emphasis upon revising subsidies, addressing overvalued exchange rates, change of use and production of energy and less excessive regulation. Structural adjustment was based on the premise that borrowing countries would agree to such principles and member states such as the USA would continue to support the IDA at US$4 billion per year as initially agreed (McNamara in Fried and Owen 1982: 11). By his own admission, McNamara stated

> These structural adjustments are going to be painful. In essence, they will require cutting back consumption from what would otherwise have been possible and reallocating the resources saved by this process to an expansion of exports or a substitution if imports.
>
> (McNamara in Fried and Owen 1982: 8)

Structural adjustment lending and the Bank's role as primary lender to Africa were secured in the 1981 Berg Report. The Berg Report was the Bank's 'Accelerated Development in Sub-Saharan Africa: An Agenda for Action' report headed by Elliot Berg and published on 16 August 1981. The report argued that the subcontinent's lack of development was the result of corruption, inefficiency and excessive regulation. The post-colonial state was seen as corrupt and bloated and 'less state, more market' was the only solution (Harrison 2004: 63). The Berg Report became 'the dominant source of economic and policy analysis for sub-Saharan Africa. Not only the amount of aid, but also the objectives, rationale and conditions attached to all aid' (Sender 2002: 187). The report supported and strengthened the Bank's role and justification as the leader of policy initiatives and development responses in sub-Saharan Africa. By 1989, 89 structural adjustment loans had been agreed between the Bank and African states. Failure to succumb to structural adjustment would result in failure to secure finance or debt rescheduling and subsequent isolation from the world economy (Harrison 2002: 56–57). African countries borrowed heavily from the Bank's long-term loans to pay off IMF short-term loans, thus increasing a spiral of debt (Mallaby 2004: 106). These long-term loans were made on set conditions that led to a decline in civil servants in all aspects of the state, an increase in the private sector's role in provision and service delivery (Sender 2002: 194), job losses, reduced good subsidies on goods, economic slowdown, minimal welfare provision and little political voice for states and their populations (Woods 2006: 158). In many African countries, where the public sector was the largest employer, structural adjustment led to mass unemployment. For example '[i]n Uganda, a World Bank-supported retrenchment programme had cut the public employee list from 320,000 to 150,000 between 1990 and 1995' (Harrison 2002: 62). Job losses in the public sector had a particularly negative impact upon health services with provision becoming intertwined with cost-cutting measures, over equity in provision and severe understaffing (Poku 2002: 531; Whiteside 2002: 191–192). The long-term consequences of which have been severely debilitated health systems within countries in sub-Saharan Africa, ill equipped to address the HIV/AIDS pandemic. States and donors have hence been playing catch-up to strengthen the health systems undermined by structural adjustment as health issues such as HIV/AIDS emerge.

The health agenda

It was in the context of McNamara's presidency and the beginnings of structural adjustment lending that health came on to the agenda of the Bank. For McNamara the 'health of man' was a central component of socioeconomic development (World Bank 2008a). In July 1979 the executive directors of the Bank first approved lending to the health sector (World Bank 2008a). Previously to 1979, health only existed as a constituent element of other projects and country strategies. The Bank had established a partnership with the WHO previously in 1971 on water sanitation and supply, and also entered into partnership with the WHO, United Nations Development Programme (UNDP) and the Food and Agriculture Organization (FAO) to raise funds to combat river blindness in Benin, Ghana, Ivory Coast, Mali, Niger, Togo and Burkina Faso (World Bank 2008a). Despite the board's decision in 1979, it was not until the late 1980s that the Bank became directly linked with healthcare through its co-financing of health sector programmes, and indirectly through the socioeconomic impact of structural adjustment, and neoliberal reform in partnership with the IMF. Directly, the release of the Bank's 1987 *Financing*

Health Services in Developing Countries: an agenda for reform and 1989 *Sub-Saharan Africa: from crisis to sustainable growth* led the Bank to increase its role in health operations. These health operations were very specific. The issue for health reform in poor countries as the Bank saw it was to balance the need to alleviate demands and pressures on existing health systems while not increasing public expenditure (World Bank 1987). The Bank proposed a new approach to healthcare based on the role of the private sector – within which NGOs were firmly situated – and the individual: states should (i) charge user fees for government health facilities as 'individuals are generally willing to pay for direct, largely curative care with obvious benefits to themselves and their families'; (ii) provide insurance or other risk coverage for individuals and their families to buy; (iii) use non-governmental resources effectively; and (iv) decentralise government health services (World Bank 1987). Indirectly, structural adjustment led to the reduction of healthcare provision through a decline in hospital expenditure and staffing, the introduction of service user fees to be paid by the individual, and responsibility taken away from the state to the individual (Ugalde and Jackson 1995: 537). These policies shifted policy-makers away from the concerns of the community and placed the onus upon households to address health problems (Loewenson 1995: 55–56). The impact of these policies was most acutely felt where the focus of the Bank's health activities were based: sub-Saharan Africa. These operations did not exist in isolation of wider trends within the Bank at the time. The 1989 report on sub-Saharan Africa had two significant implications for health: (i) it advocated the need to double expenditure on healthcare and (ii) it was the first time the Bank introduced the concept of good governance, stating that the underlying problem in sub-Saharan Africa was 'a crisis of governance' in the political, economic and social aspects of the term (World Bank 1989; Williams 2008).

Privatisation of healthcare services and the subsequent emphasis placed on the individual facilitated a rise in community and non-state provision of healthcare services (Lee and Goodman 2002: 97–98; Owoh 1996: 216) that was encouraged and, in parts, financed by the Bank. Community provision of healthcare services can be traced back to the emphasis placed upon community involvement in primary healthcare within the 1978 Alma Ata Declaration and marked a decline in the dominance of biomedical-centric models. (Rifkin 1986: 240). The logic went that community involvement increases the amount of funds to reach the poor through greater geographical coverage, wider uptake, at less expense to users (Gilson and Mills 1995: 219). This has led to a shift in focus towards community empowerment rather than changes in the prevalence of particular diseases (Laverack and Labonte 2000: 256). Community empowerment within health policies exists in relation to specific groups, i.e. health promoters, home-based carers, etc., with emphasis upon strong community attachments and local knowledge (Labonte and Laverack 2001: 115). This model of healthcare planning became widely adopted by international actors and donors (Zaidi 1994). At the same time, the Bank was able to position itself at the centre of this community model through demonstrating its comparative expertise, funding capacity and leadership (Buse 1994). Community models of development focus both donor and state activity on giving tools and resources direct to the community as a means of individuals own-ing and identifying those initiatives that act to the betterment of their personal and societal development. In regards to healthcare, this involves channelling funds directly to local providers of healthcare, be it palliative care or the development of local health centres. Community groups articulate their main health priorities in partnership with local government structures and donors such as the Bank. Community as the focus of CSO engagement and as a form of implementation procedure for Bank projects was thus not new within the MAP when it was intro-duced 20 years later or specific to HIV/AIDS. Community and individual respon-sibility was embedded in the working practices of the Bank since its first forays into healthcare provision in the era of structural adjustment.

Civil society emergent

The consequences and impact of structural adjustment upon the structure of developing states and issues such as healthcare provision (or lack thereof) and the rise of community provision facilitated an upsurge of civil society activity as a whole, not just in relevance to the health sector. The decline in state provision at the cost of the private sector and to the individual facilitated a gap in the delivery of basic needs. This gap led to an emerging shift of CSOs traditionally involved in advocacy campaigns towards service delivery and transnational campaigns. CSOs utilised the increasing controversy surrounding structural adjustment to open up space for engagement with the Bank through the establishment of the Multilateral Development Bank Campaign, which highlighted issues surrounding the Bank's role in development. The CSOs that engaged with the Bank during this time were predominantly INGOs that targeted the Bank through network advocacy, member state support and highlighting the Bank's impact on domestic policies around the world (Nelson 2002: 378). Campaigns at this stage did not represent the collec-tive action programmes representative of a more global civil society, but were marked by acknowledgement of the issues by individual organisations. A more comprehensive assessment of the impact and outcome of structural adjustment was to follow.

The emergent criticism of structural adjustment and focus on the Bank during the early 1980s was mainly ignored by the Bank (Sender 2002: 194). In 1982 the Bank established a World Bank–NGO committee to foster dialogue with non-state actors and monitor opposition (O'Brien *et al.* 2000: 29). The committee presented a formal channel in which CSO leaders could meet with World Bank President and senior managers annually to discuss various issues.[4] Project planning and implementation partnerships became enshrined in 1989, when the Bank issued a directive to significantly increase NGO involvement in projects. However, this involvement did not include CSOs in decision-making forums or policy devel-opment (O'Brien *et al.* 2000: 29). Despite the non-governmental sector being recognised in areas such as healthcare, the first free-standing NGO-implemented project was approved on 21 March 1989 as part of the Togo Credit Grassroots Initiative. This project provided financing to NGOs; technical support services, such as improvement of monitoring and evaluation; assistance to the government's development division; and support to the community for implementation and capacity (World Bank 2005: 200). This one-off project reflected trends already evident within the Bank's operations, that of the need to involve community-based organisations in its projects with little recognition of those international NGOs which seek to target and criticise the Bank. This set a specific precedent within the Bank of using local, community-based forms of civil society as its non-governmental component of projects to the exclusion of those organisations that target and criticise the Bank. For the role of the Bank, civil society was about low-cost service provision.

This level of CSO engagement reflects the Bank's ability to manage change within the international system. At the collapse of the Bretton Woods system the Bank shifted its attention towards structural adjustment lending that both reflected the dominant economic interests of its member states and heightened borrower state dependency. Key to such a shift was the agency of McNamara, who maximised his close relations with the US administration to expand financing to developing countries and the international bureaucracy of the Bank, and then redirected the focus of the Bank in line with the international economic objectives of the late 1970s. This pattern of change and policy relevance comes to be one of the key explanatory factors of why the Bank involved itself in the HIV/AIDS response: maintaining its relevance by looking to new development issues, and expanding its relevance at a time when it can develop a leadership role within the international system. Recognising the emergence of CSOs, the Bank demonstrated tokenistic gestures towards international NGOs to acknowledge the limited impact they had at this time, and created community components within many of its in-country programmes as a means of promoting transparency. These gestures were constructed and sidelined by the Bank. Thus, engagement during the 1980s was not only conditioned by the Bank, but CSOs themselves were a by-product of the socioeconomic system the Bank had been so influential in creating and maintaining. This has been acutely felt and promoted in the field of healthcare reform.

The 1990s: CSO engagement and the health Bank

The current expression of multi-sectoral governance reform and the involvement of CSOs within the Bank is the result of internal and external factors. Externally, the structural adjustment critique had united global civil society and demonstrated the power and resurgence of CSOs, and had led to the inclusion of community-based civil society actors within the Bank's projects. High profile campaigns against the Bank and Bank-specific projects such as the Sardar Sarover Dam Project in India and the Polonoreste Project in Brazil,[5] culminated in the '50 years are enough' campaign and created political space in which CSOs could operate. Campaigns were structured around specific projects that had adverse consequences for the environment and communities in which they operated or were targeted against the ideology and view of development processes advocated by the Bank. CSOs had become better organised and mobilised. Organisations deployed new advocacy tactics for targeting specific project officials, sympathetic staff members and gaining media support. The mushrooming of various global networks mobilised groups on specific issues pertaining to the Bank, saw a growth in global inclusion and increased organisation capacity. CSOs became more sophisticated in their approach to the Bank and views of wider political processes and access to such processes.[6] Those CSOs able to shape their objectives in the Bank's working language on development, establish personal relationships, and demonstrate a similar institutional working culture gained greater direct leverage than those who lacked the skill, capacity or desire to do the same. Crucially, those CSOs that adopted the 'boomerang' pattern of engagement, depicted by Keck and Sikkink (1998), in which CSOs circumvented the Bank and the host state of particular projects to target member state governments, specifically the USA, enacted greater change within the Bank.

From the inception of the World Bank–NGO Committee in 1982 to the mid-1990s, Bank initiatives to absorb CSO criticism were practically non-existent. The Bank suffered from institutional inertia. This inertia stemmed from the Bank's inability to adapt to criticism arising from economic crises and the growth of an increasingly interconnected, organised and targeted 'global' civil society. The presidents during this era (Barber Conable 1986–91 and Lewis Preston 1991–5) failed to acquire and maintain confidence of this emerging form of civil society, the Bank's member states and, crucially, borrowing countries. Despite establishing the Inspection Panel in 1993, President Lewis Preston paid only lip service to CSOs and was widely condemned within the '50 years is enough' protest (World Bank 2007b). Member state commitment declined under CSO pressure and wider scepticism surrounding the Bank's ability to effectively fulfil its mandate. Doubts over the Bank's effectiveness arose out of the Wapenhans Report (World Bank 1992), which identified a lack of quality in the Bank's projects in terms of both implementation and supervision, with one-third of the Bank's projects being identified as problematic. As Williams (2008: 81) argues, these problems and issues were not new to those targeting the Bank, but what was new was the Bank's willingness to officially acknowledge the problems and crucially not to blame the state but the culture of the Bank. The Bank had become marred by bad governance, corruption, failing projects, lack of funds and competition from rival UN agencies. These factors culminated in external and internal pressure on the Bank to become more accountable and transparent to those it affected. Thus, although CSOs were a catalyst to increased transparency, such demand arose from the wider institutional rot prevalent within the Bank at the time and the need for good governance not only within borrower countries but within the Bank itself.

Reflecting the importance of strategic leadership, the selection of James Wolfensohn as World Bank president on the 16 March 1995 was a crucial factor in the Bank's shift towards widespread implementation of the Bank's good governance agenda and the inclusion of CSOs within the working practices of the Bank. At the time of his appointment, discontent with the Bank from both inside and outside had reached a peak. Wolfensohn maximised this peak to shift the Bank's approach to policy and practice that emphasised a change in institutional approach which would focus upon development, aid and the relationship between the Bank and borrowing countries (Stiglitz 2003: 122) through an emphasis upon good governance. Wolfensohn confronted the Bank's staff, placing renewed emphasis upon counter-corruption mechanisms and refreshing the Bank's approach to development with the creation of three technical working groups in which staff members would be situated: (i) Human Development, Poverty Reduction and Economic Management; (ii) Private Sector Development and Infrastructure; (iii) and Environment, Rural and Social Development (Rich 2002: 33). Bank effectiveness through better managed and implemented projects in light of the Wapenhans Report was to occur through a more holistic partnership with borrowing countries and wider inclusion of CSOs as a means of promoting good institutional and project transparency. Each of these managerial principles was to be operationalised through the Comprehensive Development Framework (CDF).

The CDF is the Bank's flagship programme under Wolfensohn and the most holistic practical application of the Bank's good governance reform agenda. According to the Bank, the CDF 'emphasizes the interdependence of all elements of development' and is based upon four pillars: a long-term, holistic approach to development; country ownership of the design and implementation of its own development strategy; country-led partnership; and a strong focus on results (World Bank 2007c). The CDF is an approach to development that was implemented through poverty reduction strategy papers (PRSPs). PRSPs combine an individual country's macroeconomic, structural and social policies and the financial 'needs' of the country to attain growth and poverty reduction. The main ethos of the PRSP process is that they are drawn up by the Bank 'in partnership' with governments, civil society actors and other development agencies such as the IMF (World Bank 2007d). The underlying assumption of the CDF/PRSP process is an apparent shift away from the stringent conditionalities of structural adjustment to become more accommodating of an individual country's needs. The Bank sees the inclusion of all aspects of the state, civil society and the private sector as an effective means of promoting checks and balances and democratic forms of participation: the very fundamentals of the good governance agenda. In engaging with states and CSOs, the CDF and PRSPs would be based on a partnership, thus there would be less need for conditional lending or economic incentive.

A main component of the CDF was the reassertion of the Bank's position as a leader of development knowledge. The Knowledge Sharing Programme that underpinned Wolfensohn's commitment to 'The Knowledge Bank' was established to promote the sharing of information within the Bank, with its development partners and with states. The role of developing countries is intrinsic to the 're-appropriating and adapting knowledge for development' (Stiglitz 2001: 209) in terms of the 'right knowledge' that would fit in with the culture of the Bank. The Bank viewed its role as 'scanning globally' to identify effective methods and procedures for alleviating poverty and then playing a 'brokerage role' in facilitating learning practices and procedures between countries. Wolfensohn's vision saw the Bank's main purpose as establishing best liberal practice in a sea of differing approaches and practices within development. These approaches could be expressed through the CDF processes and on specific development issues such as HIV/AIDS. Of importance to the Bank's knowledge agenda is that it recognises the utility of knowledge and agenda-setting in past Bank operations, and unlike other institutions within the UN is able to put its knowledge claims into action through the funding of projects and government initiatives and financial support. The Bank is able to frame its ideas in such a way as to become the norm operating principle within development, as counter to the negative connotations of structural adjustment, there are few states or international organisations that would openly disagree with the need and pursuit of good liberal governance, irrelevant of what this form of governance may mean in practice for the Bank. It was this process that underpinned the Bank's approach to HIV/AIDS, and established its foundations as the agenda-setter for the global response.

The Bank's reinvigorated approach to CSOs under the CDF reflects its positioning as a model for best practice. Wolfensohn signalled his intentions towards CSOs from the outset of his presidency with a visit to Mali, where he met with community groups, NGOs and government officials (Mallaby 2004: 101). Since this visit, Africa has become a central focus in the design of the CDF, with Uganda's Poverty Eradication Action Plan providing the basis on which to build the CDF. Mallaby suggests that Wolfensohn thought the idea that you should give Africans control and encourage NGO participation arose from the bitter experience with structural adjustment and an over-arching need for CSOs to make states accountable and transparent. At the centre of the good governance agenda was the notion that the failure of weak governments to implement structural adjustment showed that the key blockage to development was not absence of good policy prescriptions, but a lack of the political will needed to put good policy in place (Mallaby 2004: 218). Thus what you had was Wolfensohn advocating not so much a substantive shift away from structural adjustment, but rather the same policies with added participation and reach. Where there was will, economic incentive would not be necessary. CSOs were central to communicating the governance reform of the Bank within the local community and the state within sub-Saharan Africa. CSOs would participate as a means of generating the political will for reform, as long as this will was based on liberal forms of governance. This era marked the first full integration of CSO activity within the Bank.

Based on the reforms undertaken by Wolfensohn and the central role CSOs play within the governance reform agenda of the Bank, the Bank operates engagement with CSOs through five media: (i) consultation, (ii) dialogue, (iii) partnering, (iv) direct funding and (v) a Community Outreach Program in Washington DC. Dialogue and consultation is carried out through consultation meetings such as strategic policy workshops; 'electronic dissemination tools' (e.g. video conferencing through the Development Forum), e-newsletter and web-based exchanges; and CSO attendance at the Bank's annual spring and autumn meetings. Consultation is viewed by the Bank as a 'more structured exchange' in which it is involved in 'active listening'. This is interpreted as the Bank considering – and in some instances providing feedback on – external comments. This consultation refers to general Bank practice as well as project-specific work. The main examples of such consultation have been within the PRSP process, the Heavily Indebted Poor Countries (HIPC) initiative and annual World Development Reports. Involvement within the annual meetings refers to discussion within seminars, and informal dialogue meetings with the president of the Bank and managing director of the IMF. The Bank's official documents suggest that the purpose of this engagement is to promote outreach and the quality of projects through the promotion of transparency, accountability and 'public understanding of the Bank's work' (World Bank 2007e). Hence the Bank not only wants to promote good governance in borrower countries but to present an image of good governance within the culture and practices of the institution itself.

Funding of CSOs is either direct from the Bank's headquarters or through a particular project. Direct funding occurs in partnership with other donor agencies, through community-driven development projects which refer to either the annual community-driven development account of US$1 billion that is disbursed directly to community groups on an annual basis (World Bank 2007e) or through country-based projects such as the MAP. CSOs are able to compete under the Bank's procurement guidelines to provide goods and services, become vendors, assist in monitoring and evaluation activities, become contracted by governments to provide technical assistance or train project personnel.

Since the reforms introduced by Wolfensohn in the late 1990s, the World Bank's engagement with CSOs is structured through three engagement teams at the country, regional/departmental and global levels. There are 40 staff members disbursed within country level offices as civil society country staff; 40 'regional' staff who work in Washington as part of the civil society group in various regional units; and the global civil society team that co-ordinates each of these structures by 'formulating institutional strategy, providing advice to senior management, undertaking research and dissemination, and reaching out to CSOs at the global level'. Of the 120 civil society team members, 80 are based in Washington DC. All have different areas of special interest and backgrounds. It is the Civil Society Group and Civil Society Team which are of concern in this section. The main role of the civil society team is to co-ordinate the Bank's overall CSO engagement practices and policy, work on strategy and advise all Bank staff on how to engage effectively. Key to this is the role of the president. Wolfensohn's preference for and widespread inclusion of CSO engagement within the good governance agenda meant it was a priority to establish strong links between Wolfowitz – and subsequently Robert Zoellick – and CSOs early in their presidency.[7] The advice of the civil society team to the Bank president focuses upon 'identification management', i.e. identifying the key NGOs in a specific sector, setting up meetings, negotiating and 'knowledge management participation'. Knowledge management refers to monitoring CSO output on the Bank through scanning 60 'of the leading websites' and producing an e-digest on civil society that reflects the key points and issues raised by CSOs on all issues relevant to the Bank.[8] The overall management of the World Bank's activities and its management of public perception have led to a large growth in the communications sector.[9] Engagement with CSOs thus continued to be based upon a sophisticated system of absorbing external criticism through structured dialogue with forms of global civil society, and funding and support to local community groups.

Complementary to the civil society team, Wolfensohn introduced a spectrum of specialist units to engage with a range of civil society actors that loosely fit under the remit of the civil society team, but were seen to necessitate specialist subsections within the social development department such as foundations, community foundations and faith-based organisations. The community foundation unit was established as a means of facilitating these actors as a sustainable development tool through building the Bank's knowledge of their utility, capacity and potential.[10] In a similar vein, the main role of the development dialogue on the values and ethics unit is to educate Bank staff of the utility of these organisations and facilitate partnerships through setting up meetings, provision of an information centre and attending conferences.[11] Social action funds are a central mechanism for enhancing in-country accountability structures as a part of creating demand for accountability. These funds fit in with the Bank's approach to demand side governance and social accountability within the PRSP process.[12] However, these funds have the overall aim of bringing governments to account, as opposed to the Bank itself. The inclusion of these various units reflects Wolfensohn's development ethos that the concept was so wide-reaching that it required the introduction of multiple actors with different skills to encompass all the various issues.[13] Fundamentally, it showed that to institutionalise widespread governance reform, the Bank needed to engage with multiple sectors of society that may not be addressed by the funding of community groups and the state alone: the fundamentals of a multi-sectoral approach to governance. For example, the roles of religious and faith-based organisations are essential components and often difficult stumbling blocks to the full adoption of the Bank's governance reform. They thus, for the Bank, need to be brought into dialogue and participate in 'knowledge sharing' as much as possible to align with the Bank's reform agenda.

Since the Bank's widespread adoption of these CSO engagement practices, the Bank has presented itself as an institution of best CSO practice within global governance: multi-sectorality is very much an extension of this. The level of integration was not caused by CSO activity but by Bank recognition of the need to change and adapt to criticism so as to secure financial and political support from its member states to continue its operations. Integral to understanding this has been Wolfensohn's effective management of CSOs within the wider framework of good governance. Wolfensohn acquired the confidence of Bank staff, member states and key influential CSOs through the statement of a clear ideology based on supplementary evidence and sustained supportive majorities.

Civil society, sector-wide approaches and health

The issue of health became a central part of Wolfensohn's comprehensive approach to development and good governance. Wolfensohn consolidated the Bank's growing role in public health to articulate key strategies for prominent health issues that affected development, most notably HIV/AIDS. During the 1980s the Bank's funding to healthcare had expanded, and Richard Feechem, the then director of the Bank's Health, Nutrition and Population sector, had used healthcare as a means of diverting negative attention away from structural adjustment (Abbasi 1999b). Financial commitment coupled with problems associated with the WHO enabled the Bank to present itself as a non-political organisation at the centre of global health policy (Buse 1994). The culmination of this was the Bank's strategic focus on health within its flagship World Development Report (WDR) 1993 *Investing in Health* (Buse 1994; Lee and Goodman 2002; Owoh 1996*)*. WDR 1993 was interpreted by those working in public health as a means of embedding the Bank's market-driven approach to welfare (Owoh 1996: 216). It articulated the need for privatised healthcare, widespread use of user fees, minimal state interference and the role of the market (World Bank 1993). Using health as the focus of the Bank's flagship publication makes a clear statement of both the Bank's role at the centre of global health, and its commitment to privatised forms of healthcare in developing countries.

The decline of health provision through state welfare and the introduction of new forms of co-financing and user fees by the Bank allowed it to make claims to knowledge and expertise in health reform (Buse and Gwin 1998: 666), and consolidate its role as a central actor within global health (Lee and Goodman 2002). Combined with the decline of the WHO as a result of internal wrangling and confusion about its mandate – discussed in more detail in Chapter 5 – the Bank was able to enlarge the space for decision-making and influence within global health policy-making through its 'unrivalled financial resources' and the 'top-down nature' of health policy reform at the time (Lee and Goodman 2002: 109–110). The Bank used its supposedly 'non-political' specialised status and lending expertise within the wider body of the UN to assume this position as opposed to its main rival body, the UNDP (Buse 1994: 98; Ugalde and Jackson 1995: 530). Important to understanding the MAP, the health agenda promoted by the Bank was one of individual responsibility, minimal state inclusion, decentralisation and the primacy of the private sector. The role of civil society within this was located in the realm of the private sector as a cheap and efficient form of service delivery, and a means of addressing the 'crisis of governance' within the health sector in sub-Saharan Africa. Locally based community groups had thus already come on to the Bank's agenda as a means for promoting its own particular brand of good governance.

Changes towards civil society inclusion and the promotion of good governance in the Bank were reflected in trends within healthcare. Criticisms of the impact of structural adjustment upon healthcare systems and internal Bank reviews of the effectiveness of its health policies led to a slight adjustment to the economic liberal values underpinning its health interventions during the late 1980s and early 1990s. Simply put, health services had not improved as the Bank had previously thought, and in some countries were on the decline. The Bank's explanation for this was that it had not taken account of the systemic conditions or infrastructure needed for improvement, i.e. there was a lack of good governance. This recognition combined with wider reform packages occurring within the Bank during the late 1990s led to a refocus of the institution's global health policies towards systemic reform of the role of the state and privatised provision, targeted interventions and most notably a 'sector-wide' approach (Buse and Gwin 1998: 666). This sector-wide approach was the foundation for multi-sectoralism within the HIV/ AIDS response and developed some of the central principles of the Bank's trends towards community-driven development, inclusion and good governance. Sector-wide refers to the need to involve all aspects of the public and private sectors and the individual in the provision of healthcare. Nothing different from the Bank's previous forays into health reform so far. However, the difference here was the sidelining of emphasis or the perceived emphasis placed on user fees, conditionalities and the role of individuals within this. Central to this perceived change in the direction of the Bank was Richard Feachem, the Director of Health, Nutrition and Population (1995–9), who, according to a series of articles by Kamran Abbasi in the *British Medical Journal*, directed attention away from user fees and structural adjustment and towards issues of sustainability and working relations with other international actors such as the WHO (Abbasi 1999a,b). The Bank entered into partnership on healthcare reform with the UN as part of the UN Special Initiative for Africa in 1996 and with the WHO and SmithKline Beecham on a programme to eliminate elephantiasis in 1998 (World Bank 2008a), as well as numerous other projects at country level.

Over the last 10 years the Bank has developed these sector-wide models through its 'soft' approach to conditional lending and as part of its wider good governance strategy that prioritises government 'ownership', community 'participation', a 'sector-wide' approach to health and new forms of lending. This outreach towards the WHO and UN, and the shift of focus towards sector-wide approaches did not mark a significant change for the Bank as the private sector, civil society and the individual remained paramount. Issues of market-oriented practice in promoting efficiency within healthcare systems, the shifting role of the state to make way for privatised provision and the introduction of non-state actors as the main service providers within healthcare remain pertinent to understanding of the Bank's role within global health. It is these factors, trialled in the introduction of user fees and private sector delivery in the 1980s, then rebranded as sector-wide approaches under the wider processes of governance reform from the mid-1990s, that underpin the MAP and its consolidation of good governance.

The Bank's role in HIV/AIDS: the MAP

The MAP encapsulates the central components of good governance reform within the Bank and the culmination of the Bank's earlier forays into global health. This is evident in the emphasis it places upon comprehensive approaches to development issues through government ownership, health knowledge and engagement of communities as the principle form of civil society. There are three key factors which have precipitated the emergence of the MAP. The first explanation is that the MAP was a natural progression of the Bank's previous involvement in sexual reproductive health and family planning. Previous to the MAP, the Bank had mainly approached HIV/AIDS as part of wider family-planning issues. During the 1990s, neither the World Bank World Development Reports nor the UNDP's Human Development Reports had considered the long-term effects of HIV/AIDS development in sub-Saharan Africa (Barnett *et al.* 2001: 369). Up to this point it was the WHO's Global Programme on HIV/AIDS (GPA) that presented the global response to the epidemic (Barnett and Whiteside 2002: 74). The Bank had formally marked World AIDS Day in 1995 and reaffirmed its investment of US$700 million to HIV or other sexually transmitted infection (STI) prevention but had not prioritised HIV/AIDS specifically (World Bank 2005: 239). The Bank did have three HIV/AIDS projects, in India, Zimbabwe and Brazil. The India project in 1992 had little success, with the Bank wanting to fight stigma and denial and the Indian government preferring to prioritise blood safety. However, despite the project's approval, the Indian government remained dissatisfied. The Bank's second HIV/AIDS project up to this point was in Zimbabwe in 1993, which involved a freestanding loan to pay for STI treatment. However, this project had been implemented with minimal research into the spread of the disease (Mallaby 2004: 316). Further to these specific projects, the Bank had started conducting research into the epidemic with the release of its 1997 report 'Confronting AIDS: Public priorities in a Global Epidemic', which focused on a concept of how the Bank should move forward,[14] involvement in the launching of the AIDS Vaccine Task Force in April 1998, and partnership with MTV and UNAIDS' 'Staying Alive' project (World Bank 2005: 256–260). These initiatives, however, were isolated issues or country specific and not part of or reflective of a wider HIV/AIDS agenda by the Bank. The Brazil project however was marked as a success story, principally for the role of good governance, and thus became the framework in which future Bank HIV/AIDS policies would be built.

The three World Bank–Government of Brazil AIDS and STD control projects are often seen as the successful model on which the MAP was developed. The first project ran from 1993–8 and had the over-arching objectives to reduce HIV incidence and strengthen the public and private institutions responsible for STD and HIV/AIDS control through a focus on public sector governance and reform (World Bank 2004a). Key to this was the role of the Brazilian government in raising awareness and funds and establishing an appropriate infrastructure for HIV/AIDS control. Different from the MAP, the first project was very much health based as opposed to multi-sectoral in the emphasis placed on the role of the Ministry of Health and health professionals in developing services for HIV/AIDS patients and monitoring the illness and associated opportunistic infections (World Bank 2004a). A central part of the project was the role of NGOs in promoting behaviour change and an emphasis upon the institutional development for an effective HIV/AIDS response that could be sustained at the local, municipal level. Bank lending would be conditional on the government developing 'institutional innovations' and expanding capacity to implement the programme (World Bank 2004a). The second AIDS and STD Control Project, 1998–2003, prioritised similar areas as the first: reduction in HIV incidence and strengthening of public and private institutions (World Bank 2004b). The project again focused upon HIV/AIDS as a health issue, by assessing the performance of the health system and emphasising the need for an expansion and improvement in diagnosis, care and treatment (World Bank 2004b). The third project, 2003–7, again developed the main themes and objectives of the first two. However, the emphasis upon the 'national response' and the decentralised role of NGOs and the municipalities had greater recognition within the over-arching objectives of the project (World Bank 2008b). The project was also more progressive and encompassing than other global initiatives of the time in the targeting of high-risk groups, condom promotion and the development of needle exchange programmes for injecting drug users as well as home-based care and the protection of rights of people living with HIV/AIDS (World Bank 2008). These three projects were seen as a success for the following reasons. First, the project established an HIV testing and treatment system, which became the model for anti-retroviral treatment (ART) provision in a developing country. Second, the role of government leadership in terms of commitment and political openness and the focus on decentralised decision-making was seen to elicit positive results in breaking down barriers to stigma and discrimination. The Ministry of Health was already committed to taking action, and from the Bank's perspective its relationship with the government was open and transparent and based on political will. Third, there was a commitment to combating HIV/AIDS from all aspects of civil society.

The Brazil projects did influence the establishment of the MAP in the sense of a wider awareness of what works in the setting of a particular country. The success of the project was integral to the board of the Bank recognising HIV/AIDS as an issue worth funding and support in Africa. The MAP reflects the Bank's success in Brazil in the recognition that the Bank has a specific knowledge on HIV/AIDS interventions that emphasise government leadership, decentralisation and NGO participation. However, the MAP lacks two significant ingredients to the Brazilian model: existing government willingness and ministry of health leadership. The MAP seeks to create government leadership without the necessary evidence of political will, and does so by adopting a multi-sectoral approach that removes HIV/AIDS from the health sector and the introduction of neoliberal economic incentive as a means of liberal reform. John Garrison, senior civil society specialist of the Bank's civil society team, was instrumental in the Bank's involvement with the Brazil projects. Garrison's central role in this project was on facilitating CSO capacity in formulating proposals and implementation. He indicates that it was the Bank that pushed for civil society inclusion 'but then later on as the programme began to open, then it just took off and the Bank didn't have to do much more'[15] within the Brazil project, a trend similar to that of the MAP. Thus while the Brazilian model provided the basic component framework of the MAP, the Bank modified it to be more participatory of civil society, and inclusive of all elements of the state beyond the health sector. In other words in promoting state ownership, civil society inclusion and adapting the Brazilian experience to fit in with the Bank's own development knowledge, the Bank took the Brazil model and added more good governance.

The second catalytic factor leading to the emergence of the MAP was a chance meeting between two Bank staff members, Debrework Zewdie and Hans Binswanger, on a bus returning from a staff retreat in 1997. Binswanger, an AIDS activist within the Bank, was committed to community-driven development. Zewdie was an Ethiopian Doctor who worked on public health and had witnessed the effect of HIV/AIDS on sub-Saharan Africa. After being approached by the governments of Ethiopia and Kenya for financial assistance to help fight HIV/AIDS, Debrework Zewdie 'raised the flag' of the crisis to the board of directors. At this stage, Zewdie had to convince the board that (i) the Bank had done little to fight HIV/AIDS; (ii) the Bank is a development agency and HIV/AIDS is eroding the past 50 years of development, it is therefore the Bank's business; and (iii) community support is key to tackling the epidemic.[16] In other words, Zewdie framed the issue in the language of comprehensive development and agenda-setting to align HIV/AIDS with the Bank's priorities. Despite the prevalence of these issues, the board was not initially forthcoming, as Jacomina de Regt, Sector Lead Specialist for Social Development, Africa Region, describes:

> I recall one leadership team meeting where she had gone in, she (Zewdie) had given a speech and she basically walked out in tears saying 'you guys don't care', 'you guys don't care' and this had an enormous impact. I mean this is a female saying that you feel like you shouldn't be doing, it wasn't in the meeting itself but it was after the meeting in the corridors where she was stood with tears in her eyes saying 'I don't think it makes any difference to any of them'. That was something I remember as having an impact on the people who saw her so passionate, so committed and so disappointed by this blah blah blah that we gave her at the end. So we had a regional vice president who actually did listen to her and did give her more of a leadership role and she also got to Wolfensohn, one way or another... how she got to Wolfensohn I don't know... she seems to be on a mission, and in that sense she's a self-made leader of this, of this whole AIDS thing.[17]

Three months later Zewdie and Binswanger and a team of three other staff members had drafted the MAP as a concept that would only go to the board once, as an adaptable programme loan where the Bank would commit US$1billion to the overall project and the vice president for the region would approve individual credits to individual countries. The concept of this process was grounded in knowledge that the process of inception to implementation within the Bank could take anywhere between 6 months to 3 years. As HIV/AIDS was seen to elicit an emergency response, this new approach to Bank funding was approved. The announcement of a new HIV/AIDS strategic plan was launched in September 1999 and the first US$500 million MAP funds for 'MAP-1' were approved the following year. MAP funds were available to any country in sub-Saharan Africa that had a national strategic plan to fight HIV/AIDS; a national co-ordinating body; and a commitment to directing 40–60 per cent of funds to CSOs. In MAP-1 countries were able to choose from three types of funding: 100 per cent grant, credit with 0 per cent interest or a loan with interest (World Bank 2007a).[18] The project was an institutional first for the amount of money committed to the project, and demonstrates a new flexibility to funding responsive to the needs and pressing issues of individual countries. An adaptable programme loan would ensure all countries would have access to the funds, and all subsequent HIV/AIDS programmes would follow the same structure.

The story of Zewdie, Binswanger and Brazil is still perpetuated by the Bank. However, the influence ascribed to these two staff members is overemphasised when considering the size and clear hierarchy of the Bank's bureaucracy. The role of Zewdie and Binswanger as agents within the Bank provides an insight into the black box of decision-making within the institution; they are also important catalysts to getting the MAP onto the Bank's agenda. The case of Zewdie and Binswanger and the role of Brazil are important factors for understanding why the executive directors of the Bank came to recognise HIV/AIDS as an issue that is central to its operations and a bankable project that it should invest in. Nevertheless, the expression, structure and application of the MAP are very much grounded within the Bank's wider good governance and health agenda.

The prescriptions that countries had to adopt in receipt of MAP money stemmed from the Bank's wider institutional development, culminating in the third explanation of the origins of the MAP: the good governance reform agenda. The MAP encapsulates the central features of the good governance reform package: partnership, state ownership, sharing of knowledge and civil society inclusion. It is intrinsically linked with the Bank's previous history of demonstrating its relevance through ensuring borrowing-state dependency, manipulating change in the international system and ensuring member state support. The Bank took the successful elements of the Brazilian projects and adapted them to fit within its over-arching liberal commitment to good governance reform. The MAP ensures dependency by reaffirming its role as lender of last resort by offering the first multi-sectoral financing of an HIV/AIDS project by any international organisation. This, in turn, ensures member state and international system support, as the Bank demonstrates its unique ability to identify and design a project that builds upon existing responses to the epidemic at subcontinent scale and reaffirms the Bank's commitment to a holistic approach to development and its position at the centre of development knowledge. Central to the Bank's ability to do so is the role of key individuals manipulating each of these factors to the project's gain.

Community as the central basis of civil society inclusion within the MAP does not represent a shift in the Bank's approach. The Bank has used community groups as central components of its operations since structural adjustment in the 1980s, and within public health since the 1978 Alma Ata Declaration. The community element of the MAP has not arisen out of a commitment from individuals such as Zewdie and Wolfensohn, but is grounded within sector-wide approaches to health practised by the Bank since the 1980s. What is different about the MAP however is that it embraces a wider process of governance reform that is not just limited to the economy and the state, but encompasses the individual and the community. Good governance and the MAP brings the state back in to where it once was within the Bank's founding principles of partnership. The MAP represents the reproduction of liberal processes of participation, inclusion and transparency at every level of state, society and the individual that are achieved through neoliberal economic incentive. This has been seen in general trends within the Bank's approach to global health but not at the financial level, geographical spread, and over-arching ambition of the MAP. The MAP thus represents the most intrusive extension of the Bank's good governance agenda in sub-Saharan Africa. The success and ability of the MAP is however constrained by the institutional contradictory antecedents of both the project and the governance reform agenda itself: the need to put states at the centre of the Bank's activities while opening up the Bank to non-state actors and emphasising the central role of the community and sector-wide approaches, and, despite an emphasis on liberal forms of development, the use of *neo*liberal incentive to implement reform.

Conclusion

This chapter has explored the institutional foundations of the World Bank's multi-sectoral agenda for HIV/AIDS by mapping where the agenda comes from as a means of explaining what the agenda looks like. The Bank's health agenda is firmly rooted in the process of good governance reform that has been a central operating principle of the Bank since its inception. The state and the community are as fundamental as the economy in the promotion and realisation of governance reform. The antecedents of multi-sectoralism are grounded in the Bank's ability to adapt and change in response to internal and external criticisms by affirming its commitment to its founding principles of development and state partnership. Change occurs through a process of perceived inclusion of external non-state parties, structured in such a way as to include local communities in borrower countries and exclude larger NGOs that have leverage and access to the Bank. The second manner in which change occurs is through the reassertion of the Bank's position as a leader in development knowledge. Health has been a central component of this need to adapt to maintain relevance; however, the Bank's record on health policies also demonstrates how in practice the Bank really has only made minor adjustments rather than substantive institutional change. The Bank's health policy has long involved emphasis on private provision and a form of multi-sectorality, which under good governance reform has become consolidated and widely applied within the MAP. The Bank is able to set the global HIV/AIDS agenda, by shifting the perception of HIV/AIDS as a health issue to understanding it as a development concern. The Bank is then able to apply its good governance approach to carrying out development through significant multilateral funds and claims to knowledge. Multi-sectoralism and the Bank's role in HIV/AIDS are not new, and have not come from a wider recognition of the need for more participatory decision-making but rather should be understood as a natural progression of the Bank's original mandate for reconstruction and development. Good governance sees the application of this initial mandate to not only bringing the state back in to the economism of healthcare reform, but emphasises the role of the community and the individual in the application of this reform. This reform is based upon the central tenets of liberalism, with the role of the neoliberal free market very much at the fore. For the Bank a problem like HIV/AIDS can be addressed by first using the similar model of state leadership that was such a success in Brazil, but then adapting such a model to fully include civil society actors and individuals to promote transparency and accountability in decision-making while maintaining the primacy of the market economy, i.e. *extended* good governance. The problem here is that on application this type of good governance reform leads to contradictory outcomes and is often only achievable through the provision of economic incentive, particularly in sub-Saharan Africa, particularly in HIV/AIDS governance. As Chapter 3 shows, this is most acutely evident with the application of the MAP to the state.

3   Owning HIV/AIDS

The state

At the centre of the World Bank's commitment to multi-sectoral interventions into HIV/AIDS is the state. As every HIV/AIDS epidemic around the world has shown, it is impossible to fully address the disease and its impact without the state acknowledging the problem. Similarly, as the Bank's development orthodoxy has shown, good governance reform cannot work without fully incorporating various parts of the state, most notably the president or prime minister and the Ministry of Finance. Thus, to address HIV/AIDS through a specific form of governance reform based on ownership, responsibility, transparency, participation and accountability, interventions must focus a significant amount of funds and initiatives on the infrastructure of state institutions. Within the MAP it is the role of the president, Ministries of Health and the National AIDS Councils (NACs) that are the focus of such reform. These areas of the state in sub-Saharan Africa carry out the following functions in regard to the MAP: co-ordinating the national response, providing leadership and direction in articulating national strategic plans and breaking stigma, and, crucially, engaging with civil society groups. For the Bank, interventions are based on helping states develop their capacity to fully acknowledge and respond to the impact HIV/AIDS is having upon its population. However, as this chapter will show, these state-based interventions have mixed rates of success. The state response is often fraught with problems of capacity, bureaucracy, corruption, confusion and institutional rivalry. Although some of these problems are endemic within specific states, the application of multi-sectoralism and the Bank's governance reform agenda has exacerbated and in some cases created them. The state structures established as part of the MAP and the problems associated with them reveal the contradictions inherent to the application of the Bank's governance reform agenda and the problem of enacting change and ownership through economic incentive.

This chapter provides substantive evidence of what the World Bank's HIV/AIDS governance reform agenda looks like in practice at the level of state institutions. It pursues this aim by first looking at the national translations of the Kenyan, Tanzanian and Ugandan MAPs to mark out any specific institutional differences. Second, the chapter considers the role of presidents and the construction of 'the war on AIDS'. Third, the chapter outlines the role of the NACs and their decentralised counterparts, before focusing on the Ministry of Health and the Ministry

of Finance. Fourth, the chapter then assesses some of the constraints and problems associated with the state-led response to HIV/AIDS, and the mechanisms
introduced to address these issues. Fifth, the chapter draws together what these
functions and problems say about the Bank's HIV/AIDS agenda and governance
reform more generally. The chapter argues that the Bank has made the state key
to effective HIV/AIDS governance through the introduction of new state structures that have come to embed its multi-sectoral agenda. However, these structures and the application of multi-sectoralism are driven by neoliberal economic
incentive as opposed to a will or intent on the part of the government. Where
the state is found wanting the Bank has introduced the role of local civil society
actors as forms of private service delivery. This has resulted in confusion about
ownership, transparency and governance of the national HIV/AIDS response, and
consequently a large amount of funds being channelled to the response with little
co-ordination, direction or national identity of each country's strategic plan for
combating the disease.

National translation of the MAP

The importance of the state is evident in the World Bank's consistent reiteration
that the MAP is a state-based project. According to the Bank, each state is to own
its MAP project by participating in its design and decision-making about how
funds should be spent and what issues should be prioritised. However, fundamentally, the structure, ideology and purpose of the project remain the same in each
country. Each of the three countries adheres to the central principles of the MAP:
(i) evidence of a strategic plan designed in a participatory manner; (ii) existence of
a high-level co-ordinating body with broad representation of all sectors; (iii) government commitment to quick implementation arrangements, including channelling grant funds directly to CSOs and the community – nominally 40–60 per cent
of MAP funds; and (iv) agreement by the government to use multiple implementation agencies, especially NGOs and community groups, in the response (World
Bank 2000a–e; World Bank 2003a–d). The three projects, the KHADREP, the
TMAP and the UACP, all have a near-identical working structure and institutional
agencies. Each has a National HIV/AIDS Council established under the MAP, the
National AIDS Control Council (NACC) in Kenya, the Tanzania Commission for
HIV/AIDS (TACAIDS) in Tanzania, and the Uganda AIDS Commission (UAC)
in Uganda, and decentralised agencies working within local government. These
three HIV/AIDS councils demonstrate an adherence to the multi-sectoral tenets of
the MAP through their apparent commitment to participation with non-state actors
and the private sector, the importance of government ownership, and the need to
involve multiple sectors of the state in the governance of HIV/AIDS (World Bank
2000a–e; 2003a–d).

The blueprint nature of the MAP is reflective of the ahistorical approach to
governance reform Harrison describes wherein the Bank ignores different social
and political demographics between different states. As this chapter shows, this is
true of the MAP. There are, however, minor nuances to how Kenya, Tanzania and

Uganda interpret the MAP's main framework. The contexts and country-specific differences suggest each of the countries' individual MAPs as being government owned and designed, as they resemble slight deviations from the overall framework of the MAP.

Kenya

KHADREP in Kenya was one of the two original MAP projects. As such, KHADREP reflected the central principles and objectives of the Bank at the time of the MAP's inception: rapid disbursement of funds to the community and breaking the silence surrounding HIV/AIDS. These two factors were paramount at the time of KHADREP's implementation and were prioritised over targeted outcomes.[1] The rapid disbursal and widespread response led to US$50 million being channelled to 6,000 community groups.[2] The originality, scale and speed of the response undermined the Bank's ability to monitor the funds or have targeted interventions. Since the inception of KHADREP there has been a growth of multilateral and bilateral donors to HIV/AIDS with shifting priorities and funds. As a result, the Bank has drawn up the Total War on AIDS (TWOA) project as a MAP-2 intervention. The TWOA represents a more structured intervention that moves away from the central principles of the MAP, as enshrined in the KHADREP, and targets activities in line with the Kenya National AIDS Strategic Plan (KNASP) (National AIDS Control Council 2005a). The NACC decided the priority areas and objectives of the TWOA and then referred them to the Bank for approval. The key aim for the TWOA is to 'fill a gap where nobody else wants to go' by targeting critical areas with the overall aim of reducing infection rates.[3]

Uganda

The ethos behind the UACP is similar to that of the KHADREP. Despite the existence of high-level political support in Uganda, which was not present in Kenya at the time of the MAP, the UACP was still based on the over-arching objective of a massive increase in the community response to the epidemic. The UACP is a decentralised model loosely based upon a previous District Health Service project in Uganda.[4] Different from Kenya and Tanzania, the UAC was established in 1992, previous to the MAP or 'The Three Ones'.[5] However, under the UACP, the Commission undertook a major overhaul, with a massive increase in funds and the hiring of new staff from other line ministries within the Uganda civil service, many of which had been working on the Bank-sponsored Sexually Transmitted Infections project.[6] This overhaul was mainly funded by the Bank. In comparison with Kenya and Tanzania, Uganda is a much smaller country, therefore the scope of the project is smaller and access and capacity building more straightforward. In addition to geographical space, the UAC and the UACP differ from the Kenyan and Tanzanian projects as the UACP does not cover the whole of the country. Northern Uganda does not fit under the remit of the UACP because of the ongoing conflict between the government and the Lords Resistance Army (LRA). HIV/ AIDS work in this area is covered under the Northern Uganda Social Action Fund (NUSAF). Although the UAC is still active, the UACP closed in 2006 without a MAP-2 project or alternative Bank funding to replace it.

Tanzania

The TMAP was the latest of the three MAP projects to be implemented. The project differs from the UACP and the KHADREP in its introduction of regional facilitating agents (RFAs) to co-ordinate the response at the regional level, and its subproject the Zanzibar Multi-Sectoral AIDS Project (ZMAP) complete with semi-autonomous AIDS Council, the Zanzibar AIDS Commission (ZAC).[7] Both of these councils are sustained by government funds, not World Bank funds, as in the case of Kenya and Uganda. A key point of contention in Tanzania is the disproportionate amount of funds channelled to the public sector instead of CSOs. Although this is also evident in Kenya and Uganda, it was only expressed by CSOs as a problem in Tanzania.[8] Tanzania differs from Kenya and Uganda in its history of being relatively closed to outside donors, particularly INGOs.[9] As a result, compared with countries such as Kenya and Uganda, which have a strong INGO presence, in Tanzania there are only 19 INGOs that are considered to have 'any credibility.'[10] TACAIDS has differed slightly to the UAC and the NACC in showing some evidence of resisting advice from the Bank. For example, TACAIDS refused to appoint a financial management company to handle MAP funds, instead agreeing that the money would be channelled through the Ministry of Finance, as well as challenging the Bank on funding delays and over-bureaucratic procedure.[11]

The slight adjustments to the MAP made by each state suggest a degree of autonomy in interpreting the over-arching framework. However, much of this difference can be attributed to the timings of each of the projects. All three projects were in the 'emergency' phase of MAP-1 and MAP-2, where the Bank placed emphasis on getting the money to the ground and 'learning by doing' (World Bank 2007a). The slight differences between the three projects can be used as evidence of ownership and the Bank responding to state needs. However, as the rest of this chapter will show, minor changes made to the MAP model and country-specific variations should not detract from the significant patterns of change and reconfiguration pursued by the Bank at the state level. This is evident not only within those organisations ascribed to addressing the HIV/AIDS epidemic in a specific country, but also within senior government office and the role of the executive in leadership.

Presidents and the war on AIDS

The adoption of the Bank's HIV/AIDS projects and the success of state-led interventions are dependent upon the role of the president. Since the inception of the MAP, and the increased availability of HIV/AIDS financing, presidents within sub-Saharan Africa such as Mwai Kibaki of Kenya, Jakaya Kikwete of Tanzania and Yoweri Museveni of Uganda have all called for a 'war on AIDS'. Museveni was unique in the leadership role in combating HIV/AIDS at the outset of his presidency, which has since become a key component in Uganda's labelling as a 'success story' in the fight against HIV/AIDS. Explanations of why Museveni adopted such a role are blurred. A popular argument and Ugandan rumour is that at the time of Museveni's rise to power through a military coup in 1985, soldiers and civilians began to exhibit symptoms of HIV/AIDS. Aware of the fragility of his power, and – according to rumours in Uganda – under the advice of Fidel Castro, Museveni sought to encourage voluntary testing and counselling first within the army and then within the wider aspects of society as a means of maintaining political stability. What is not rumour, however, is how Museveni's willingness to talk about HIV/AIDS and a leadership role led to wider financial commitments and support from the donor community.

Presidents must be seen to commit to combating stigma and be seen to be taking the epidemic seriously in order to receive donor funding and approval from the international community. Those presidents and states that are willing to declare 'war' against the epidemic are seen as appropriate countries in which to invest resources and hence become prioritised by institutions such as the World Bank as models of best practice or 'good' reformers in terms of intervention. To acquire the label of 'good' HIV/AIDS reformers, presidents must be seen to do the following. First, they must declare a 'war on HIV/AIDS'. This has been done effectively by the Kenyan government in the labelling of their second MAP project, the TWOA, as 'total war on AIDS.' The emergence of the TWOA follows on from several speeches by President Mwai Kibaki, who has often used 'war on AIDS' rhetoric as a means of signalling his leadership and willingness to break stigma surrounding the epidemic. This is the second component of the president's role; they must show prominent leadership in breaking stigma. In July 2007 as part of a drive to get people tested in Tanzania, President Jakaya Kikwete and his wife Salma Kikwete took a public voluntary HIV test with the president announcing 'In the war against HIV/AIDS, voluntary testing is the first line of defence' (Mwamunyange 2007). However, Kikwete is one of the few leaders in sub-Saharan Africa to take such a prominent test. Other leaders address issues of stigma through working to promote cultural change. For example, Prime Minister Raila Odinga has been influential in promoting male circumcision as an additional means of reducing HIV transmission among the Luo community in Kenya by meeting with the Luo Council of Elders and admitting to having the operation himself. Hence, leaders must not only speak out on such issues, but, third, must be seen to lead by example. Fourth, as a central element of multi-sectorality, presidents must show willing towards civil society actors. In practice this often translates to photographs with civil society groups to mark World AIDS Day and emphasising the need to involve every aspect of the community within public speeches or pronouncements on HIV/AIDS.

As the various examples indicate, there is a general willingness for state leaders to perform these functions of good HIV/AIDS governance. However, apart from a few isolated incidents of leading by example and rhetorical statements that would appear typical of elected officials, there is much to suggest there is little substantive commitment to addressing HIV/AIDS, particularly in regard to thorny issues for African states such as homosexuality and the status of women. Homosexuality is illegal in Kenya, Tanzania and Uganda, which is not problematic for the states' leaders, as for them it does not exist. For example, following his earlier leadership in breaking stigma and addressing Uganda's HIV/AIDS epidemic, Museveni has since stated that 'Uganda has no homosexuals'. Not stopping there, Museveni has gone on to speak about the disease as 'not a serious sickness', and people who become infected with HIV as 'instead of becoming an asset you become a burden' (Global AIDS Alliance 2007). Museveni's claims have come into much criticism by HIV/AIDS campaigners across the world, but have not received significant criticism from HIV/AIDS activists in Uganda. Although other Presidents have not been as outspoken as Museveni, homosexuality denial remains and the underlying socioeconomic drivers of the epidemic such as women's access to property rights go unaddressed, and issues such as mandatory as opposed to voluntary testing and testing within the armed forces remain contentious within government policy.

The wives of presidents have similarly been looked on to perform leadership roles by engaging in awareness-raising activities such as the International Women's AIDS Run. However, as with the case of Museveni, this role has also been accompanied by controversy. For example, in 2006 Lucy Kibaki caused a debate in Kenya when she suggested young people had no need to learn about condoms as a means of protecting themselves against HIV/AIDS as they were not effective forms of prevention (BBC 2006). Similarly, Janet Museveni has spoken out against educating young people about condoms, with some reports suggesting she has argued that condoms cause AIDS (Human Rights Watch 2005). Presidents have done as much as possible to distance themselves from such claims, but the statements of leaders wives attract attention from the media, and, crucially, international donors.

The role of presidents is instructive about the role of the state within the Bank's wider HIV/AIDS governance reform. Presidents perform the functions necessary to present themselves as 'good' leaders of HIV/AIDS governance, by using the rhetoric of war, and presenting a public example in specific areas of HIV/AIDS prevention, treatment and care. However, such 'good' reform is often lacking in any real substance, with presidents performing a ceremonious role in HIV/AIDS leadership while failing to address some of the key drivers of the epidemic. Similar to problems with the full implementation of structural adjustment, leaders show a general willingness to address the issue of HIV/AIDS based upon multi-sectoral principles of good governance while remaining relatively closed off from any real change. This in itself could be seen as evidence that the Bank's influence upon changing the behaviour of the executive towards HIV/AIDS is limited. However, the role of the executive in endorsing national strategic plans drawn up in line with the central tenets of the MAP and the positioning of the National AIDS Councils within the Office of the President/Prime Minister suggests otherwise.

The National AIDS Council system

Each country's MAP is organised through the NAC system. This system is loosely organised around the NACs operating at the national level, District HIV/AIDS Councils (DACs) organising HIV/AIDS responses at the district or ward level, and community or village AIDS councils or initiatives at the community level. Alongside these HIV/AIDS councils are line ministry-specific HIV/AIDS committees or control units with the principle role of mainstreaming the epidemic through the activities of the state. It is the responsibility of the NACs to co-ordinate the activities of this system, as well as work with the Ministry of Health and develop partnerships with CSOs. It is through the NAC system that the Bank is able to apply its own form of good governance reform to the HIV/AIDS response. This occurs through the establishment of norms of good multi-sectoral governance within the system, the structuring of national strategic plans to mainstream and develop such norms in practice, and the sidelining of the Ministry of Health as the principle state actors in the national HIV/AIDS response.

What are the NACs and DACs?

The NACs are governmental bodies, predominantly located within the Office of the President or the Office of the Prime Minister, with the primary responsibility of co-ordinating the national response to HIV/AIDS and managing the MAP. The role of the NACs has developed over the course of the implementation of MAPs in different countries. The main role of the NACs is to co-ordinate the national response to HIV/AIDS by identifying those CSOs that should receive funds, strengthening the DACs, working with partners to articulate the national strategic plan, mobilising partners and working with line ministries and donors in strengthening capacity and filling the gaps in the national response to HIV/AIDS.[12] The Bank promotes the NACs as being the owners of each respective project.[13] The Bank views ownership as the main method of project sustainability as it makes governments articulate the response and push the agenda themselves. Key to this is the ability of governments to recognise and 'internalise' HIV/AIDS as their own problem.[14] As such, the NACs have the overall responsibility of CSO engagement through the selection and co-ordination of funding and dialogue, with the Bank absolving itself from responsibility through the reiteration of government ownership.

The methods of CSO relations deployed by the NAC system reflect the Bank's central approach to engagement: funding, dialogue and feedback, partnerships and networking. Engagement under the MAP has two tracks: the first is of NGOs at the national level, and the second is of community groups at the community level. In contrast to the 5,000–6,000 community groups funded under each country-specific MAP, on average 25 NGOs are funded at the national level in each of the three countries studied. The difference between a community group and a national NGO in this context is that national NGOs operate across the country whereas community groups work in a specific, smaller local community.[15] Access, funding and feedback from community groups to the Bank occur within a decentralised governance structure through the DACs. These agencies function as the intermediaries between the community and the NACs, and the implementers of the community component of the MAP. The DACs plan the district's response to HIV/AIDS in line with the national strategic plan, draw up and manage the district HIV/AIDS budget, facilitate community sensitisation and awareness raising of the MAP, design and issue the call for proposals, disburse funds to the community, conduct monitoring and evaluation of funds, and feed information back to the NACs and the Bank.[16] The DACs are responsible for the co-ordination of all CSOs active in one area: they should be aware of their coverage, activities and outcomes. The average DAC in Uganda is supposed to co-ordinate 10,000 CSOs, 500 of which they supervise under the Community HIV/AIDS Initiative (CHAI).[17] The number of DACs per country varies with size and the government, but the scope of CSOs they cover is approximately the same.

As district representatives of the NACs, the DACs work in close association with their national counterparts. The NACs are responsible for the training and monitoring of the DACs, and sensitising them to the issue of HIV/AIDS and community engagement through the provision of workshops, information materials and funding.[18] The NACs approve the overall funding allocation to the community under the respective community components of the MAP. All activity at district level is reported to the NACs through quarterly reports. The NACs visit the district at least annually to assess any problems or gaps in training or capacity or to conduct workshops within the community. The DACs are involved in wider co-ordination, discussion groups, such as annual reviews, and national planning.[19] Of those DACs interviewed, the majority described their relationships with the NACs as good and supportive.[20] These representatives view the NACs as an extension of the Bank and the MAP but still reiterate an interest in the Bank visiting and interacting with the DACs directly.[21]

The NACs designed the frameworks through which CSOs engage. In Tanzania, Joseph Temba, the Director of Policy and Planning TACAIDS, and Rustica Tembele, Director of Community and District Response TACAIDS, describe how the concept for the Community Action Fund (CAF) existed prior to the MAP, and that once in receipt of MAP funds, the Fund came to fruition as a result of TACAIDS–Bank consultation.[22] The Community HIV/AIDS Initiative (CHAI) in Uganda was drawn up independently of the Bank. This was the same in Kenya and in Tanzania.[23] The three community elements of the MAP – CHAI in Uganda, the CAF in Tanzania, and the Kenyan HIV/AIDS Community Initiative – demonstrate clear similarities between each other and the recommendations outlined within the MAP. Despite claims that these programmes existed in theory before the MAP, they were designed by the NACs that came into being after the MAP and reflect the project's main objectives.

Central to the operations of the NACs and DACs is each country's national strategic plan. National strategic AIDS plans are put together in collaboration with the NACs, Ministry of Health, CSOs and international donors such as the World Bank. On average each strategic plan is applied to a 4-year time period.

Each plan typically begins with a foreword from the president/prime minister reasserting the need to continue efforts in the war on HIV/AIDS. The plans outline the central challenges and priorities of each country's epidemic; the core principles of the response; and methods of implementing and financing the strategy. Key to this is an over-arching strategic vision that all aspects of the state must come together to work towards combating HIV/AIDS. Each plan has a results framework based upon planned results, deadlines and delivery strategies. The framework clearly indicates which part of the state is the lead agency in delivering these results and their state-based partners. The strategic plans exist separately to the MAP but they exhibit several similarities in their over-arching objectives and strategic vision, particularly in the number of non-state actors involved in preparing the document and the emphasis upon the need to adopt a multi-sectoral approach that sees HIV/AIDS as a development problem not a centralised health issue. The plans, as with the NACs and DACs, adopt the language of multi-sectoral participation, ownership, partnership and accountability as operative norms of good HIV/AIDS governance. The adoption of multi-sectorality and the need to draw up the plan in partnership with multiple agencies have only been present within national strategic plans, if they existed at all, since the arrival of the MAP.

The World Bank, UNAIDS and the NAC system

The Bank sees itself as a liaison officer that facilitates the government's involvement in HIV/AIDS and moderates the design of projects so that there is a fair system of checks and balances between different levels of governance. Further to this, the Bank provides assistance to the NACs in establishing systems and structures, and supervises the implementation of the MAP.[24] The relationship between the Bank and the NACs is very close, with each party viewing dialogue as participatory, fair and balanced.[25] The success of such a relationship is the result of individual personalities, professional relationships and backgrounds. The task team leaders contributing to the MAP are predominantly economists with health specialist backgrounds.[26] For example, Albertus Voetberg, the World Bank Senior Health Specialist in Kenya, has been attributed by many to be the key individual to translate the MAP from principle into practice as a result of his presence, commitment and dedication.[27] In regard to the NACs, a common perception of TACAIDS is that nothing would happen without Joseph Temba, the Director for Policy and Planning: 'there isn't anybody really except for Joseph Temba'.[28] Temba responds to this claim by suggesting he is TACAIDS' focal point and that at TACAIDS' initial inception the organisation only had three members of staff, therefore the work of others can go unrecognised.[29] The lack of individual in-country presence is seen as problematic by some organisations, as they find it difficult to establish a working rapport and ongoing partnerships with such people.

In viewing the NACs as their natural counterpart to co-ordinating the HIV/AIDS response, UNAIDS has played a central role in strengthening the capacity of the NACs. UNAIDS strengthens the NACs' capacity through advocacy work, sharing strategic information, monitoring and evaluation, promoting stakeholder, nominally CSO, inclusion and resource mobilisation, with the overall aim of making sure the NACs are able to deliver on their objectives in line with each country's strategic plan.[30] Other UN agencies complement UNAIDS by offering issue-specific work, such as the United Nations Fund for Women (UNIFEM) assisting in the integration of gender into the NAC planning processes. Futures Group, who have a contract with the UK Department for International Development (DFID) to implement and co-ordinate their HIV/AIDS work, operate in line with NAC structures and participate in the multi-donor institutional reviews of the NACs. This commitment to working through and strengthening the capacity of the NACs by multiple donors and international agencies demonstrates the widespread recognition the NAC system has as the central state actor within the governance of the disease. What is significant about this recognition is the multi-sectoral approach to HIV/AIDS governance that the NACs embody in their emphasis on participation, ownership, decentralisation and civil society inclusion. The role of the NACs sees the removal of HIV/AIDS from the health sector. Ministries of Health still have a crucial role to play in the state governance of the HIV/AIDS response, yet their functions and roles are effectively managed by the Bank so as to limit their over-arching influence on the HIV/AIDS agenda.

Ministries of Health

In all three countries, the Ministry of Health provides the technical arm of the response: addressing medical issues of anti-retroviral therapy (ART), opportunistic infections, voluntary counselling and testing (VCT), prevention of mother-to-child transmission (PMTCT), procurement, logistics, and technical support for hospitals and health centres. Each of the Ministries of Health, except Uganda, has a special HIV/AIDS agency: National STD and HIV/AIDS Control Programme (NASCOP) of Kenya; National AIDS Control Programme (NACP) in Tanzania; and Zanzibar AIDS Control Programme (ZACP) in Zanzibar. However, these agencies were not seen as suitable actors in which to co-ordinate the response because of a commitment to non-health-based responses and the problems faced by Ministries of Health across the region. In Tanzania, the Ministry of Health reflects the knock-on impact of structural adjustment discussed in Chapters 1 and 2, with a large number of health staff positions under-filled. Managerially, Ministries of Health are seen as inefficient throughout the world. These systems are strengthened with WHO technical support, resource mobilisation, training materials and policy guidance.[31] However, the HIV/AIDS sections of the Ministry of Health remain clinically oriented with few sectoral ministries accepting their authority. The Bank uses the clinical focus of the Ministry of Health as justification for the establishment of the NACs. For the Bank, the state needed to have a regulating body that prioritised a multi-sectoral approach to HIV/AIDS alongside the health sector dimension.[32]

The shift of HIV/AIDS from a health issue to a development one is conducted at the state level in a strategic manner so as to not fully alienate the Ministry of Health. Central to the Bank's good governance reform is the full willingness of the state to own or adopt such reform. This needs to be throughout the state, and thus inclusive of the Ministry of Health. The Bank attempts to achieve this by not abandoning the health sector altogether in terms of HIV/AIDS interventions but providing assistance on technical support, procurement and supply chain issues, and a general commitment to strengthening health systems (World Bank 2007g). These functions however tend to be *ad hoc,* and there remains no over-arching project that commits to health sector strengthening in HIV/AIDS delivery as the MAP. An example of the Bank's *ad hoc* interventions can be seen in the area of anti-retroviral drugs. The shift in focus towards ART provision has seen an uptake of people on treatment but is marred by its lack of sustainability. A central problem with ART is the absorptive capacity of the existing structures: an understaffed Ministry of Health means there are fewer people to help administer the drugs effectively, there is little accurate data on who is infected with HIV, their CD4 count and therefore who is requiring the drugs. Transport is problematic with rural areas being virtually inaccessible, and the majority of people with HIV/AIDS live in rural communities with limited access to treatment and care facilities, e.g. 45 per cent of the population in Tanzania have access to health services.[33] A major concern of the NACs is how to sustain such treatment without the funding of the US President's Emergency Plan for AIDS Relief (PEPFAR) and within the irregularities of the Global Fund, as it cannot be afforded by the majority of the population in East Africa or the governments.[34] In such cases it is often the Bank that steps in to provide *ad hoc* support.

In practice the Bank's involvement in the health aspect of the HIV/AIDS response through *ad hoc* interventions in procurement and the operations of the Ministry of Health have several repercussions for the effectiveness of state level HIV/AIDS governance reform as confusion about agency mandates, institutional rivalry and capacity issues become evident. Similar to the role of the president within states, the application of the MAP shows a disjuncture between the rhetoric of HIV/AIDS governance adopted by the state and the practical ramifications of such governance reform.

Ownership and implementation: problems and contradictions with the NACs

Since its inception within the MAP, the NAC system has suffered several problems. The first of these is perhaps the most obvious: that the introduction of any new government agency with a large mandate would face institutional bureaucracy and a problem with capacity. However, this problem has been compounded by evidence of corruption and subsequent frustration and mistrust between the NACs and DACs and those bodies they are meant to partner: CSOs, donors and the Ministry of Health. Underlying each of these problems has been a discrepancy over the NAC mandate to both co-ordinate the national response and implement the MAP. This discrepancy arises from the practical application of the good governance approach to multi-sectorality, which promotes a specific form of ownership and partnership reform that is both contradictory and counteractive in practice.

Bureaucracy and capacity

Upon implementation, the structures and processes of the NACs were cumbersome and bureaucratic. As management units, they added an additional layer of bureaucracy to already complex government–donor relations. The levels of day-to-day bureaucratic inertia range within the NACs. TACAIDS seems consistent in its processes, deadlines and ability to keep appointments; UAC follows a similar pattern in consistency and transparency, yet could be problematic in terms of deadlines and appointments; however, the bureaucratic structures of the Kenyan NACC resemble a complex *ad hoc* system of protocol that is seemingly without process or procedure, varying by the day. Access to information depends on who you engaged with in the NACC, with some individuals being open; some changing the requirements necessary as if they were making them up, and other representatives denying any knowledge of individuals or previous processes.[35]

The institutional capacity of the NACs has been marked by underfunding, lack of staff and a rapid accumulation of responsibility. For example, as Nick Southern, Country Director of Care International Tanzania, puts it 'TACAIDS is still put upon in this country … its just volume of expectation … it is simply the expectation of that organisation, and that doesn't mean they deliberately don't fulfil that requirement, its just unrealistic', with TACAIDS mandate being 'the Mother of all deliverables'.[36] Initially established to manage the MAP, the NACs now have the responsibility of bilateral basket funds, the Global Fund and co-ordinating all HIV/AIDS activities in-country. Capacity issues are the responsibility, not the fault, of the NACs. Fault lies in the design and responsibilities placed upon them by international donors, principally the Bank, and CSOs arising out of the empowerment and government ownership models advocated by such donors. The need for one co-ordinating body within the response, the rapid demands of funding disbursal, preference towards CSO funding not government funding, and the multiplicity of actors involved in the response, all place stress upon the NACs' capacity and confuse their initial mandate. International organisations such as UNAIDS and CSOs view this as a result of their inability to delegate responsibility to their partners, such as the Ministry of Health.[37] Staff members within the NACs are targeted as lacking the skills and ability needed to support the community and partner CSOs effectively. As the World Bank suggests, the NACs are not bureaucratic, they are just new institutions with the responsibility of disbursing funds rapidly without systems and procedures clearly in place. Added to this, the NACs then have to manage a different set of procedures under the different funding requirements of donors.

Problems with capacity and bureaucracy have been most acutely felt within the DACs. The emphasis upon rapid disbursement under the MAP led to the DACs being established with little understanding of the issues, mechanisms of governance, community engagement or training to address these gaps in knowledge. One community group – Kenya Orphans Rural Development Programme (KORDP) – complained the DACs had not even heard of common issues such as psychosocial support[38] and that they were disinclined to engage with them. The DACs are understaffed and underfunded. The existing staff members lack sufficient training and all are dependent upon funding to conduct any form of CSO engagement. Management and disbursal of funds leaves minimal time and ability to co-ordinate activities within the district, the DACs central role.[39] The burden of the DACs and their limited ability to manage such burden results in the slow disbursal of funds and a lack of absorptive capacity within the communities themselves.[40] Despite the large sum of money being channelled to HIV/ AIDS, little reaches the community, as the structures do not exist to get it there. As with the case of the NACs, the introduction of new donors and different funding structures overwhelms the DACs. As Morris Lekule of TACAIDS described, 'LGAs [local government authorities] working in collaboration with CSOs wasn't our culture.'[41] MAP funds earmarked to 'familiarise' DAC staff with the concept, were in effect training to teach them the 'operationalisation of a multi-sectoral approach.' As such, every level of DAC–CSO engagement is 'determined by the centre.'[42] This has been a continuing problem for the MAP, and the responsibility has primarily been placed with the NACs to address the barriers to successful implementation. Significant sums of the MAP have gone to building the capacity of DACs or restructuring their existing frameworks. This funding is not just Bank money, but has come from other multilateral donors. For example, with the MAP ending in Tanzania in 2009, Round 9 of Global Fund money is being targeted through TACAIDS to strengthen the district response and local structures in addressing HIV/AIDS. This is money that is also supposed to be earmarked for local community groups and national NGOs.

Corruption and allowances

A further problem with the capacity and bureaucracy of the NAC system has been that of corruption and allowances. The perception of corruption presents a powerful obstacle to trust and collaboration between the NACs and their partners. Corruption has only been evident in Kenya and Uganda. In 2005, Uganda was tarnished by the Global Fund's withdrawal of support resulting from the discovery of the mismanagement of funds by an independent audit conducted by PriceWaterhouseCoopers. The Global Fund suspended all of its five grants to Uganda until the Ministry of Finance had established a structure that would ensure effective management of the funds (Global Fund 2007). This issue has since been rectified, and the Global Fund was quickly re-established in the country. Accusations of corruption are not commonly linked to Uganda, and the Global Fund issue was minor in comparison to the problems experienced by the Kenyan NACC and the country's wider reputation for corruption.[43] Levels of misappropriation were such that national NGOs alleged the then head of the NACC – Margaret Gachara – was reputedly paying herself KSh2 million (approximately £13,500) out of MAP funds earmarked for the community. This allegation was supported by the *Lancet*, which revealed the total sum of Gachara's financial impropriety was obtaining US$315,789 (approximately £157,894) in salary (Siringi 2004: 193). The embezzlement of funds resulted in a severe delay in disbursement and, subsequently, the implementation of the MAP. The corruption scandal led to all senior NACC management having to reapply for their jobs, removing the NACCs funding decision-making capability, the then Head of the Council being imprisoned and an external audit conducted by PriceWaterhouseCoopers. The NACC continues to face accusations of preferential treatment to CSOs of similar tribal identity and there are claims that 'there have been bigger thefts than that of the NACC',[44] although there is no clear evidence of this happening.

The Bank has been very vocal about the issue and has adapted a pragmatic view to such corruption, acknowledging its existence and shifting the focus on to how to address it. Albertus Voetberg, the ex-task team leader for the Kenyan KHADREP project and regional Bank representative for HIV/AIDS, explains how he addresses the issue:

> There is no question about whether there is corruption in the government, it is not even an issue. Even in the World Bank the question that should arise should not be whether there is corruption, the question should be what to do about it, and if you make bold statements that there is no corruption or is, you miss the point, and that I think is the biggest problem that we many times have this problem of a government that is not very proactive in addressing it, they seem to hide it, or ignore it, or deny it than coming out into the public and saying of course there are bad apples. There are 5,000 communities that receive funds I am actually very happy that there are only four that are corrupt. But we know that they are there, so the question comes how do we find them? What do we do about them? But if you say there is no corruption then to me it's useless talk. It puts people on the wrong footing, everybody knows there's corruption. Also in the World Bank we have an investigation unit, everyone knows there is corruption so we better find it. That is the attitude that we would like to see.[45]

Clear incidents of corruption are straightforward to acknowledge and signify an intention to address. Contentious issues that are not necessarily corrupt but point to a degree of unfair practice such as allowances are a much thornier issue for the World Bank. Allowances are a contentious issue within the bureaucratic nature of the DACs. Allowances exist to a degree in Kenya and Uganda and are widespread in Tanzania. Allowances are payments supplementary to wages. There is no clear definition of what they pay for, but in general reference to the DACs they are claimed when DAC representatives attend meetings away from their headquarters and/or go on community visits. Some organisations use them as a means of increasing staff salaries without pushing them into a higher tax bracket. Within the context of HIV/AIDS, allowance costs for attendance at meetings, food and community visits are required by DAC officials at the approximate amount of £20 per day. This is a barrier to effective community empowerment as the money paid to the DACs under allowances often comes directly from funds earmarked for community delivery, which in turn restricts the budget for community visits and direct engagement.[46] Allowances contradict the purpose of the DACs, as their existence acts as the only incentive for DACs to carry out their main responsibilities, representing a wider problem in the culture of those who work within them.[47]

These problems have been widely recognised by donors, NGOs and governments alike.[48] Donors such as USAID view these requirements as an allowable cost to be included within a specific project's budget whereas other donors do not.[49] The majority of donors treat it as a grey area open to interpretation at the local level. Governments will not restrict allowances, as they are similarly benefiting from their existence, whereas donors do not address the issue because they see it as an overt breach of sovereignty. International agencies such as the WHO see it as a government issue[50] and vice versa. Government officials either defend them or are pragmatic about the situation. The NACs are realistic in their awareness that unless you pay them, nothing would happen at the district level and that those meetings attended would only be the ones to pay allowances.[51]

The issues of corruption and allowances are not new or specific to HIV/AIDS and the MAP. However, apart from clear incidents of corruption, allowances remain unaddressed within the project. This is problematic as they present a barrier to the NACs and DACs fulfilling their function of engaging with CSOs and enhancing their participation within the MAP. CSOs and community groups that are in need of support are aware that the NACs and DACs have the money, and are in some cases using it for allowances that are supposed to be their very job. This does not help address a longstanding mistrust that has existed between the government and CSOs in each of the three countries. Bureaucracy complicates transparency and perceptions of NAC activity and thus does little to dispel CSO concerns or improve relations between the NACs and the communities they are meant to be working in partnership with.

NACs and CSOs

A 'healthy mistrust' exists between the NACs and the local community groups and national NGOs that represent the main forms of CSO within the MAP. This is despite the majority of CSOs interviewed in Tanzania and Uganda stating their support for the NACs and Kenyan respondents giving a more balanced view, with 9 per cent of those interviewed saying the NACC was good, and 19 per cent expressing it was bad. Discontent is more in evidence when exploring the CSOs' views in more detail. The research shows that mistrust is based upon specific CSOs' views that the NACs are political entities conditioned by wider government spending plans and objectives or a political institution that distorts outcomes and achievements to make the government look successful. Such views reflect traditional divisions between the government and civil society in East Africa. CSOs, such as the National Guidance and Empowerment Network of People Living with HIV/AIDS (NGEN+) in Uganda, prefer not to be involved in the UAC partnership committees, as once involved they have to agree to government policy and its financial and political 'monopoly' of the AIDS agenda under collective responsibility, when in certain instances the government acts against the needs of people living with HIV/AIDS.[52] Other CSOs interpret the actions of the NACs as directed by donor demands, and that for governments to realise their objectives in the response to HIV/AIDS they must be more dynamic in the management of such demand. Competing demands reduce the NACs disposition to actual governance of community empowerment, thus reducing the already limited space for social activity that exists in East African society.

The perceived bureaucratic nature of the DACs has engendered frustration rather than collaboration with CSOs of all forms.[53] CSOs have to establish relationships at every level of decentralised government and with all members of the DACs to achieve any outcome from engagement. Successful interaction is dependent upon the individuals that participate in dialogue and meetings, their objectives, outlook and personal relationships. DACs refer groups with specific concerns to the Ministry of Health and vice versa with little co-ordination between the two or established protocol about referrals. As is discussed in more detail in Chapter 4, CSOs feel that mistrust could be better managed by CSOs through improved co-ordination, presence within the community to gain first hand experience of the problems CSOs face, greater publicity of their work and the promotion of transparent funding methods to get rid of 'briefcase NGOs.'[54] These factors would minimise mistrust and as a consequence strengthen the response at the national level.

Who owns HIV/AIDS? The Ministry of Health and institutional rivalry

The fractious relationship between the NACs, DACs and the CSOs they are supposed to partner can similarly be applied to the NACs' relationship with Ministries of Health. Despite the Bank taking token measures to include the Ministry of Health within elements of its HIV/AIDS strategy, the shift in focus from a medical to a multi-sectoral response to HIV/AIDS has resulted in contention between them and the NACs. A particular source of contention was an overlap in implementation and an unclear delineation of roles and responsibilities.[55] George Tembo, Associate Director of UNAIDS, describes the turf wars and friction at the outset of the MAP, 'the Ministries of Health were initially the leaders of the response, they were the ones who were leading everything, then we started talking about the multi-sectoral approach, then the Ministry of Health felt threatened, "oh you're taking our turf" so there's friction.'[56]

A great force for contention was over who had ultimate authority over the national response, principally arising out of who had greater funds. In terms of authority, an anonymous representative of USAID in Uganda described the Ministry of Health as 'pissed' that they did not house the UACP; and Awene Gavyole, the WHO's HIV/AIDS focal point in Tanzania, explained 'there is some sort of "I am the authority and I am the technical person".'[57] The conflict between these two agencies is widely recognised as problematic in that they do not work together generating further overlap and distrust.[58] However, despite suggestion of conflict, representatives of the NACs and the Ministries of Health acknowledge a degree of initial animosity[59] but then consistently state their co-operative relationship, as Rustica Tembele of TACAIDS describes the relationship, 'for me, we are just a wedding.'[60] This commitment to providing a united front is normally done by both representatives of both parties issuing examples of their joint working practices and interlinkages between staff and committees.[61]

Divisions between state agencies and the balance governments must strike between international initiatives and national priorities are made more complex by the mushrooming of non-state actors, and the impact their presence within service delivery has upon the functioning and role of the state. The decline of the Ministry of Health as a result of the introduction of the NACs is characteristic of the Bank's governance reform, in which it promotes bodies within the executive and stresses new forms of ownership as replacement to existing structures and political cultures. However, bilateral money and the 'old guard' political structures of the state promote competition, but not the sort the Bank promotes. Underpinning this problem is a general confusion as to what the reformed NAC system should be doing – implementing or co-ordinating – and whether it really owns the MAP.

Ownership, confusion and compromise

Confusion as to the NACs' mandate exists over their role as co-ordinators of the national response and implementers of the MAP.[62] Representatives of the NACs, the World Bank and UN agencies all stress that the NAC's role is co-ordination not implementation.[63] However, in articulating the strategic plan, selecting those CSOs to receive MAP funds, monitoring and training the DACs, and strengthening public sector responses, the NACs are heavily involved in operational implementation. Initially the NACs were not supposed to engage in such activities, but the demands of the MAP resulted in them doing so, MAP-1 established the NACs as implementers and MAP-2 reinforced this role.[64] The NACs present their roles as co-ordination, but on further enquiry admit that they have become involved – unintentionally – in implementation. This presents a conflict of interests, confusion and overburden on the part of the NACs, rendering them unable to perform either co-ordination or implementation successfully. As co-ordinating bodies, the NACs should not house projects, as it contravenes the legal mandate by which they were established within the Office of the President/Prime Minister. This is problematic in the NACs wider relations with CSOs, as in implementing the project the NACs are directly competing for funds with the project's traditional implementation partners – CSOs. As one CSO characterises the situation 'how can you referee when you are a player?'[65]

The relationship between problems in funding mechanisms and the DACs are underpinned by the same contradiction between ownership and conditionality evident within the NACs. DAC staff members in all the countries considered acknowledge the influence of the MAP and World Bank priorities, yet reiterate ownership of the project through design of district HIV/AIDS work plans and the fact that, as Robert Okumu of Tororo District Council, Uganda, describes, 'all issues come from down here, at the District operational level, so that is why the District issues now we say is *our* strategic plan and *our* framework.'[66] However, the DACs did not exist prior to the MAP. District HIV/AIDS work plans are designed in partnership with the NACs under the guidelines of each specific national strategic plan, which represent the key principles of the MAP in each of the three countries studied. The DACs resisted CSO engagement, but had to agree to a CSO component of the district HIV/AIDS work plan in order to receive any funds.

The key factor that underpins the problems surrounding NAC capacity and their mandate is the discrepancy over ownership. Contrary to Bank and NAC affirmations of government ownership of the MAP, such ownership is articulated and directed by the Bank. Neither NACs nor CSOs were engaged in the design of the project as the MAP was a general framework within which country-specific variations would be designed and implemented in-country by states. The objectives and CSO engagement structures within the Kenyan, Tanzanian and Ugandan MAPs were created by the Bank. This is evident in two ways. First, the Bank used the MAP to establish or re-craft the NACs. The UAC in Uganda technically existed previous to the MAP but underwent an institutional reform and is now fully funded by the Bank under MAP funds, the NACC in Kenya is funded by the Bank and only existed in discussion paper form before the MAP, and TACAIDS in Tanzania was established under the MAP but is supported by government funds.[67] In Mozambique, a co-ordinating body already existed within the government; however, the task team leader of the MAP had to keep to the overall blueprint and insisted on establishing an additional body and subsequently causing friction with the government. If the government had refused it would have not received the badly needed funds.[68] In the UAC, once work-plans were articulated they had to be approved by the Bank; when the CSO proposals were reviewed the UAC prepared recommendations for the Bank's approval; and once the MAP was accepted, the UAC had to sign an agreement to support CSOs. In Tanzania, TACAIDS found the US$34 million out of the US$50 million MAP budget earmarked to line ministries disproportionate to that of the community fund. However, the Bank has not changed its position on the funding.[69] In all three cases the state level response to HIV/AIDS was relatively inactive. The central objective of the Bank was to use MAP funds to give states 'the push that was needed' to facilitate a high-level political commitment.[70] Thus not only did the Bank use the MAP as a catalyst for the NACs inception, it promoted an agenda that structured NAC practice alongside Bank good governance reform principles. Upon implementation of the MAP at country level, governments did not have a role in articulating the project's main objectives. Governments are only able to articulate the agenda by choosing to accept the terms and conditions of the initial contract.

The main example of Bank design of the structure and practice of the MAP is the requirement of channelling 40–60 per cent of MAP funds to CSOs. Such a requirement was heavily resisted by each of the three governments who have little practice of CSO engagement fostered by mutual distrust and dislike. As such, the Bank made governments recognise the use CSOs had in the national responses to HIV/AIDS and the need to adopt a new approach to development work.[71] The Bank was able to make governments recognise the use of CSOs and adopt suitable mechanisms of engagement through the promise of desperately needed funds. Hence, the imposition of the CSO principle and the NACs under the MAP represented stringent conditionalities. In July 2009, the Bank threatened to withdraw funding from its HIV/AIDS programmes in Nigeria unless they upgraded their HIV/AIDS committees to full agencies (Rabiu 2009). Keen to dispel any use of conditionality on account of its association with controversial structural adjustment policy, ACT (AIDS Campaign Team) Africa avoided the issue by stressing that requirements such as the implementation of the NACs were 'not a conditionality, if you read the MAP what it says is to put the co-ordinating body at the highest level of government, what did we mean by that? It's that it should not come under the Ministry of Health.'[72] Instead, the Bank preferred to characterise such influence as 'arm twisting' or working with NACs to 'remind them ruthlessly' of their role.[73]

Perhaps the most interesting evidence as to the lack of NAC ownership of the MAP can be found in the Bank's reticence to admit to being involved in the project, specifically its design. The Bank's eagerness to stress its benevolent role has, in one example, culminated in Nadeem Mohammed, Senior Operations Officer from the Bank's ACT Africa asking for the Bank's logo to be removed from any of the Uganda AIDS Commission's work by stipulating 'this is your programme, your initiative, we don't do anything, we just mobilise funds to allow you to do what you do, so next time don't put on the World Bank logo, it's just your programme, you are working, I'm just monitoring.'[74] When asked how the UACP was devised, Peter Okwero, the World Bank's task team leader in Uganda, responded 'I can't really say how it developed, it just came by itself. When we were sitting, it was never, the Bank did not come with any idea, I don't think the government came with any particular idea.'[75] The Kenyan Bank team were adamant that 'the Bank has no objectives behind the TWOA, it is the government, we are supporting the government. That's the point, and don't forget it.'[76] The task team leader for Tanzania provided a more contradictory response to the question of ownership, suggesting it should be the Tanzanian government that designs the project, but in practice it is always the Bank,

> the preparation has to be with the country. Actually the project should be prepared, ideally it should be prepared by the government, ideally, you know, we are not preparing the project as a Bank, I mean this is, but in most cases you find that it is the Bank preparing, doing most of it, it is supposed to be the government preparing a project and the Bank assisting, providing you know, assisting the country to prepare a project, so that there is ownership of that project, right from the word go and throughout the implementation and even after implementation. So that is how it should look like but for most of the projects of the Bank you will find that because of the capacities of the country er, a lot is being done by the Bank.[77]

The issues of bureaucracy, institutional rivalry and CSO distrust facing the NAC all in part stem from this problem of ownership. The NAC system is effective in adopting the language of the Bank. However, these norms and language have very little substance. With an issue as contentious as HIV/AIDS it is reasonably straightforward for states to give the perception of 'good' reformers in their use of good governance language. However, these states are preoccupied with the need to present this image of good governance with little substantive action. Ownership cannot be induced within a state from the top down. Especially when the method in which such ownership is implemented is in abstraction of existing government systems. The method of governance reform adopted by the Bank is ahistorical in its blueprint structure and lacking in any awareness of existing political and social cultures. This discrepancy over the perception and implementation of reform and an ability, not a will, to govern on the part of the state is the central contradiction of achieving liberal good governance through neoliberal economic incentive that in regard to the HIV/AIDS response is leading to divergent outcomes to the Bank's initial agenda, and, as the next chapter shows, not necessarily positive consequences for communities affected and infected with the disease.

Unblocking bottlenecks and private sector inclusion

The Bank and the NACs are aware of some of the problems the NAC system faces, and as the previous section shows attribute these issues to general teething problems with the project. A degree of bureaucracy is inevitable within a project the size of the MAP and its use of state agencies and structures as the main channels for CSO engagement. A simple way of avoiding such bureaucracy would be to engage with fewer groups and focus on the national level alone, which would then undermine any form of community participation in the system. A further alternative would be to fund community groups directly with no state intervention as in the case of PEPFAR. However, the Bank is mandated to work in partnership with states. To work independently of states would undermine any long-term commitment to building infrastructure and the means to address the epidemic independent of foreign aid. Criticism of state-based intervention is often more to do with the level of distrust that has traditionally existed between CSOs and the government than with the MAP itself. According to Adam Lagerstedt, World Bank Senior Health Specialist, the Bank interprets community awareness and complaints about the lack of funding as a good sign that communities are beginning to take ownership of the response and thus will incentivise the government to take action. Task team leader of the MAP in Uganda, Peter Okwero, emphasises that despite some of the CSOs' misgivings concerning the community component of the MAP, the project has succeeded in motivating the communities where other community focused projects have failed.[78] The Bank does, however, have to be seen to be taking action to address some of these concerns. With the MAP being a flexible long-term commitment and a flagship programme for the Bank, there is considerable emphasis on the MAP to perform well.

For the Bank and the NACs the main problem is not the discrepancy over ownership or contentions within state ministries but the lack of good governance in delivery at the local level. Funds were not being delivered to the community quick enough, and, for the Bank, the bottlenecks to implementation and full engagement of the community were firmly located within the DAC system. Recognising these problems, the Bank introduced minor adjustments to the MAP that brought the private sector into the NAC system where areas of state intervention were seen to be failing. In Kenya, the Bank took grant-making powers out of the NACC and situated them in a separate body – the Joint Inter-Agency Co-Ordinating Committee. The Joint Inter-Agency Co-ordinating Committee is made up of 30 per cent government, 30 per cent development partners, 30 per cent civil society and 10 per cent private sector.[79] Its primary role is to assess CSO funding proposals and make recommendations to the NACC and the Global Fund.[80] The introduction of the Committee took decision-making of CSO funding out of the principle responsibility of the state and made it more multi-sectoral in its composition. However, as Chapter 4 shows, the composition of such committees tend to reflect the usual suspects within the civil society component that are seen as 'good' actors within the response in their alignment to donor and state-led priorities and the language of governance.

Minor adjustments to the NACC in Kenya were accompanied by more substantial changes at the district level. In Kenya, the DACs in their initial incarnation were dismantled and replaced with District Technical Committees, which to all intents and purposes fulfilled the same role but with greater emphasis upon addressing the difficulties and technicalities of channelling money to the communities. These committees are assisted by Provincial AIDS Control Councils, which co-ordinate the response at the regional level and provide support to the new District Technical Committees and the NACC. Training and consultation was conducted by UNAIDS and the NACC so that each agency was able to better understand their role.[81] The most substantial adjustments, however, were made to the TMAP project with the introduction of RFAs.

Regional Facilitating Agents (RFAs)

RFAs act as intermediaries between the Tanzanian AIDS Council, TACAIDS and the decentralised multi-sectoral AIDS committees to disburse funds to the community and manage CSO inclusion. They operate as an extension of TACAIDS' mandate, thus increasing the working capacity of the MAP at the national and district level. The RFAs see their central role as facilitators of community participation. However, such facilitation would be limited to only those organisations which had a record of sound implementation in HIV/AIDS-specific activities. The geographical size of Tanzania combined with the bureaucratic nature of local government limits the ability of the already overstretched NACs to assist districts and communities in capacity-building and institutional support. Hence, the central role of RFAs was extended beyond the perceptively straightforward task of funding disbursal to the much more complex job of improving the structures through which such money would flow. RFAs thus became responsible for building the capacity of the regional secretariat, the Local Government Authority (LGAs), the DACs and the community, as well as overseeing and co-ordinating the overall implementation of the MAP community component.[82] Technically the RFAs would operate through the pre-established government structures of district (DAC), community (CMAC) and village (VMAC), observing the key gaps in provision and identifying ways in which to build capacity in such areas based upon the CSO Mapping and Capacity Assessment Tool designed by TACAIDS.[83]

RFAs are made up of a combination of organisations from civil society, predominantly large international NGOs and the private sector.[84] TACAIDS and the Bank found RFA selection to be 'one frustrating process' compared with the initial selection of CSO funding under the MAP.[85] This process adhered to the Bank's procurement and international competitive bidding guidelines and subsequently took 14 months to complete. Technical proposals received by the RFAs require both screening by the government and prior review by the Bank. A call for applications from NGOs, consultancy firms and the private sector for 11 positions was placed in the major newspapers within Tanzania with applications being 'subjected to scrutiny' by the Tanzania Central Tender Board.[86] The selection criterion was weighted to favour national organisations. However selection was also dependent on groups having pre-existing capacity and resources.[87] Many local organisations were therefore disadvantaged when competing for funds with larger INGOs and private companies that sourced funds from outside the country. Some RFAs had to borrow money from elsewhere to secure their position and achieve their objectives. Stigmata Tenga of ST Associates, (RFA for Arusha and Mara) claimed that Action Aid (RFA for Coast, Dodoma, Morogoro and Singida) borrowed money from the UK Department for International Development (DFID) to fund their activities under the TMAP.[88] When asked if that resembled an unfair advantage, the Bank's response was 'they cheated', as a central expectation was that RFAs already had the capacity to implement the project.[89] The RFAs that won the contract attributed their selection to experience in managing and co-ordinating large-scale projects; close working relations with the government and the Bank; HIV/AIDS-specific regional expertise; familiarity with resource mobilisation and disbursement; reputation; and knowledge of HIV/AIDS, community responses and the culture of the Bank.[90]

RFAs build capacity by mapping the number of CSOs in the area, their activities, shortfalls and successes. Throughout the mapping exercise, RFAs work with the DACs and community is suggesting successful models for implementation and the monitoring of projects and project appraisal. The purpose was to identify the gaps in implementation and to look for ways to facilitate wider participation in areas that were lacking. These two functions combined lead to the subsequent disbursal of funds to communities. These exercises are conducted by an assessment team that examines all activities and approve or decline funding to CBOs based upon the NACs directives and evaluation criteria. Mapping is conducted in line with the principle tenets of the CSO Mapping and Capacity Support Tool, designed by private consultancy firm GTZ for TACAIDS. It involved a preliminary screening of a CSO (basic facts and information on their activities), how to select CSOs during field visits, guiding questions for the field visit to verify preliminary information, how to analyse data from the field, a summary of analysis of each CSO, a ranking list exercise of each of the CSOs, their weaknesses and strengths, and suggested contents for a CSO workshop (TACAIDS and GTZ 2005).[91]

Central to the work of the RFAs is the notion that they are an extension of TACAIDS 'their eyes and ears', and are working for the country not private interest.[92] As such, they are a main actor within the promotion of the Bank's multisectoral HIV/AIDS agenda. RFAs engage with TACAIDS through an initial orientation workshop in partnership with the Bank, and subsequent quarterly reports and meetings wherein they discuss problems and opportunities and share information with other RFAs.[93] Each RFA interacts with the wider HIV/AIDS response structure at the regional level with regular meetings with the District Medical Officer and the Ministry of Health. Further to their meetings with TACAIDS, each of the RFAs is visited by a representative from the World Bank or the United Nations Development Programme (UNDP) to monitor their progress. GTZ – a German development corporation and RFA for Mbeya and Rukwa – resented being visited by the UNDP and not the World Bank, mainly because the UNDP representative had little experience of HIV/AIDS.[94] Despite these visits, report writing and CSO engagement strategies, the RFAs have led to confusion and distrust among the DACs and communities they are supposed to engage with.

Initially the role of the RFAs was not fully introduced to those agents and communities they were supposed to be working with. For example, one RFA was meant to begin operations on 2 January 2006. However, the letters of introduction to the Community Multi-Sectoral AIDS Committees (CMACs) and DACs that they would be working with were relayed by TACAIDS, thus leading to complications, inconvenience and greater delay.[95] The lack of introduction combined with discrepancy about their role led to an initially fractious relationship between the DACs and the RFAs. The initial idea behind the RFAs was for them to facilitate the DACs engagement with the community. However, because of the problems with the DACs, the RFAs had to then train the DACs without the necessary funding to do so efficiently, thus leaving the RFAs with less money and infringing on their time and capacity to fulfil their main roles of co-ordination and mapping. The RFAs successful in delivery are those with large support systems behind them and the presence of pre-existing funds to operationalise the project. Organisations such as GTZ (RFA for Mbeya and Rukwa) and Care International (RFA for Kigoma and Tabora) thus have greater capacity than smaller consultancies, such as ST Associates (RFA for Arusha and Shinyanga), whose only work is to be an RFA. As Stigmata Tenga from ST Associates argues 'it is becoming a very huge work, it is becoming a very huge work.'[96] The RFAs are not supposed to engage in implementation, but are meant to facilitate the DACs visiting the community, map activity and strengthen feedback structures. It is assumed that the DACs 'will listen and follow the RFAs in what they want them to do;'[97] however, the prominence of allowances, and distrust over the RFAs usurping their role, reduces the smoothness of transition.

The RFAs have reduced the decision-making capacity of the DACs and replaced their role as dispenser of funds to the community. Some RFAs admit to such tension[98] whereas others are keen to deny its existence 'I think we are very encouraged by the, you know the warm, warm, warm reception.'[99] The relationship between the RFAs and the DACs is crucial as they are the main structure of funding and feedback for the community. Issues are discussed at the lower levels and then fed back to the RFAs by the DACs assessment team of two CSO representatives and two local government representatives. However, if there is no clear line of engagement between the DACs and the RFAs, concerns and issues are not fed back to decision making. The tensions between the RFAs and the DACs and the protracted selection process – between 9 and 14 months depending on who was asked – increased the time it took to implement the community component of the MAP as opposed to speeding up delivery. This delay has been felt by many of the community groups interviewed[100] who saw it as unfair that for this period people in the NACs, DACs and RFAs had been receiving a salary for disbursement to community groups while such groups saw nothing.[101] This problem is compounded by the distances between districts within certain regions. TACAIDS claim the majority of RFAs have five staff members, but the majority of those interviewed had three, project manager, social scientist and medical specialist, who run the risk of spending all their time travelling.[102]

The delayed disbursement of funds under the RFAs and tensions between them and the DACs have led to a mixed reaction within the community. The system is seen as not working and frustrating, as one CSO representative states, 'we ourselves have knowledge' that is not engaged with.[103] The prevailing view of community groups is that they would prefer to engage directly with TACAIDS 'these RFAs, we don't want them'[104] and have finances directly channelled to the people it means to affect. Some organisations have felt ignored by RFA activity, being promised funds that they never received, and noting that the community members they worked with had never heard of the RFAs. Other groups praised the work of the RFAs, thinking they had thorough work plans and a good level of community engagement in which everyone sits together and discusses the issues facing the region. Opinion on the RFA is therefore very much dependent upon the region, the community group and whether they are involved within the MAP.

The introduction of the RFAs presents a further dimension to debate surrounding ownership of the MAP. The concept for the RFAs did not stem from the community, the DACs or the NACs, it was introduced by the Bank. Willingness to admit the Bank's involvement depended on the person and their position. Notably the only official interviewed who admitted the Bank's influence was Joseph Temba, Director of Policy and Planning in TACAIDS.

> They were introduced by the Bank, actually. Initially we had all the money, the World Bank's money, the TMAP fund, for the council … here the Bank says well government are not very good collaborators with the private sector and NGOs so we better have them, some of the RFA to support them, where TACAIDS give money to and then they can give back to these NGOs.[105]

The NACs maintained the right to decline their involvement. For example, in contrast to mainland Tanzania, the Zanzibar and Pemba archipelago declined the involvement of RFAs, despite the ZMAP being a part of Tanzania's overall TMAP. The ZAC decided the notion of RFAs costing US$800,000 a year 'felt ridiculous' as Zanzibar is geographically small and for every dollar they gave to the community they would have to give another to the RFA, which is unnecessary.[106]

The Bank's response to the problems with the NAC system suggests the following about the implementation of its good governance reform agenda for HIV/AIDS. First, that it is the Bank that is the driving force for change at the state level when institutional problems and bottlenecks arise. The Bank's response is to develop the multi-sectoral element of the NAC system by introducing formal structures in which international donors, large international NGOs and the private sector have direct access to decision-making within the MAP and the wider framework of the national HIV/AIDS response. Second, these structures do not necessarily alleviate some of the problems and inertia in community delivery, but as the relationship between the DACs and RFAs demonstrate, they often compound such problems. Some communities felt that funding distribution was worse under the RFAs than before with just the various multi-sectoral committees. Third, the introduction of the RFAs reflects the way in which the Bank ignores the cultural difference of the DACs and the local government infrastructure to the wider governance reform in which it attempts to enact. Fourth, when states fail to implement multi-sectoral governance reform, the Bank turns to the private sector. In occupying a role as the extension of TACAIDS, the RFAs introduce such an additional layer of private service delivery and bureaucracy into the wider processes of the state.

Conclusion

The application of the Bank's multi-sectoral governance agenda within the state suggests that the state remains central to any form of effective HIV/AIDS governance or reform. This centrality, however, hinges upon the state's ability to effectively implement HIV/AIDS-specific governance criteria. These criteria are full CSO inclusion, the removal of HIV/AIDS from the health sector and into the Office of the President/Prime Minister and a willingness to perform a go-between function for the Bank and the community. The Bank has implemented such a strategy though the introduction of the NAC system of governance. Despite the UAC in Uganda existing prior to the MAP, the NACs are Bank designed. They carry out the main functions of the Bank in introducing a liberal form of governance to the HIV/AIDS response. Where the NACs seem to be lacking or demonstrate some form of 'bad' governance, the Bank increases the role of the private sector – in which civil society is firmly positioned in this instance – and development knowledge and expertise to address the state's shortcomings. The problem with this is that underlying all these new institutions and adaptations to the system is a disjuncture to the presentation of 'good' governance and good governance realised. Presidents and the NACs have become adept at adopting the governance language of participation and ownership, but in practice this led to discrepancies over mandate, confusion and a lack of any real progress in co-ordinating the HIV/AIDS response or implementing the MAP.

The lack of good governance in practice at the state level, i.e. state ownership, transparency and accountability, fundamentally arises from the fact that the states do not fully own the MAP. The MAP is a global, blueprint project that only allows for minor changes that fit into its over-arching multi-sectoral remit. It ignores pre-existing systems of governance and establishes the new NAC system under the rubric of the need for multi-sectorality as an emergency response to a complex issue. This approach, however, overlooks the fundamental social and political cultures of the state that not only have the responsibility for the disease's governance, but feed into the socioeconomic factors that drive the epidemic. The approach is ahistorical in that it fails to acknowledge both the political character of the country it operates in *and* previous problems the Bank has faced in implementing projects in sub-Saharan Africa, where willingness of the state does not exist. There is a willingness to respond to HIV/AIDS within the state, not necessarily, however, in accordance with the multi-sectoral approach the Bank is promoting, hence the Bank has to incentivise multi-sectoral change within the state through economic means.

The role of the state in the MAP suggests the following about the World Bank's multi-sectoral agenda for HIV/AIDS. First, the state occupies a central role in implementing this agenda. The successful implementation of the agenda within the national and local government suffers from several contradictions within the Bank's wider governance reform agenda: the need to promote forms of ownership, accountability and transparency within the state emanating from the control and influence of the World Bank in Washington. Second, in establishing institutions at every level of the state and reproducing the language of multi-sectoralism and governance norms, the Bank is able to use the state to embed and perpetuate this agenda. The role of the private sector and CSOs are crucial within this. Third, state leadership is not a natural phenomenon within HIV/AIDS governance, and as such is driven by economic incentive to enact change and generate ownership. This leads to several problematic outcomes and discrepancies over ownership, participation and accountability within the state. As the next chapter shows, these discrepancies often lead to a delay in funding disbursement, isolation of civil society organisations in decision-making and distrust of state structures. Furthermore, the application of governance reform is not limited to the state but is applied to the community level, where neoliberal economic incentive for multi-sectoral forms of HIV/AIDS intervention have complicated relations within communities and the local response to the disease. It is the inclusion of community groups and individuals within the Bank's multi-sectoral approach to governance reform within the MAP that fully embed its agenda for HIV/AIDS.

4 Constructing multi-sectoralism
The community

The inclusion of CSOs, nominally national NGOs and community groups is integral to the application of the Bank's multi-sectoral agenda for HIV/AIDS. Civil society groups have long been at the forefront of HIV/AIDS campaigning since the early 1980s in the USA and UK, and civil society–government partnerships have become the norm for interventions in combating the disease. Contrary to common understandings of the role of civil society within global governance, it is not international NGOs or transnational networks that occupy the main role of engagement with the Bank or the NACs. For the Bank it is individuals and groups within local communities across sub-Saharan Africa that have thus far educated people on methods of prevention and cared for people infected and affected by the disease. These groups thus come to be at the centre of its multi-sectoral agenda. The Bank's approach is that if you offer funds to such groups you can support existing activities and facilitate wider awareness of HIV/AIDS and participation from every aspect of society in combating this. At the heart of this multi-sectoral approach are the governance reform values of efficiency and market-based delivery and incentives, government accountability, the need for an open and transparent civil society and the role of the individual. Community groups and the individual are the central arenas in which the Bank can fully embed its agenda for HIV/AIDS. The application of this multi-sectoral agenda leads to mixed outcomes, notably the emergence of an HIV/AIDS-specific service industry within local economies and individual behaviour. In sidelining transnational advocacy networks and INGOs and offering financial incentives, civil society becomes an arena of commercial activity that is bounded within the governance regimes inherent to the NAC system of HIV/AIDS governance.

This chapter looks at how the Bank goes beyond the state to fully embed its multi-sectoral agenda within the community and the individual. It does so by first outlining the main mechanisms or civil society engagement within the MAP at the national and community level. Second, the chapter explores some of the problems and limitations of engagement put forward by the community groups and NGOs the MAP seeks to include, before considering how the Bank has organised the MAP in such a way as to disperse influence and accountability. Third, the chapter focuses on the role of the individual and mechanisms developed by the Bank to change individual behaviour and choice. The chapter then draws together what the

Bank's multi-sectoral agenda means in practice and why it matters for the global HIV/AIDS agenda. The chapter develops the arguments made in previous chapters to suggest that in emphasising a multi-sectoral approach to HIV/AIDS, the Bank has constructed a form of liberal governance achieved through *neo*liberal incentive. The economic impetus for civil society inclusion and individual behaviour change has led to the formation of a market of HIV/AIDS CSOs involved in service provision. As such, CSOs are motivated by financial gain rather than the promotion of transparency and accountability within HIV/AIDS governance, which undermines any long-term initiatives to sustain the in-country response to the epidemic once the funding no longer exists.

Putting multi-sectoralism into practice

The main priority of multi-sectoralism within the MAP is community empowerment through the funding of community groups and national NGOs. The methods of encouraging multi-sectoral participation within the MAP reflect the Bank's wider approach to civil society engagement: funding, dialogue and feedback, partnerships and networking. Engagement under the MAP has two tracks. The first is of NGOs at the national level, and the second is of community groups at the community level. In contrast to the 5,000–6,000 community groups funded under each country-specific MAP, on average 25 NGOs are funded at the national level in each of the three countries studied. The difference between a community group and a national NGO in this context is that national NGOs operate across the country whereas community groups work in a specific, smaller, local community.

The methods of engagement used by the Bank fit within a particular interpretation of community-driven development, rooted in the idea that communities are best placed to generate projects and ideas for policy as they can identify the main issues and means to address them.[1] The MAP has no clear objectives or criteria which community groups must fulfil, other than an overall strategy to direct funds to a vast array of groups so as to cover all aspects of the response, and an upsurge in community participation, ownership and sponsorship to address the epidemic as comprehensively as possible. Key to this is the community's ability to hold their governments to account for how they have addressed HIV/AIDS and to facilitate widespread support for tackling the epidemic.[2]

The MAP differs from alternative approaches to multi-sectoral community-driven development favoured by other donors. The first alternative outlines the key objectives of a particular programme and issues a call for proposals based on clear guidelines and gaps that need filling. This approach is reflected within the US PEPFAR project. The second conducts a baseline survey of a community's needs, current activities and capacity, so as to identify the key factors required in a project and stipulate the approach most fitting to these needs and a community's ability to plan their own responses.[3] The MAP is much more *ad hoc* and less stringent in this regard. Differing approaches are all based upon the same model of decentralised governance based upon field offices and regional representatives conducting the majority of community engagement.[4] Decentralised working structures promote the message of a community-based response to the epidemic to the furthest outreach in rural East Africa, and thus mobilise the population. The MAP is distinct in that it lacks a results-based approach to engagement, yet it acts within the commonly accepted processes of decentralised governance. This is an interesting departure for the World Bank, as in contrast to bilateral and multilateral donors such as PEPFAR, which will not fund specific projects associated with the promotion of condoms and abortion, there is technically no area of HIV/AIDS prevention, treatment and care that the Bank will not fund. Funding is the main mechanism of promoting multi-sectorality within the state. It creates a specific form of multi-sectoralism based upon market principles of competition and efficiency in delivery as opposed to advocacy.

Funding

Funding of CSOs under the MAP is between £30,000–50,000 per national NGO and £2,500 per community group, disbursed quarterly on an annual basis by the NACs and the DACs.[5] The selection procedure is based upon calls for funding proposals placed in each individual state's mainstream press at the beginning of the project by the NACs. These calls for proposals stipulate the criteria NGOs have to pursue. For more rural communities and people without access to newspapers, initial community access and mobilisation is conducted through posters, meetings and targeting key people within communities as 'community mobilisers.'[6] According to the Bank, calls for proposals are 'published in such a way that anybody can see it. Even if there are a few people who can read, there are enough people who read to be able to tell the other ones if the paper is up there'[7] in local market stands and community meeting points. Once funding proposals are submitted directly to the NAC or DAC, they are assessed for project duration, type of activity, overhead costs, targets, need and allocations of responsibility among staff members.[8] This criteria, however, appears to be adaptable on implementation. When questioned about the formal stipulations for funding, few CSO and community officers within the NACs could respond fully to the question – often giving a convoluted answer, or changing the subject. The World Bank only becomes involved in the selection of CSOs when approval is needed for sponsorship of over £50,000.[9]

Though not specified by the NACs, or the working documents of the individual MAPs, each country funded a range of multi-FBOs.[10] FBOs are prioritised by the NACs and the Bank for their close links to, and trust within, the local communities in East Africa. In the early stages of the epidemic, churches and mosques were active in caring and educating within the congregations and wider communities in which they were based. FBOs have been less involved in treatment provision, monitoring and evaluations, and in some cases promoting the ABC of prevention – Abstain, Be Faithful, use a Condom – yet their capacity to reach people has led to targeted FBO interventions by donors.[11] Further to the inclusion of FBOs, each of the three MAPs considered directed funds to organisations working with the armed services.

Activities at the national and community level are based upon the standard five thematic areas of care and treatment: prevention and mitigation of new infections, improvement on quality of life for people infected with HIV/AIDS, support and co-ordination, mitigation of socioeconomic impact, and civil society and private sector engagement. These five thematic areas include activities such as home-based care work; orphans and vulnerable children (OVCs) programmes, such as paying school fees, memory boxes; psychosocial support for people with HIV/AIDS and people affected by HIV/AIDS; prevention methods; peer education through mediums such as drama and dance, community workshops; voluntary counselling and testing (VCT); and mitigation of socioeconomic impact by establishing income-generating projects. The scope of the activities depended on the size and capacity of the group, with many groups having expanded to conduct a range of activities.[12] Interviews with community groups suggest that the majority of funding disbursed to the community is for training programmes. Training occurs from the top down. Community groups are trained in home-based care, counselling, peer education and basic methods of prevention of mother-to-child transmission (PMTCT) in the first instance by INGOs and NGOs.[13] The community groups then utilise these skills to train and 'sensitise' other members of the community. The result is that most community activity focuses on training, while issues of delivery in health services, education and psychosocial support remain unfulfilled. Activities take place across the country with a heavy concentration in areas with high infection rates, most notably Kisumu in Kenya, Iringa and Mbeya in Tanzania and Kyotera in Uganda. Most of those NGOs funded under the MAP have a base in the capital cities with additional offices throughout each individual country.

The majority of community groups interviewed began as issue-specific organisations, but responded to growing needs in the community by expanding and adapting their practices. Those organisations that expanded their practices were able to attract wider funds, as donors perceived them to have a more holistic approach in responding to the epidemic, and it is more cost-effective to fund one group that engages in multiple activities than various different organisations. Expansion of practices, however, requires greater funding in the first place. Thus organisations seek a range of funding in order to attract additional funding. The cyclical nature of this excludes smaller community groups that do not have the means to provide a small amount of seed money to expand their operations, or may have limited access to other, slightly larger organisations that may assist with this. One of the community groups interviewed expressed a desire to change the organisation's status to become a registered NGO so as to attract more prestige and recognition within the wider policy community, and thus more funding.[14] This co-dependency between expansion and funding is felt acutely by many of the community groups interviewed, and is seen as one of the main limitations to their expansion and ability to deliver services to the community.[15]

The range of activity encompassed by the MAP is both wide and varied. The corollary of this is the existence of taboo areas that few organisations address. These are homosexuality, intravenous drug users (IDUs) and commercial sex workers (CSWs). Homosexuality is illegal in Kenya, Tanzania and Uganda. The status and stigma surrounding homosexuality in these countries makes it difficult to target effectively such high-risk behaviour or for individuals to collectivise around the issue and represent themselves in wider policy-making arenas. Estimates as to prevalence rates among homosexuals in Kenya, Tanzania and Uganda is unavailable in the WHO/UNAIDS' epidemiology database – but globally it is estimated that men who have sex with men make up 5–10 per cent of people living with HIV/AIDS (UNAIDS 2009). Men who have sex with men are an important area of concern, as it is estimated that only 40 per cent have access to healthcare, and because of taboo are often married and thus pose a risk to their partners (UNAIDS 2009). When asked if they confronted unsafe homosexual sex, interviewees would respond in a similar way to how Presidents were shown to in Chapter 3, by denying the existence of homosexuality in East Africa, considering it a 'foreign term' that 'somehow does exist' but is not common, or refusing to address the question within their wider work as it is contrary to their religious beliefs.[16] Those who were willing to address homosexuality either considered the stigma surrounding the issue a struggle with little return or so shrouded in stigma and secrecy it was impossible to know where to start.[17] Very few of the peer educators interviewed said they would address homosexuality, with only a select number discussing it when approached by an individual confused by their feelings.[18] Despite the taboo surrounding homosexuality in each of the three countries considered, the NACC in Kenya volunteered an interest and commitment to targeting men having sex with men and women having sex with women as vulnerable groups.[19] Homosexual advocacy or care groups are unable to mobilise as well as people living with HIV/AIDS because of the stigma and illegality surrounding their status. This limits their influence within civil society. What it does not limit, however, is their efficacy in targeting the Bank. Whereas some managers of the MAP in Kenya were doubtful of the return, others asserted the Bank's interest in tackling taboo areas such as homosexuality in MAP-2.[20]

The mobilisation of commercial sex workers and CSO work has increased slightly, but remains limited within the region. This is despite widespread recognition of their high-risk status. Kenya Voluntary Women's Rehabilitation Centre (K-VWORC) was the only CSO interviewed (or evident in the region) to specifically engage with commercial sex workers. Elizabeth Ngugi, the founder of K-VWORC, has promoted the cause of commercial sex workers and in so doing has secured support from the World Bank and UNAIDS.[21] The majority of K-VWORC's success has been the result of Ngugi's ability to attain such support. Groups such as the International Red Cross, working with intravenous drug users, are similarly confronted by a similar pattern of stigma and denial.[22] According to one interviewee, USAID would not touch either commercial sex workers or intravenous drug users 'with a barge pole' because of neoconservative ideology and their contentious standing with US voters.[23] This presents a dilemma for the Bank in balancing its recognition of the importance of addressing issues such as HIV transmission through homosexual sex and the stigma surrounding it, with not wanting to be seen to force the issue upon the NACs or civil society. The problem thus becomes how to incentivise governments and community groups to acknowledge and address these issues in a considerate and non-discriminatory manner. The Bank is progressive in its acknowledgment of the need to address a multitude of social taboos; however, it stumbles over issues of how to address them.

Since being recognised as an issue pertinent to high prevalence rates of HIV/ AIDS, women and gender has become a target issue for many CSOs. Of those CSOs interviewed, 60 per cent in Uganda, 48 per cent in Kenya and 37 per cent in Tanzania had what they classed as a gender component to their work. However, on closer inspection it became evident that the issue of 'women and gender' meant women only, and wider sociocultural issues of 'maleness', women's rights, sexuality and gender-based roles remained ignored and, to some extent, taboo. For a large number of those CSOs interviewed, having a gender component only meant advocating equal opportunities and having female members in their organisation.[24] Some CSO representatives felt that the gender issue had gone too far, with little equality for men and rising discontent for women's groups, as Vincent Kalimire from the Foundation for African Development puts it:

> I'm not so much opposed to the women's movement but I don't appreciate the women's organisations approach to addressing gender concerns. They are just looking at women's concerns, to me I am looking at the situation of HIV/ AIDS, you look at it broadly, yes it affects women, but these issues are also related to men because we are inter-related and therefore we cannot promote one line. If you think about issues and leave out men and you don't enter into dialogue, then you don't achieve much. Our women's movements, or the so-called gender activists they're not really gender activists, they're women, but for example from the approach, when organising activities we are aware of so called, structures in our society and I believe we cannot have representation in our community because most communities have fewer women than men, but at least 6 men to 4 women, that is what we encourage, that you can always get into your programme, otherwise if you start using it as a club, as an exclusive club, men sit alone, women sit alone, then you cannot achieve much, it is a greater benefit to bring them more closer. Also the women's movements are based in town here, they don't look at the issues affecting women, the real problems that affect women down at the grassroot, but the whole thing is about power.[25]

Interviews with non-HIV/AIDS-specific women's groups in Kenya suggest that the Bank is seen as somehow not being interested in gender concerns.[26] However, the Bank does recognise HIV/AIDS as becoming an increasingly feminised epidemic through the disproportional impact it has upon the socioeconomic status of women, and in so doing many CSOs working under the MAP are addressing the issue.[27] These CSOs are addressing issues such as empowering women to become economically independent of men; staging educational events for women and men such as football matches where issues such as gender and HIV/AIDS are discussed during intervals; land rights campaigns; men- and women-specific clubs;

intensified counselling and sensitisation for couples; improving female education; and involving men in prevention of mother to child transmission work.[28] Contrary to the previous opinion of Vincent Kalimire from the Foundation for African Development, the main message of these activities is effectively summed up as 'let's give credit to women but still involve men.'[29] This attitude is being adopted by the NACs as well as the DACs, but it remains a major challenge. Problems with land rights, education for girls, women being able to disclose their status to their partners, domestic violence and participation of women remain pertinent taboos.[30]

The activities funded by the Bank suggest the following of the MAP. First, that it tends to fund in a standard manner that disburses a specific amount of funds quarterly and to thematic areas that are similar across the global response to HIV/AIDS. FBOs and military organisations are central components of this. Second, the Bank shows a willingness to fund any project related to HIV/AIDS, no matter the controversy surrounding it. This highlights a central contention within the MAP and the Bank's agenda: how hard the Bank can or should push or incentivise to address concerns that are seen as non-existent or too taboo within the state and civil society. The Bank can do so through funding conditionalities or through dialogue and consultation. The effectiveness to which in part depends on how multi-sectoral decision-making within the MAP is in practice.

Feedback and dialogue

According to the Bank, a commitment to open dialogue, where no-one is excluded, is central to the MAP and transparency within HIV/AIDS decision-making.[31] In each of the case study countries, feedback from MAP-funded NGOs and community groups occurs through a combination of submission of quarterly reports to the NACs, networking, speaking to the NACs and DACs, issue-based focus groups and steering committees, and national partnership meetings. At the community level, quarterly meetings are held within the district in which recipients of MAP funds discuss their activities, the problems in implementation and put questions to the DACs.[32] The most direct form of dialogue is through issue-based steering committees and annual partnership meetings. The annual partnership meetings comprise World Bank MAP task team leaders, NACs, UN agencies, donors such as USAID and the UK Department for International Development (DFID), INGOs, NGOs, CBOs, DACs and line ministries, such as the Ministry of Health (National AIDS Control Council 2005). These annual meetings are the result of feedback from the July 2005 International AIDS Society Rio Conference, in which participation in decision-making and dialogue was articulated as a problem for CSOs. Their purpose is to summarise and feedback on the year's activities, to promote discussion between the groups and to prioritise for the following year. The NACs are primarily responsible for their organisation and CSO participation, but work in partnership with UNDP and UNAIDS.[33] UNDP and UNAIDS assist with the NACs capacity to articulate who is relevant to participation and how to reach those not involved.

Steering committees or Management Co-ordinating Groups are organised around issues of concern within the HIV/AIDS response. Any CSO is free to attend such meetings. The outcome of discussion within these meetings forms the basis for agenda formulation and decision-making within the annual partnership meeting. Tanzania differs slightly to Uganda and Kenya in that, first, the meetings are a relatively new concept, and, second, input into the review meetings is not conducted by these groups but is carried out by consultants who conduct evaluations of the strategic plan.[34] In Uganda, INGOs and regional NGOs involved with the NAC participate in the Strategic Partnership Committees within a specific INGO HIV/AIDS community entity. This entity becomes self-co-ordinating, with a steering committee that meets monthly. The purpose of these entities is to support the Chair of the UAC and work within the objectives articulated for them under the national strategic framework.[35] Similar to the management co-ordinating groups that work together ahead of the Joint Annual HIV/AIDS Programme Review (JAPR) in Kenya, these entities feed back to an annual partnership forum in which their objectives for the following year are established.

Dialogue at the community level differs from that at the global and national in the use of direct partnerships between the DACs and community groups. Partnerships occur through joint planning meetings and operations. The groups partnered by the DACs are notably national or international NGO representatives, such as the AIDS Support Organisation (TASO) in Uganda and World Vision, and the heads of particular community-based networks, such as Kimara Peer Educators in Tanzania, who prove their utility through longevity and direct links to the community.[36] Bank representatives – nominally task team leaders – visit communities quarterly. Unstructured forms of dialogue occur through Bank task team leader quarterly visits to different community groups and impromptu partnerships, such as representatives issuing awards at a football tournament designed to educate young people about HIV/AIDS. Of the community groups interviewed none had engaged in unstructured dialogue (dialogue that was not report-writing) with the Bank.

Under the MAP all forms of direct engagement between the Bank and CSOs occur through either the in-country task team leaders or the project's management team: AIDS Campaign Team Africa (ACT Africa). ACT Africa engages in dialogue and consultation with CSOs on the following levels: regional meetings, feedback from in-country task-team leaders (TTLs), and through international meetings and conferences such as the biennial International AIDS Conference. Direct interaction between ACT Africa at the global level and CSOs occurs through regional meetings. The first of these was to perform a rapid survey of CSO opinion in the design stage of the MAP. Within the design stage, a CSO advisory committee was established in Kenya and Ethiopia in which – according to the Bank – every perceived sector affecting HIV/AIDS was represented.[37] During the meeting, ACT Africa introduced the organisations to the concept of the MAP, its central components and the eligibility criteria to receive funds. This model has subsequently been repeated in 29 other countries in receipt of MAP funds. CSOs were not involved in the design stage of the MAP, but were consulted before implementation as a means of gaining legitimacy for the project.

The second form of direct engagement between ACT Africa and CSOs occurs through topic-specific annual meetings to discuss lessons learnt and future strategy. Participation within such meetings is dependent upon a quota established by the Bank for both state actors and CSOs.[38] Dialogue at the global level is heavily dependent upon the ability of in-country intermediaries – the task team leaders – to channel CSO opinion through set feedback structures. The task team leader must relate information to their specific Human Development Sector Manager, positioned in ACT Africa, who in turn reports back to the vice-president for the Africa Region. The only other form of global engagement in this regard is ACT Africa's training of task team leaders on how to implement certain procedures; how to improve dialogue with CSOs; and how to better monitor and evaluate funding disbursement.[39] In each case, there is little explication of the purpose of dialogue, with consultation being an end in itself. Dialogue and consultation between the global managers of the MAP and the CSOs involved in the project is not common. Where it does exist it is to infer validity and CSO ownership of the project.

The Bank, NACs and DACs are generally seen as open and willing to partner all those with resources and listen to national NGOs as long as they fit within a certain theme or objective of the time.[40] However, the number of CSOs funded under the MAP and the constraints on the National AIDS Councils outlined in Chapter 3 present various technical difficulties in engaging with the Bank. Dialogue and consultation at the global level is predominantly the remit of INGOs. Hence, a key mechanism of national NGOs and community groups gaining wider recognition and representation within the NACs has been the formation of networks.

Networks

Networks between local community groups and national NGOs provide a simple solution to problems of scope and inclusion faced by the directors of the MAP. They facilitate widespread participation, offer expertise in issue-specific areas, are seen as having good links with the community and for donors are administratively easier to deal with. This recognition has seen a rise in networks and organisations seeking to group themselves under wider umbrella organisations with expanding mandates and an increased involvement of INGOs. Community groups in particular have recognised the utility of networks as a means of influencing decision-making. Community groups are keen to stress their wider interactions through joint referrals, combining services, and mutual stakeholder meetings as a way of demonstrating their efficacy and thus securing greater funding from donors.[41] Participation and co-ordination is generally seen as relatively balanced in terms of who is represented and the division of labour from the perspective of national NGOs.

The most sophisticated form of network that has emerged in East Africa is people living with HIV/AIDS networks. The introduction of networks of people with HIV/AIDS shows clear evidence of governments and donors taking note of CSO feedback. Networks such as the Global Network of People Living with HIV/AIDS (GNP+) and the International Community of Women Living with

HIV/AIDS have demonstrated much power and leverage in other parts of sub-Saharan Africa, specifically South Africa; however, the scope and organisation of people with HIV/AIDS networks has been much more varied in East Africa. The AIDS Support Organisation (TASO) in Uganda is the main source of people with HIV/AIDS representation within the country and has enjoyed relatively consistent access to, and standing within, the Uganda AIDS Commission and wider donors. Donors and governments have recognised the utility of people with HIV/AIDS representation within discussion and decision-making forums, which has resulted in directives to establish national networks within Kenya and Tanzania.[42] The concept of people with HIV/AIDS representation ranges from one individual or one organisation representing people living with HIV/AIDS at the national decision-making level. In Kenya, the National Empowerment of People Living with HIV/AIDS (PLWHA) has come to be the main representative of the network[43] and within Tanzania efforts to establish a similar forum have been undertaken. These forums follow similar patterns of HIV/AIDS networks and establish links with INGOs and international forums, such as the Global Network of PLWHA and the National Association of PLWHA, United States.

International non-governmental organisations and the private sector

INGOs are recognised as partners of the MAP but no INGO is directly funded under the project. INGOs working within the field of HIV/AIDS in East Africa have the comparative advantage over NGOs of experience, flexibility and established partnerships that open up more informal, direct linkages with the NACs. Despite not receiving MAP funds, they do work within the overall structure of the national response; through partnerships with the Ministry of Health and the NACs.[44] For the Bank, the inclusion of INGOs is the responsibility of states, but at the global level they would not be included within engagement.[45] Partnerships between INGOs, NGOs and the NACs are diverse and the nature of relationship depends on the organisation. INGOs and regional NGOs, such as African Medical and Research Foundation (AMREF), support and participate in the NACs as well as other government ministries through sharing technical support, training institutions and assistance in aspects of implementation.[46] INGOs, such as OXFAM, were initially invited to speak on the MAP and participate in action plan discussions in Uganda.[47] In contrast to the sustained campaign against the Bank by a select number of INGOs, criticism and awareness of the MAP is practically non-existent. Those who criticise the MAP and argue that its funds should be channelled into alternative modes of funding, such as the Global Fund, do not know or ignore the inner workings and general principles of the MAP, labelling it a 'retrofit multi-sectoral project.'[48]

Central to the ethos of multi-sectoralism is the inclusion of all aspects of state and society: the private sector thus comprises an integral part of the MAP. In relation to the MAP the private sector refers to for-profit organisations, separate from the state and community groups and national NGOs. The private sector can thus refer to national companies or community social enterprise initiatives. ACT

Africa places the private sector under the all-encompassing term of civil society.[49] The role of the private sector has increased within ACT Africa, with the group fostering relationships with business coalitions, conducting private sector workshops and issuing guidelines for effective private sector work in the HIV/AIDS response (World Bank 2007f). The MAP funds a select number of private sector organisations at the national level that engage in programmes internally within companies, educational networks, corporate social responsibility, e.g. getting Johnson & Johnson to subsidise certain provisions, and strengthening NAC and government systems within the remit of the national strategic plan.[50] The role of the private sector has been promoted within the Bank generally, and has seen increased significance under the MAP. This has, in turn, been identified by the NACs who recognise their limited success in engaging with the private sector.[51] The NACs have educated and trained specific service sectors such as taxi drivers, engaged with the private sector in municipal council meetings, identified complementary activities and promoted private sector coalitions among national companies.[52] Private sector integration nevertheless remains *ad hoc* and less integrated within the MAP in comparison to that of national NGOs and community groups.

The mechanisms of implementing the Bank's multi-sectoral agenda for HIV/AIDS governance suggest a straightforward, financially driven approach that seeks to facilitate as much participation as possible. However, these mechanisms are structured between the global, national and local community level in such a way as to limit influence and access to decision-making. They also overlook one of the central components of civil society for the application of good governance: the promotion of transparency, representation and holding states to account. Funding and structured exchanges limit this. The economic impetus thus suggests a more financial, market-driven neoliberal approach to governance as opposed to a more holistic liberal agenda. It is the dichotomy of wanting to promote the main tenets of liberal good governance through neoliberal means and incentives that becomes the main site of contestation for the Bank. This is evident in the main misgivings and problems associated with the application of multi-sectoralism within a constructed civil society.

The problem with constructing multi-sectoral civil society

As Chapter 3 suggests creating a multi-sectoral system of HIV/AIDS governance leads to problems within the state in Kenya, Tanzania and Uganda, which have pre-existing structures, culture and power relations. The application of such a system to civil society is even more complex. At the cursory level there are the problems and limitations of funding and feedback felt by those actors the MAP looks to fund. Multi-sectoralism is undermined by problems in funding transparency and utility, the purpose of feedback mechanisms, the types of CSOs that participate in dialogue, and divisions between CSOs and networks. Each of these factors weakens and limits the influence of CSOs upon decision-making and their ability to articulate their own agendas within the remit of the MAP. However, similar to problems with the state, these issues are symptomatic of deliberate structural features of how the MAP is organised and run, and the contradictions inherent to constructing processes of liberal governance reform through the principles of good governance. This section considers the problems with funding, feedback and inter-CSO collaboration identified by those CSOs interviewed within the research.

Funding

The MAP has been subject to criticism regarding its funding mechanisms which, the Bank would argue, are the result of needing to disburse funds rapidly and to a wide range of actors. CSOs accuse MAP-funded projects of being undermined by the following. First, due to a delay in the disbursement of funds, some organisations experienced a delay of 6 months, with a drawn out process of feedback reports and blame being apportioned to the Bank and the NACs respectively.[53] Community opinion suggests the central obstacle to effective engagement has been the short-term nature of funding. Funding is too little, too late,[54] and there are procedural complications in accessing funds. A delay in disbursement between projects or within the quarterly payments can result in problems such as people with HIV/AIDS being unable to access ART, and thus falling unwell, and a lack of legitimacy and trust between these groups and the communities they work with. Grants only pay for the activities themselves but not for the running costs of such activities, such as staff salaries, utilities or volunteer costs – many of whom are people with HIV/AIDS and see volunteer work as their only source of income.[55] Community groups sponsored under the MAP often end up with operational projects but no funds to continue to support them beyond their first year of operations. As one member of a community group describes the situation, 'it's tough, very tough'.[56] For example, the National Council of Women in Kenya received 2 years' funding from the MAP that was supposed to be active from June 2003 to April 2005. The money did not arrive until July 2004, resulting in the project having to be shortened in scope and coverage.[57] This is problematic, as community groups come to rely on funds and plan accordingly. Explanations for this delay were linked to problems with corruption within the NACC and thus the restructuring of the KHADREP and the NACC in response to the allegations. The mass sensitisation work conducted under the MAP has led to community awareness that the money is there, but the general perception is that the money has not reached the community: 'in the final analysis, has it actually reached the sick?'[58] This issue presented the main concern of the community groups interviewed: where money from donors and the government goes.

Community groups offer two explanations as to why the money was not reaching them. The first is the presence of 'briefcase NGOs' that present high standard proposals, receive the money and then disappear.[59] The second explanation is failure of the DACs to be transparent and accountable to those organisations they engage with. Communities funded under the MAP are sometimes unclear about the disbursement process at the district level. They do not feel represented by the DACs and do not see a clear feedback structure from their report-writing, questionnaires or community visits.[60]

The problem of the DACs and the NACs presents a second area of contention within the funding procedure of the MAP. The Bank defends delays and community confusion with a pragmatic stance to working with government structures and multiple organisations in a short period of time, 'it's a real nightmare with issues from the Bank now coming to this new institution: I mean, what do you expect?'[61] Yet if the Bank was truly responsive to community needs it would not necessarily fund through the NACs. The Bank's commitment to the NAC system leads to it being seen as very 'demanding of partners' in its monitoring of activities and need for report-writing and feedback.[62] In comparison to other donors that operate outside of the state structure and fund CSOs directly, the Bank's state-led approach is viewed as cumbersome, overly bureaucratic and as a consequence lacking in any form of sustainability.[63] The majority of CSOs interviewed either were or at some point had been distrustful of the NACs and government, thus preferring their non-involvement within engagement mechanisms.[64] CSOs who are advocating against the government on certain issues, e.g. homosexuality, see it as a contention to then receive funds from governments that legislate against their existence. This issue presented a further concern about their general relationship with the Bank. Many of the CSOs wanted to engage directly with the Bank and receive more information from it, yet the Bank maintains its role as a silent partner under the rubric of state ownership.[65]

The expansion of national NGOs under the MAP resulted in a third problem, organisations began to compete over which was the expert in particular areas of the response. This fostered greater competition over who had claims to knowledge and therefore greater claim to influence decision-making within the NAC structures. Community groups see funding access and dialogue as dependent on knowing 'the tricks of getting the money' and having 'someone who will push for you.'[66] When drawing up initial project disbursement plans, district officials identify the groups known to them that they already have a working relationship with. Knowing such groups can be the result of effective advocacy work, a clear presence or personal relationships, as, in one instance, attending the same school.[67] There is little transparency in terms of who received funds and why. This is compounded by the complexities of funding and donor fatigue. These claims are often less about who has specific expertise, but more about the positioning of organisations within the NAC structure or who shouts the loudest.

Problems with funding of CSOs reveal as much about civil society actors within the MAP as they do about the project and the Bank. The US$10 billion annually directed to HIV/AIDS relief and the existence of multiple CSO activity suggest there is an abundance of funding. Often, those groups that flagged the issue of funding had received money from the MAP and were submitting proposals to other donors. One of the main interests of community groups working in HIV/AIDS is to secure funds for their projects, and thus compete with other groups, and stress the need for more funding in line with their own interests. The issue of funding is pertinent for all community groups involved in research; however, problems associated with allocation and disbursement may be overemphasised. Issues of what activities are funded are also in part the responsibility of community groups. None of the MAP community initiatives stipulated the need to fund specific activities, thus arguably if all the activities funded are training it is because of what community groups specified in their project proposal. A greater problem with funding is the absorptive capacity of community groups themselves. MAP representatives in Kenya and Tanzania stipulated that should the funds be disbursed effectively, further funding would be made available by the Bank.[68] Issues with disbursement are part the problem of DAC infrastructure, but also part community group infrastructure. Criticism of state-based intervention is often more to do with the level of distrust that has traditionally existed between CSOs and the government than the MAP itself. The level of intricate problems associated with the MAP shows the ability of community groups to hold government agencies to account, and push for increased transparency, indicating the emergence of an effective civil society and fulfilling one of the MAP's central objectives. The degree to which these actors perform such an accountability function, however, is limited by their lack of full participation in feedback and dialogue with the NACs, DACs and the Bank itself.

Feedback and dialogue

Problems of feedback and dialogue between CSOs and the architects and managers of the MAP – the Bank and the NACs – are evident from the initial inception of the project to its standard processes of report-writing and review meetings. The level of CSO consultation at the outset of each individual MAP suggested by the NACs and the Bank is questionable. Of all the CSOs interviewed during the research, none had critically engaged in the design process of each project. When asked retrospectively about the design process, some organisations would say they were aware money was coming that would be specifically directed to CSOs, but were not involved in the manner in which the money was structured or prioritised.[69] Similarly, in the case of the TWOA project in Kenya, of those organisations questioned – specifically those CSOs which were often engaged within governmental and international organisation decision-making and the Kenyan MAP the KHADREP – the majority had not been consulted about the TWOA, were confused as to what it was or had not even heard of it.[70] ACT Africa was keen to reiterate that CSOs were engaged at the beginning of each project. However, this engagement occurred after the main principles of the project were drawn up. Consultation with those groups the Bank would affect was thus more a process of consent than collaborative design. The groups involved were those familiar to the Bank, not necessarily those that would receive funds under the MAP.

Since the implementation of the MAP, the ability for CSOs to feedback problems of funding and bureaucracy is limited by narrow dialogue based upon report-writing and annual discussions. Feedback and dialogue is seen as a one-way process in which the CSOs inform the Bank's representatives – the NACs – on their activities, but the NAC does not reciprocate by informing CSOs of Bank activity. Dialogue is not perceived as being 'real'. As the worker of a MAP-funded CSO, Patrick Ogen, Youth Alive Uganda, argues, the NACs and the Bank need to visit projects to witness first hand the day-to-day problems they face:

> Send someone to see what challenges you are having, what's happening, and can we have a partnership, a real partnership, with the donor here (gestures to table) and the CEO of an organisation here (gestures across table) to compare notes, and the donors have their weakness, they bring reporting formats, jargon, you know, there are certain things you must mention, you are the person to make up the standards. So even the evaluation too must be developed together, you are giving me your money, how do you think it should be evaluated and then you take, then you have dialogue.[71]

Of those CSOs funded by the MAP and interviews as part of research, only one group in Tanzania had direct unstructured dialogue with the Bank, compared with two in Uganda and four in Kenya. Representatives of the NACs and DACs are required to visit communities every quarter and the Bank representatives make *ad hoc* field visits, yet there is little open engagement or discussion. The majority of CSOs interviewed stated they had not been visited by the Bank.[72] For many CSOs this was problematic, as to them the Bank had no conception of some of the difficulties they faced, such as providing receipts for small purchases and accessing information on the internet.[73]

Many of the groups that took part in research did not feel the presence of the MAP at the community level and believe the majority of activity to be conducted by other donors.[74] Despite contributing to the capacity of smaller organisations, the community component of the MAP is viewed as unsustainable.[75] Community groups are pragmatic about the role of the Bank in direct engagement and see themselves as 'too tiny' to be visited by the Bank, and when asked would gesture with their hands that the Bank 'was somewhere up there' with little contact with the grassroots.[76] This is viewed with disappointment. As one member of a community group in Kenya, suggests 'they remain in their ivory towers yet they have so much to offer communities.'[77] The general attitude of the local communities and the wider issues facing the MAP can be summarised in the following quote from the head of Kimara Peer Educators, Pfiriael Kiwia,

> if they would be serious, it can work, if they were really serious. Serious in terms of if they now want to use the agencies, they should at least say these are agencies with a proper structure, and they, like advocate for some sort of network which would facilitate more feedback to them, these are the problems that came out and we're going to solve them this way, face to face, and the project would have this kind of impact on the community. Otherwise if they are not really serious, it's like they have created employment for some people.[78]

Where discussion exists between CSOs, the NACs, DACs and the in-country Bank representatives, there is no clear follow-up structure or requirement for how information arising from such discussions is then fed into the wider priorities of the MAP at either the local or national level. The limited dialogue between the Bank, NACs and nationally funded NGOs leaves the Bank open to accusations of treating CSOs as low-cost service providers. CSOs are aware of feedback mechanisms, but are less informed about stakeholder meetings and direct dialogue. When this was put to the Bank, representatives responded to the question by avoiding it.[79] One way of addressing these concerns has been to open up dialogue into steering committees and annual review meetings; however, similar to patterns of funding and structured dialogue, these meetings only really hear from the usual suspects familiar to the NAC system and the donor community.

Despite the ambition of the Bank and the NACs in terms of scope, the main source of unstructured dialogue with CSOs – the annual partnership meetings – suffer from a number of issues. The meetings are driven by the Bank.[80] There is no clear feedback between decisions made in the working groups or the annual meetings and actual policy and strategic aims. For example, in Kenya the 2005–6 national strategic plan was to be launched after the JAPR based on the findings of the meeting; however, the plan was widely available before the meeting – as a final format, not a draft – and was launched the next day, with little time for additions arising from the meeting. The annual meetings therefore resemble little more than an additional layer of consensual feedback sessions arising from the steering committees.[81] The steering committees preceding the annual meetings suffers from narrow geographical representation and serve to reinforce perceptions that decision-making forums are capital city based.[82] This factor is limited by the level of engagement within the meetings.

Observation of the JAPR in Kenya suggested a hierarchy of participation: World Bank TTLs and UN Agency representatives sat at the front of the meeting; only two of the eight chairs were CSO representatives – one of whom was Elizabeth Ngugi from K-VWORC, a popular figure among the donors; a delay in the start to the meeting, followed by a drawn out report, limited discussion time; English was the working language of the meeting, and all documents preceding the meeting were only available in English; the TWOA as a significant introduction to the Kenya response to HIV/AIDS was only mentioned, in passing, once; and the majority of representatives left after lunch.[83] The greatest problem with such discussion forums is that the participants represent the usual suspects who tend to be regularly engaged on such matters. This can range from networks such as TASO in Uganda, the Kenya AIDS NGO Consortium (KANCO) in Kenya and the National Council of NGOs (NACONGO) in Tanzania, specific national NGOs and FBOs, or particular individuals such as Elizabeth Ngugi of K-VWORC.[84] Those organisations that the NACs are aware of, and have good working relationships with, are the CSOs, who receive greater support in terms of institutional visits, are aware of procedure, are consulted on future policy and are often guaranteed funds.

The issue of the usual suspects presents a further problem for Bank–CSO engagement under the MAP, in that these organisations are not just limited to dialogue but are also receiving funds under the MAP. Organisations participating under the MAP often admitted to having prior relations with senior members of the NAC or the Bank. These prior relations could be that they attended the same school, have staff members that previously worked, or continue to work, in the NAC or Bank, acted as a consultant to the government prior to the MAP, or work for the Ministry of Health.[85] Each of these organisations openly admits that these relationships were significant factors in their receipt of funds, as Patience Talugende, Director of ISESWU – a CSO that received funds under the UACP, suggests 'it was easy for me in the Ministry, because there are projects there, it was easy for me to hear about the funding.'[86] This opens the Bank and its NAC partners up to accusations of nepotism. Inclusion of the usual suspects represents a difficult tendency to break. UNAIDS and the World Bank have responded to the problem by building the NACs capacity to identify CSOs through certain forums: technical skills, identifying gaps within networks, and umbrella organisations.[87] How such capacity is built remains unclear. As suggested previously, one option has been the development of networks, yet in practice such networks are similarly dominated by the usual suspects and divided over who has legitimacy and full access to the NACs, DACs and the Bank.

Networks and problems with inter-CSO collaboration

Partnerships and networking between CSOs is seen as key to effective HIV/AIDS response by the majority of national NGOs interviewed.[88] However, what 'partnership' means in the context of HIV/AIDS and the MAP is often interpreted differently by CSOs, donors and the government. Whereas some organisations view it to be complementing existing activities, training or information sharing – for example, one organisation provides school fees for orphans and then works with another to provide food for the group of orphans – others have come to take on the World Bank's concept of partnership, that which is borne out of a financial relationship.[89]

The leverage of in-country advocacy people with HIV/AIDS networks presents a further limitation to effective engagement. Efforts to establish and sustain people with HIV/AIDS fora suffer from two central problems. The first problem is the perceived negative attitude and continued stigma shown to people with HIV/AIDS by certain members of national NGOs and governments. For example, whereas TASO employs a policy of positive discrimination, wherein people with HIV/AIDS are given preference in available jobs within the organisation, other CSOs such as the AIDS Information Centre in Uganda face accusations of extreme prejudice for not letting volunteers with HIV/AIDS sit with them when eating or have a representative on their board of trustees.[90] The second problem relates to disputes surrounding which organisation or individual is best positioned to represent people with HIV/AIDS. Evidence suggests that such in-fighting and who has the right approach to addressing HIV and AIDS has long been a feature of the responding to the disease in the UK and USA (Berridge 2002; Shilts 1988). Networks and the formation of advocacy groups in sub-Saharan Africa are thus no exception to this. This level of in-fighting becomes increasingly problematic when positions of responsibility have financial reward. The problem of hierarchy and status has led to a stalemate in the establishment of a working PLWHA forum in Tanzania. TACAIDS has been working to establish a Council of People Living with HIV/AIDS (PLWHA) since

2003 through assistance in the writing of the constitution and providing funds for the council. However, conflict between two national NGOs – SHDEPHA+ and TANEPHA – has prevented any progress. As the representative of WAMATA, the CSO appointed by TACAIDS and UNDP to address the situation, describes 'a headache, and the headache is about personalities ... there are two guys there who are rating their popularity' the escalation of this conflict allegedly resulted in the chairman of TANEPHA hitting the treasurer of SHDEPHA+, who was the wife of his rival; the chairman of SHDEPHA+ is now suing the chairman of TANEPHA.[91] Such a situation has led to exasperation on the part of TACAIDS, as the representative of civil society and private sector response within the organisation, Hashim Kalinga describes: 'these people are ... I despair with them',[92] and the World Bank Tanzania MAP TTL, 'certain individuals trying to make money out of their problems ... they are fighting over resources ... I have heard the complaint from TACAIDS that they are really giving them a lot of trouble'.[93]

The responsibility of establishing a forum for people with HIV/AIDS has subsequently been transferred to UNDP because of its relatively apolitical status and influence.[94] There is evidence, however, that such in-fighting is not limited to Tanzania and is characteristic of people with HIV/AIDS forums throughout the subcontinent.[95] The case of Tanzania represents an example of frustration and in-fighting that characterises the co-ordination of such networks. The problem of hierarchy and status are not only limited to networks but are reflective of wider community meetings and discussion groups. For example, the Women Fighting HIV/AIDS in Kenya (WOFAK) 2005 annual meeting was marked by hostility from community members regarding incomplete training, a lack of access to the funding and audit reports of the organisation, and wider misgivings over the disbursement of funds. These queries were acknowledged by WOFAK's director, but those making such claims were based at the back of the crowded meeting room and excluded from direct discussion from WOFAK's central directors. The hierarchy within the organisation was evident in subtle observations of seating plans, and the moving of people from lunch tables to make way for the director of the Kenyan NACC and senior WOFAK management.[96] Participant observation of formal and informal community meetings suggest such hierarchies were not isolated to this example.

What is notable about these networks is they are very much national with little transnational networks or wider collaboration. Their leverage upon both national and international decision-making is limited and is yet to be realised in comparison to networks such as the Treatment Action Campaign in South Africa. As they stand, networks in East Africa are less to do with influence upon decision-making and more involved with efficiency in delivery of services. Sufficient skills, resources and structures for networks to fully access decision-making and dialogue remain located in the international. This limits the leverage of such institutions within global agenda-setting and targeting the directors of the MAP in Washington. One way of extending the leverage and influence of such organisations would be to establish linkages with INGOs. These linkages would potentially help develop the advocacy functions of smaller organisations as well as use the skills and capacity of INGOs to target donors and organisations such as UNAIDS and the Bank. However, national NGOs and community groups funded under the MAP are mistrustful of INGOs based on a perceived unfair advantage they have in accessing funds and where the funding goes. Select national NGOs think INGOs reduce the space in which they could operate and influence decision-making. For every INGO present within government and donor meetings, there was not a national NGO.[97] This led to the general feeling that unless you were a Northern based INGO the issues and problems you faced would not get heard, as one national NGO representative described, 'you need to have a mzungu (white person) working for you to raise and say issues.'[98] There is scope for co-ordination and complementary partnerships, yet different CSOs favour different relationships, e.g. human rights groups prefer to work with other human rights groups, regardless of their HIV/AIDS involvement or geographical location, whereas others prefer issue networking with large INGO support.[99]

Where is the Bank?

What is notable about the problems associated with the MAP is the lack of criticism community groups have of the Bank. Those that strongly criticise the Bank and the MAP are INGOs working at the national level, or other donors such as USAID.[100] According to INGOs working in Uganda, the MAP was widely dismissed by the donor community. This is in part due to the generally negative perceptions of the Bank by INGOs. The Bank is perceived as a cumbersome, bureaucratic organisation that increases rather than reverses poverty and wider development goals.[101] The levels of public relations exercises are of concern to INGOs that identify Bank civil society staff members as 'good schmoozers.'[102] Bank projects are viewed in general as problematic, specifically by INGOs, who take issue with the wider success rate of Bank projects and its ad hoc approach. As a representative of Care International, Tanzania, argues, 'best practice is not their number one primary objective ... if you look at their development work you will very rarely go to a World Bank country and see a project that has worked.'[103] Some organisations see the Bank as working at the diplomatic level as opposed to the operational level, which makes its work donor-driven and therefore hard to find a link between the two, as the Bank does 'not do the work of the poor.'[104] The Bank's conception of civil society within the MAP is seen as narrowly conceived to mean community groups only within an excessively statist approach, 'in short I think I would have to say I found the MAP project very blueprint, it was very narrowly conceived.'[105]

Despite certain concerns with practical aspects of funding, national NGOs are less overtly critical of the MAP and specifically the Bank itself. Those aware of the Bank's involvement in HIV/AIDS have a pragmatic view that their intentions were good in trying to send money to the community but 'their hands are tied due to the size of the project/policy and the 'through – through – through structures', or in other words the need to channel funds through the government.[106] Certain groups were keen to reiterate the positive effect the Bank has had in its commitment to working with the government, as, despite their misgivings, the structures are there and perceived to be working. Overall, however, the Bank is not seen as involved in the MAP by the majority of organisations interviewed. Criticism is either directed towards the MAP and the NACs or the Bank but rarely the Bank's role in the MAP. This is a deliberate function of the MAP.

The MAP is organised in such a way as to disperse forms of influence and detract attention away from the Bank. This makes participation, transparency and accountability as central mechanisms of multi-sectoralism difficult. Engagement with the Bank operates in two ways: first with CSOs funded under the MAP through the NAC system; and, second, through general engagement with the Civil Society Team in Washington as opposed to ACT Africa. The problems of the first form of engagement have been documented within this chapter. However, the over-arching problem with the realisation of full participation on the part of CSOs is that those organisations targeting the Civil Society Team are not aware of the Bank's role in HIV/AIDS. Any awareness or knowledge that they would gain is limited by a lack of networks and inter-CSO collaboration in East Africa. Those national and community-based CSOs do not have the leverage or awareness of either ACT Africa or the Civil Society Team in Washington, and thus continue to direct criticisms to the NACs. For those CSOs excluded from direct engagement with ACT Africa, the main entry point for dialogue with the Bank is the Civil Society Team. However, wider interaction between the Bank and the Civil Society Team, and other agencies of the social development sector, as a means of increasing CSO engagement remains limited. ACT Africa does not hold regular consultation meetings with other units involved in social development and the promotion of CSO engagement. There is no clear consultation mechanism in place between ACT Africa and the Civil Society Team in either the design on implementation of the MAP; these interactions were centred within the Africa Region Team. Such interaction is dependent upon individual personalities and relationships.[107] This is not surprising when looking at the history of the Bank. As Chapter 2 showed, the institution has a mandate to work with states, and although it makes minor concessions to CSOs, it is governments with which it forms direct partnerships with. The World Bank would view such structures as successful functions of good multi-sectoral governance as it is states that own and take responsibility for the project, and CSOs are holding them to account. This perspective on the part of the Bank embeds the fact that it is only a residual actor within the MAP. CSOs are unable to fully hold states or the Bank to account as they are constructed and maintained through financial incentive and there is a blurring of who is accountable for what. States are similarly unable to hold the Bank to account as their relationship within the MAP is organised around financial commitments to good multi-sectoral governance. The Bank thus operates with a lack of accountability, transparency, ownership or partnership: the main functions of the multi-sectoral HIV/AIDS response that it purports.

Multi-sectoralism in practice is about a specific brand of good governance which is economically driven. Economic incentive as the main means of facilitating multi-sectoralism results in division and competition between CSOs and the emergence of a decentralised HIV/AIDS service industry. Advocacy and consultation is structured by the state and the Bank, and organised in such a way as to limit autonomy and influence of national NGOs and community groups from the over-arching system of HIV/AIDS governance put forward by the NACs and the Bank. This points to the central contention of the Bank's governance agenda: it can create a form of civil society activity that has the structures of good governance; however, the only way to do so is through neoliberal forms of economic incentive that instead of leading to wider participation and functions of good liberal governance result in a market for HIV/AIDS service provision, with little emphasis upon accountability and transparency. CSOs funded under the MAP are effective in their use of the rhetoric of good governance, and in complaining about the structures of the NACs and DACs, yet this is limited in such a way as to hinder wider critical engagement of the state and those international organisations such as the Bank that seek to influence it. The remaining site of contestation and liberal governance reform is that of the individual.

The individual

Governance of HIV/AIDS principally refers to the governance of the individual: our bodies, our relationships and our choices or lack thereof. Thus at the centre of any agenda for HIV/AIDS interventions is how to change not only the society and culture of states within East Africa as a means of breaking stigma, educating people about infection, and caring for people infected and affected by the disease, but to address individual behaviour and choice. For the MAP and the Bank to be successful within its HIV/AIDS interventions they must go beyond influencing the state and the community and affect decision-making within the individual. The need to address 'the complex social and individual behaviours involved in HIV transmission' is fundamental to the shift away from a clinical approach to addressing HIV/AIDS towards multi-sectoralism (World Bank 2007a: 15). There is nothing significantly different about the Bank's approach to what the HIV/AIDS community calls 'behaviour change communication' but what is different are the new measures the Bank is adopting to provide economic incentives as a means of inducing a specific form of rational individual behaviour.

The Bank has begun to address individual behaviour within the MAP through established mechanisms of behaviour change communication. Behaviour change communication generally refers to the development of different approaches and messages in order to, according to Family Health International, 'develop positive behaviours, promote and sustain individual, community and societal behaviour change, and maintain appropriate behaviours' (FHI/USAID 2002). 'Appropriate' behaviour in this regard refers to increased condom use, reduced number of sexual partners, reduced stigma, advocacy and demand for information and services, awareness of risk and a delay in first sexual activity (FHI/USAID 2002). In practice this can take the form of community role plays, shared testimonials by people infected and affected by HIV/AIDS, drama productions and sporting events, government policies, peer-to-peer counselling and the media presence of PLWHA. The Bank adopts an approach to behaviour change based upon the principles of social diffusion theory that suggests individuals respond better to the experience and testimonies of community members, friends and neighbours than external experts (World Bank 2007a: 63–64). Hence for the Bank effective behaviour change must be based on local knowledge community led that 'can be supported – but not directed – from the outside' (World Bank 2007a: 64). The main implementers of behaviour change tend to be community networks and the media.

Behaviour change communication is a central function of the global response to HIV/AIDS both in breaking stigma associated with the disease and preventing increased HIV infection rates. It is thus integral to the working practices of the MAP. However, it is undermined by two contentious issues. The first is the contradiction between the Bank emphasising its supportive and benevolent role for communities to take a leadership role while promoting a form of change specific to the wider objectives of the MAP. The need for behaviour change communication has emerged from global institutions such as the Bank and not the communities that implement such behaviour. The Bank thus has to isolate those actors that do recognise the need for breaking stigma and changing individual behaviour, and then educate them on what is 'appropriate' behaviour change. Second, the incentive for such change is the threat of HIV infection. This approach assumes that the perceived risk of HIV infection is such that individuals will rationally address their behaviour in a manner to limit infection of themselves and others. However, for many people denial remains a strong barrier to understanding such risk; and for others the risk of HIV infection is something to be balanced against their existing quality of life and life expectancy. For example, if the average life expectancy for a certain country is low, individuals may rationalise that it is better to spend money on eating rather than expensive drugs and treatment; they may also prefer sexual intercourse without a condom, and hence see present pleasure as more important to their quality of life than some form of 'other' long-term suffering, especially if their life is likely to be short anyway. Rationality for the Bank and the international community is not necessarily the same as what is rational for other people. Rational human beings have a tendency to act irrationally; it is thus important for any form of liberal governance reform to provide the incentives towards a specific conception of rational behaviour.

The issue of rationality has been pertinent to HIV/AIDS interventions since the first wave of the pandemic in the USA. The behaviour of 'Patient Zero', Gaetan Dugas, has long been an area of contestation within the HIV/AIDS community. Documented within Randy Shilts' *And the Band Played On*, Dugas is depicted as being in denial as to methods of HIV transmission and his own ill health to the extent that he would have unprotected sex with multiple partners in the dark so they would not be able to notice the lesions on his body caused by AIDS-related Kaposi's sarcoma, only after proclaiming 'Gay cancer … Maybe you'll get it too' (Shilts 1988: 198). Dugas' alleged behaviour is an extreme example of denial or irrational behaviour. However, such extremes continue within the current wave of the HIV/AIDS pandemic. The main problem for the global response to HIV/AIDS to behaviour change is thus twofold: (i) how to induce change from the community when there is not necessarily willingness to do so and (ii) how to induce change when the risk of ill health or death is not a strong enough incentive. For the Bank the answer is economic incentive.

Conditional cash transfers have grown to have a central role within the Bank's healthcare interventions. According to the World Bank's report *Conditional Cash Transfers: Reducing Present and Future Poverty*, 'conditional cash transfers are programs that transfer cash, generally to poor households on the condition that these households make pre-specified investments in the human capital of their children' (Fiszbein and Schady 2009). These transfers are to act as 'social safety nets' by encouraging parents to invest in the health and education of their children. They have become the norm of poverty lending within Latin American countries, principally within Brazil and Mexico, and in recent years have been piloted in three countries in sub-Saharan Africa: Burkina Faso, Kenya and Nigeria (Fiszbein and Schady 2009). Conditional cash transfers have begun to be recognised as effective tools for behaviour change by those working in the Bank on public health and HIV/AIDS in Africa. In line with the Bank's previous experience in Latin American countries, conditional cash transfers have been mooted as a source of support for those caring for orphans and vulnerable children to encourage them to invest in their health and education. The most significant change, however, relates to the potential use of conditional cash transfers as economic incentive for behaviour change.

The Bank's role in behaviour change communication and the potential to use conditional cash transfers as a means of incentivising safe sex suggest one of the central contentions of the liberal underpinnings of the governance HIV/AIDS: how to incentivise rational behaviour within irrational human beings. Incentives such as education, peer-to-peer counselling, media campaigns and government legislation have all increased awareness of the risks of means of HIV transmission but have not correlated in a change in behaviour. What the Bank has done is thus turn to *neo*liberal principles of governance reform by introducing private economic gain as an incentive to encourage rational behaviour within individuals and community groups. This follows the same pattern the Bank has adopted within community groups. When specific incentives, such as risk of illness, suffering and premature death, fail to induce widespread support and advocacy among a population, the Bank introduces the concept of economic gain either through community sponsorship or conditional cash transfers. In the immediate context of the MAP's lifetime this form of economic incentive has several outcomes. The first is a shift within local economies from traditional forms of economic development through production in agriculture to service economies within the NGO sector. The funding towards HIV/AIDS is such that individuals recognise HIV/AIDS as a sphere in which money can be made and is in many regards more profitable than other industries. For example, when conducting research for this book, a conversation with local taxi drivers in Dar es Salaam revealed how a few were considering setting up an NGO because that way they would be paid well, have a nice house and be given a car. The second result of the Bank's use of economic incentive is the beginnings of introducing the market to governing individual behaviour. Key to the Bank's governance reform of the state and community response to HIV/AIDS is the targeting of individual behaviour. Reform of HIV/AIDS governance by the Bank thus concentrates on these inter-related spheres of interest – the state, the community and the individual – and the main operating incentive for such reform is economic gain.

Conclusion

This chapter has shown that the community is at the centre of the Bank's multi-sectoral agenda for HIV/AIDS governance reform. This in itself is not particularly new or revealing. As Chapter 2 suggests the Bank has long sought to establish relationships with community groups and it is local communities that have often felt the brunt of the HIV/AIDS pandemic. However, the MAP presents one of the largest projects of systematic inclusion of community groups within the Bank. It is the community that is constructed as a form of civil society. This form of civil society is driven by financial incentive as a means of caring and treating the sick, breaking stigma and crucially changing behaviour among individuals as a means of HIV prevention. This financial incentive has led to mixed outcomes. As the Bank hoped for at the beginning of the MAP, there has been an upsurge in community activity and widespread awareness of HIV and AIDS. However, those community groups and national NGOs funded under the MAP continue to be excluded from decision-making or any feedback into how the local, national and global HIV/AIDS response may be directed or what it will prioritise. Groups are divided over money and status. What has happened is the construction of a specific form of multi-sectoral service industry located within local communities under the label of civil society. The sidelining of INGOs and more advocacy-based NGOs in-country has silenced the critics of the Bank and led to disaggregated structures of influence, so it is unclear for those affected by the MAP how they access decision-making. Compounding this are the problems of ownership and economic incentive within the NAC system that facilitates this type of civil society.

The role of multi-sectoral civil society has not led to more good HIV/AIDS governance. Communities are unable to fully hold the government to account, and crucially the role of the Bank is not at all transparent. The problem for the Bank in instilling good HIV/AIDS governance reform is that it has used neoliberal forms of economic incentive to create liberal outcomes. What the Bank's agenda for HIV/AIDS thus comes to look like is a contention between the desire for liberal governance reform and the neoliberal economic incentives used within the state, community and the individual to attain such reform. It is this contention within the Bank's form of multi-sectoral HIV/AIDS governance that underpins the wider structures and institutions of the global response to the epidemic. The following chapter will show how the Bank's multi-sectoral governance reform agenda and the contentions within it have been exported to and promoted within global forums of decision-making, implementation and other project design.

5   Setting a global agenda

The problems and contradictions inherent within the World Bank's global agenda for HIV/AIDS are bounded within the central contention of the MAP: how to enact liberal governance reform through neoliberal means. These problems are not isolated to the MAP or the Bank itself but are endemic within the system of HIV/AIDS governance that has come to constitute the global response. The reason being that at the heart of the global response is the MAP. The previous chapters have shown how the central principles of the MAP, and thus the working practices of the Bank's good governance reform agenda, have come to shape every level of HIV/AIDS governance at the state and community level. This chapter will show how this agenda has become embedded within the global response. The MAP underpins the working practices of various UN agencies, the Global Fund and bilateral donors. New actors that have emerged within HIV/AIDS governance must align with this system. Despite the fact the various MAP projects are currently coming to an end and the Bank appearing to withdraw from HIV/AIDS interventions, in establishing the foundations of the global response the Bank continues to set its agenda through institutions that constitute global HIV/AIDS governance.

The chapter pursues its aim of showing how the World Bank has set and sustained the global agenda for HIV/AIDS by first looking at the decline of the WHO and the relationship between the Bank, UNAIDS and the UN system. Second, the chapter then looks at how the MAP underpins the central mechanisms and approach to HIV/AIDS governance of the Global Fund, before considering the relationship between the current system and bilateral actors such as the US government's PEPFAR programme and the rise of philanthropic foundations, principally the Bill and Melinda Gates Foundation. Third, the chapter explores how the problems and contentions found within the MAP at the state level are replicated at the global level of institutional interaction, and the ramifications of this for effectively responding to the HIV/AIDS epidemic. Fourth, The chapter outlines how, despite the Bank seemingly withdrawing from HIV/AIDS in sub-Saharan Africa, the Bank's influence is extending in other ways within these countries, and how the framework of the MAP continues to be exported throughout the Caribbean. As such, the chapter argues that through a combination of timing and establishing structures within health systems at the country-level through the

MAP, the Bank has established and sustained the working structures of the global HIV/AIDS response.

Goodbye WHO, hello UNAIDS: the MAP and the UN system

The Bank's ability to set the global agenda for HIV/AIDS primarily lies with its relationship with UNAIDS and the relative sidelining of the WHO. As Chapter 2 outlined, in the years preceding the MAP, the role of the WHO had began to decline as a result of leadership issues, accusations of cronyism and a general unwillingness to take risks. Kenna Owoh identifies this period as that between the 1978 Alma Ata Declaration and the 1993 World Development Report, wherein a general shift from state-organised to market-driven private welfare occurred and the 'WHO ceded leadership to the World Bank' (Owoh 1996: 213). The decline of the WHO in regard to HIV/AIDS specifically was the consequence of the end of the first multilateral programme on HIV/AIDS – the Global Programme on AIDS (GPA) – and the perceived failure of the '3 by 5' initiative to get 3 million people on ART by 2005.

In 1987 the UN designated the WHO as the lead agency in responding to the global HIV/AIDS crisis, resulting in the establishment of the GPA. Financed by the WHO's core budget and those countries that wanted to fund HIV/AIDS programmes multilaterally the GPA's priorities were to provide over-arching guidelines to states; endorse public education as a means of prevention; give advice on safe blood products; assess diagnostic methodology; and co-ordinate research into the epidemic (Lisk 2009). Underpinning this was a commitment to stigma and a rights-based approach to tackling the epidemic: the antecedents of the multi-sectoral approach the Bank would come to adopt. Despite having relative success under the leadership of Jonathan Mann, the GPA soon fell into difficulty in 1988 with the appointment of Hiroshi Nakajima as Director-General of the WHO. Nakajima's appointment saw the resurgence of a primarily public health approach to the institution's operations, and crucially attempts to reign in the spending and autonomy of the GPA (Lisk 2009). Key to this was limiting the authority of Mann and the need to mainstream the GPA within the wider structures and programmes of the WHO (Lisk 2009). HIV/AIDS was soon mainstreamed across the operations of the WHO and the GPA was rolled into a stand alone, UN co-ordinating agency: UNAIDS. The WHO since the end of the GPA has taken a backseat role in the governance of HIV/AIDS, with the exception of the '3 by 5' initiative. Launched on World AIDS Day 2003, the aim of the initiative was to have 3 million people on anti-retroviral treatment in developing countries by 2005 (WHO 2009). However, the project was labelled a failure because it did not reach its target, and was mired by contention among the WHO, WTO and pharmaceutical companies over access to treatment and patent laws under the regulations on Trade-Related Intellectual Property Rights (TRIPs). Accusations of misdirection of funds and lack of payment from its member states followed, and donor states began to seek other means of financing global health initiatives.[1] The difficulty in articulating a clearly defined health strategy by the WHO had two significant consequences for the global governance of HIV/AIDS: (i) a gap in multilateral HIV/AIDS financing left by the GPA that opened up space for the World Bank to develop its multi-sectoral agenda, and (ii) UNAIDS assumed the role of lead agency targeting the epidemic within the UN system.

The UN's central role within the HIV/AIDS response is to mobilise political and financial support and co-ordinate the response at all levels of governance. The current level of political support for HIV/AIDS is in part the response to the United National General Assembly Special Session on HIV/AIDS (UNGASS) declarations of 2001 and 2006. The first high-level response to HIV/AIDS was the inclusion of 'Combat HIV/AIDS, malaria and other diseases' as Goal 6 of the Millennium Development Goals. This put HIV/AIDS on the global agenda, but failed to secure any financial or political willing to address the issues at hand. UNGASS 2001 was the first commitment of this kind. It provided a watershed in terms of political and financial support to fight HIV/AIDS and was marked by the introduction of the concept for a Global Fund.[2] UNGASS 2006 represented a follow-up of the commitments made in 2001 and a reaffirmation of commitment at a time when both the first round of the US President's Emergency Plan for AIDS Relief (PEPFAR) and the MAP were coming to an end.[3] Securing political commitment and co-ordinating the response to HIV/AIDS has become the responsibility of UNAIDS. UNAIDS has acquired this role through its perception as a non-political agency with no funding mechanism or governmental linkages. It presents itself as an 'honest broker' that does not have a hidden agenda.[4] Technically, the role of UNAIDS is to consider how UN systems are working in-country to support such systems and to co-ordinate the various agencies. UNAIDS has aligned its working mechanisms with the MAP and its practices in-country. The NAC system of HIV/AIDS governance is one in which all international institutions commit to under the rubric of government ownership of the response to their national epidemics. Hence, UN agencies must commit to working within government structures. This occurs to varying degrees among different UN agencies; however, UNAIDS has institutionalised the NAC system through its central co-ordinating mechanisms. The principal role of UNAIDS is to co-ordinate UN efforts in the response to HIV/AIDS, hence its co-sponsors – UNHCR, UNICEF, ILO, World Food Programme (WFP), UNDP, UNFPA, UNODC, UNESCO, WHO and the World Bank – must co-ordinate their interests and programmes with the main guiding principles the agency provides.

Co-ordination occurs through two central mechanisms: 'The Three Ones' principles launched on 25 April 2004 and the Global Task Team on Improving AIDS Co-ordination among Multilateral Institutions and International Donors (GTT) on 2005 (UNAIDS 2005a,b). 'The Three Ones' advocates one strategic plan, one co-ordinating body and one monitoring and evaluation system at the national level; and the GTT, arising from the 2005 'Making the Money Work' meeting, is the tool via which the principles are operationalised.[5] 'The Three Ones' commitment to one strategic plan and one co-ordinating body reflects the main tenets and working practice central to the MAP: the one co-ordinating body refers to the NACs; the one strategic plan refers to each country's national strategic plan, which as Chapter 3 showed, tend to be underpinned by the main priorities of the MAP and an over-arching commitment to multi-sectorality; and one monitoring and evaluation system that prioritises multi-sectoral partnerships and the need for good transparent and accountable governance. 'The Three Ones' has since become *the* working principles for the global HIV/AIDS response to which all actors subscribe to. It thus legitimises the NAC system created by the Bank, and further embeds the global commitment to multi-sectoralism based upon financial incentive.

The interlinkages between multi-sectoralism and UNAIDS go beyond the parallels between the MAP and 'The Three Ones' to UNAIDS' wider engagement of CSOs. UNAIDS engages with CSOs by ensuring such actors are involved in the 'strategic planning process' where national priorities and plans are created, and ensuring regular contact and co-ordination. UNAIDS strengthens the capacity of CSOs through effective proposal writing, monitoring and evaluation, and training on how to mobilise resources. To avoid in-fighting and conflict between CSOs, UNAIDS works to establish networks and links between different organisations. Finally, UNAIDS strengthens CSO access to decision-making by involving them in the UNGASS discussions and fostering dialogue between them and national governments.[6] Commitment to government partnership and CSO inclusion as core functions of multi-sectoral governance is evident throughout the working practices of UNAIDS' co-sponsors, with perhaps the exception of the WHO. Partnerships with CSOs either take the form of formal associations within the UN system, or meeting with CSO representatives at the regional and national level, and facilitating partnership and inclusion at the state level.

Effective co-ordination is promoted through joint monitoring and evaluation mechanisms, with the majority of international organisations and governments subscribing to the Lot Quality Assurance (LQA) system.[7] Central to such co-operation is the reinforcement of the Bank's multi-sectoral approach, both through the key components of co-ordination and through actors such as UNAIDS that oversee it.[8] The extent of integration varies between countries and is dependent on a number of factors, most notably individual personalities,[9] and is presented by Kristan Schoultz, Country Director of UNAIDS Kenya, as being close and collaborative,

> we have a very particular healthy development partner network. These are our colleagues and they're also your friends, I mean we're in all the same meetings together, we're in meetings convened by each other, in meetings by government and other partners so it's quite a day to day close working relationship.[10]

The practical realities of operations suggest co-ordination is obscured by overlap leading to double-dipping of donor funds, where CSOs receive funds for the same project or activity from multiple donors, and competing organisational objectives.[11] These problems arise from donors not being open and transparent in where they are spending their money; lack of attendance at the Development Partners Group (DPGs) – a representative of the Center for Disease Control (CDC) openly admitted he did not attend the meetings and that he did not know anyone who did; and disdain for 'The Three Ones' and the working structures within it.[12] Overall 'people do not want to be co-ordinated.'[13] Underpinning these factors is the different agenda, criteria and preferred areas of intervention of each individual organisation,[14] whether a donor or a CSO. As Rustica Tembele of TACAIDS describes the work of donors,

> You find they are treading on each others' toes and yet you could see how they could. You know what I mean? It's competition, because donors also have their own agendas, they have instructions from back home, where they're coming from, that is a problem.[15]

Differing priorities and a multiplicity of actors lead to difficulty in measuring the success of specific approaches and policies. As a result, different organisations are keen to attribute success or progress to their individual interventions. Each donor wants to demonstrate their good work and authority on the subject so as to persevere with their own individual mandate at the expense of policy and project harmonisation.[16] The predominant role of UNAIDS and its co-sponsors at the national level is to co-ordinate the response, the success of which is challenged by the combination of individual personalities, perspectives and organisational leverage in a specific country. UNAIDS co-ordinates the response in each country, but at the global level of HIV/AIDS governance, it is only responsible for its co-sponsors and reflects the NACs in terms of capacity and lack of authority to enforce 'The Three Ones' over major donors. The role of UNDP, for example, varies between countries, with the Tanzania representative leading the DPG while the Uganda representative is excluded from wider HIV/AIDS structures.[17]

A specific example of the World Bank's involvement within such partnership structures can be seen in its engagement of the WFP. In Kenya the HIV/AIDS representative of WFP were unaware of the then in-coming Total War on AIDS (TWOA) project and were not invited to the Joint Annual Programme Review (JAPR).[18] Only 24 per cent of those groups interviewed had heard of the TWOA and only 29 per cent had been invited to attend the JAPR. In Uganda, the WFP tried to engage with the World Bank to see who they were funding and how they could complement their programmes and received no information; as the WFP Programme Officer Uganda Purnima Kashyap describes 'the World Bank is in a world of its own.'[19] Despite the presentation of a united front and donors in-country emphasising the need for nutritional support for PLWHA, the World Bank task team leader (TTL) for Uganda responded to such a claim by stating 'I've really never known exactly what they want to do, I know they want to support nutrition but exactly how that fits into HIV/AIDS as a programme is not very clear.'[20]

The Bank's disdain for WFP would suggest a lack of inclusion of the organisation into its wider agenda. However, the WFP is in a precarious position within the UN system: it is not a co-sponsor of UNAIDS and is often seen as a second-tiered agency in regards to HIV/AIDS. Hence, the Bank does not need to align its interests with the organisation. Rather, WFP must align itself with the Bank in order to gain wider relevance in the development partner community.

Policy alignment across UN institutions towards multi-sectoralism is only one means through which the Bank extends influence via its agenda for HIV/AIDS. The Bank is further able to extend this influence through the filtering of key actors within global health through the Bank system into other international actors working on global health. Similar to patterns with those NGOs and community groups familiar to the Bank, a select number of 'sacred cows' (Pisani 2008) or 'gatekeepers'[21] occupy the main leadership roles in HIV/AIDS governance. Many of these actors have worked in similar institutions, come from similar backgrounds and have close working relationships. For example, Richard Feachem, the first Executive Director of the Global Fund (2002–7) was Director for Health, Nutrition and Population (1995–9) at a strategic time in the Bank's arrival on the global health stage. Feachem was widely credited for bringing health issues to the fore within the Bank during the Wolfensohn reform period (Abbasi 1999a: 866–867). Bank staff are briefed in the art of 'paradigm maintenance' (Wade 1996) wherein they are employed, promoted and recognised for taking an approach to global health that fits in with the Bank's over-arching commitment to market-based, neoliberal development initiatives (Broad 2006). As is often the case within the development field, there is much cross-over between professionals in global health organisations. However, this cross-over does not signal a cross-germination of public health and a liberal approach to global health. The policy space is one-way, with market-based interventions supplanting 'public' health approaches within these organisations. What is specific about the World Bank's role in health is how it has exerted its influence and embedded its own paradigm for global health through a combination of individuals, state and community partnership.

The influence of the Bank is widely recognised by those working within the international HIV/AIDS community. When asked about whether there was a link between the MAP and 'The Three Ones' ex-Executive Director of UNAIDS, Peter Piot responded:

> Oh yeah. Definitely ... I think that historically the MAP was the first discreet international effort especially for AIDS, before the Global Fund, before PEPFAR, the concept came from 99/98, and because of the World Bank's leverage with the finance ministers and so on I think it was of tremendous help to put HIV on the agenda.[22]

Piot is not alone in thinking this. Many of those working in the international HIV/AIDS community, especially in sub-Saharan Africa, are aware of the presence of the MAP and the Bank. The Bank is present at in-country donor partnership meetings, government steering committees and UNAIDS' committee of co-sponsoring organisations. The Bank is not a passive actor within these meetings. Yet there is a curious silence as to its role and the ramifications of the project in wider discussions about the effectiveness of the global HIV/AIDS response. Institutions that offer large amounts of money often come under more scrutiny, especially when the organisation has a reputation for problematic projects like the Bank. However, the Bank (and the MAP) receives little attention because it is effective in emphasising the ownership role of governments and presenting itself as a benevolent facilitator of government activity. Moreover such is the fragility of HIV/AIDS funding that after decades of campaigning for greater funds, there is a reticence towards questioning the manner in which these funds are deployed and the long-term consequences they have for the state and community in sub-Saharan Africa. The long term is generally only considered in regard to the epidemic, not the sociopolitical context in which it is situated. The Bank engages in a specific form of quiet diplomacy that is underpinned by significant financial commitment in such a way that the state, the community and other actors, such as UNAIDS, and increasingly the Global Fund, are seen as the central mechanisms for effective HIV/AIDS governance.

The new MAP? The Global Fund

Although UNAIDS extends the Bank's agenda for HIV/AIDS governance through its role in co-ordination, perhaps the clearest extension of the multi-sectoral approach to combating the epidemic is the Global Fund. Established under UNGASS 2001, the Global Fund was presented as a new paradigm in health funding, based on CSO inclusion in the decision-making process, rapid disbursement of funds and government partnership. It was seen as dynamic in that it had CSOs present within its main governing body: on the Board of the Fund in Geneva and a large presence within the Fund's in-country operating bodies, the Country Co-ordinating Mechanisms (CCMs). This apparent dynamism, however, is merely an extension of the multi-sectoral principles established by the MAP. In effect, the Fund's commitment to multi-sectoralism, and the mechanisms it uses to respond to the epidemic are ideationally identical to the MAP and the NAC system the Bank has created. This is clear in the operations of the CCMs and the workings of the Fund in-country, and the Fund's status within the UN. The differences between the Fund and the Bank only seek to embed the Bank's influence further.

The Global Fund operates in-country through CCMs that disburse funds and co-ordinate state responses to HIV/AIDS. The Global Fund provides technical assistance and support to the CCMs, but the emphasis of operations is country-driven. The CCMs are near-exact replicas of the NACs established under the MAP: both have the role of co-ordination, mapping activity and facilitating CSO engagement (Global Fund 2007). The similarities between the two have led to the inclusion of the CCMs in some countries within the NACs. The only difference between the two structures is that 40 per cent of the CCMs should be composed of CSO representatives, which should include the presence of people with HIV/AIDS. These CSOs were either handpicked participants or the positions for CSOs within the CCMs were advertised in the local media of each country.[23] However, the central tenets of inclusion, partnership and participation resonate between the two, and there has since been a move to increase CSO involvement within the NACs. The importance of increasing knowledge of their activities within the community and emphasis upon increased participation remain central components of each project.

In the three countries examined, the CCM was included within the NACs. When conducting research in 2005–6, the NACs themselves knew little about the Fund: Uganda had had its funding withdrawn; Kenya 'is not working well with Global Fund money';[24] and Tanzania seemed to be developing a proactive approach to managing the funds.[25] When funding was withdrawn from Uganda there was little awareness of what was happening, how the funds were being assessed and when or if the Fund would return. The majority of government actors and CSOs only knew the actions of the enquiry into the mismanagement of funds through the local media.[26] The Global Fund's grants are disbursed in rounds annually. However, if the funds for Round 1 are not spent, a country cannot receive funds for Round 2. Global Fund funding mechanisms are met with frustration as there has been a delay in disbursement. For example, in Kenya, where only 30 per cent of funds were spent, access to the next round of funding was restricted.[27] This has a knock-on effect on the CSOs sponsored under the Global Fund who are dependent on the next round of funds. For example, KENWA was guaranteed that once their Round 1 contract, to sustain 450 people on ART with Global Fund money, ended it would be continued. However, because of 'structural problems' with the government the contract was delayed, leaving 450 people without ART and KENWA having to rapidly negotiate contracts with other donors.[28] National NGOs have not had a positive response to the Fund: there is a lack of information how to access funds; no clear feedback structure; and a lack of consistency in their objectives.[29] The accusation that Uganda's funding was withdrawn as a result of CSOs mis-spending funds heightened this tension.[30] Similarly in Tanzania, delays in funding and efficiency in notifying CSOs of the status of their application led to confusion, as Nick Southern of Care International Tanzania describes:

> the Global Fund, we had a letter from the post, this is an example of Tanzania, we had a letter from TACAIDS, Global Fund round 2, or 2003, so we wrote the proposal for 2002, we got a letter a year ago now that we are delighted to inform you have won the contract, and we had a hard time because the person who wrote that's computer crashed and we had no copy of the proposal, we actually had to get a copy of the proposal, that was 3 years old, no one had an idea, now when you've got those sort of things going on, then you have an absolute recipe for confusion.[31]

Since 2006 there is evidence that the Fund is working more effectively within these countries, and that it is increasingly taking on issues that were previously the responsibility and priorities of the MAP. This is supported by looking at the patterns of who the principal recipients tend to be in each country. In 2008, the principal recipients of Global Fund money for Tanzania were the Ministry of Health, the Ministry of Finance, Pact Tanzania, Population Services International and AMREF; in Uganda, just the Ministry of Finance; and in Kenya, KENWA, Sanaa Arts Promotions, Ministry of Finance and Care International. In all three cases, the Ministry of Finance is earmarked for funds. Earmarking funds for the Ministry of Finance shows a commitment to supporting state structures, which is the norm for any multilateral donor. However, combined with targeting those large NGOs that were also closely involved in the MAP, and placing an emphasis upon improving mechanisms of good governance such as ownership and participation, we begin to see evidence of a wider alignment to the MAP. Significantly, the Fund has taken on the role of strengthening the capacity and ownership of the DACs and CSO participation within these structures. For example, in conversations with representatives of TACAIDS and the Global Fund in Tanzania in 2009, it became evident that those funds earmarked for Round 9 of the funding process would be channelled to the districts to help them develop the multi-sectoral approach to addressing the epidemic. The emphasis upon Round 9 was to take over where the Tanzanian MAP had left off, with TACAIDS directing it.

Despite trends towards a convergence between the MAP and the Fund, there are several differences that must be acknowledged when suggesting an over-arching symmetry between the two organisations. First, the Fund focuses upon malaria and tuberculosis as well as HIV/AIDS. Second, the Fund has engaged with the private sector – through the Global Business Coalition and its Project RED campaign – as a means of sustaining funds in a manner that the MAP failed to. Third, despite having specialised UN status, the Fund is not a co-sponsor of UNAIDS and, fourth, it has no in-country presence; instead the Fund has representatives for specific regions, normally about five countries per person. Fifth, the Fund specifically targets large national or international NGOs as principal recipients. The logic employed is that these groups will then work with local communities as sub-recipients. Of note, it is these differing factors that have subjected the Global Fund to much of its criticism. A central bone of contention remains its lack of in-country presence. This has led to difficulties in co-ordination between the different agencies on a regular basis; minimal knowledge of what the Global Fund actually does, who they are, how they work and their intentions; and a delay in funding disbursement.[32] The functioning of the CCMs is problematic through the confusion over funding disbursal, where it goes and how it fits in with the wider response.[33] Initially, the lack of knowledge surrounding the CCMs resulted in minimal CSO participation within decision-making. Issues of tokenism and inclusion of the 'usual suspects' continue to be a problem but are at times unavoidable. For example, participation of people with HIV/AIDS has been marred by sickness and confusion over the jargon and acronyms used within such meetings.[34]

The corollary of these differences is that they are additional as opposed to counteractive functions in embedding the Bank's multi-sectoral agenda. In adopting a multi-sectoral approach to good HIV/AIDS governance, the Fund extends such an agenda to the areas of malaria and tuberculosis through the state, NGOs and, crucially, the private sector. The Fund's limited in-country presence restricts its ability to establish working relationships with both the state and the community. This can also be seen in its lack of co-sponsorship of UNAIDS. The Bank in contrast is able to present itself as a useful partner of states and UN agencies through its continued presence, and the relative stability of its funding. The Global Fund relies on funding from bilateral and multilateral partners, as does the Bank. However, the Bank's HIV/AIDS interventions draw from a larger budget of core funding to the Bank – specifically the IDA and International Bank for Reconstruction and Development – whereas the Fund is dependent upon fluctuations within the development community and funding for health initiatives. As Chapter 2 showed, it is exactly such a high profile, flexible project such as the MAP for which the IDA was established in order to generate and sustain funds. In this sense, the Bank has considerably more longevity having shown itself to be an effective lender of last resort and adaptable to changes in the global financial market. The Global Fund has not. What we thus see is the Fund embedding the multi-sectoral approach to HIV/AIDS articulated by the Bank, while not threatening the authority of the Bank's relationship with states or the longevity of the institution's role within global health.

The similarities and overlap between the MAP and the Global Fund have seen a need to delineate the functions of both institutions. The Global Fund reiterates the need for co-ordination within the global response through regional meetings between its 'natural partners', that is UNAIDS and its co-sponsors, wherein in they share knowledge and advice on technical issues. Agencies conduct joint implementation visits, and discussion forums and collaboration have transcended consultation through practical co-ordination, for example, in Burkina Faso, Fund money was delayed so the MAP stood the shortfall.[35] In 2006, the Fund and Bank published a study on their requisite comparative advantages and how their activities could complement each other and lead to wider co-ordination within the global response. For the Fund, this means maintaining its role in financing rather than implementing initiatives to address HIV/AIDS, malaria and tuberculosis, and engaging in methods of prevention and treatment procurement as opposed to health system strengthening. Health system strengthening and capacity-building is very much considered the remit of the Bank, 'its strategic and programmatic focus should emphasize this to a much greater extent and with enhanced clarity. This is fundamental to progress not merely on AIDS but to other diseases' (Shakow 2006: 6). In strengthening health systems, the report suggests the Bank should use its leadership role as a broker for large investments in health among donors and develop a 'more complementary partnership with WHO.' Crucially, the Bank should address its own internal management and promote multi-sectoral budgeting, and work with governments to build policy frameworks that facilitate the work of the Fund. The report recognises the existing problems of lack of ownership, alignment with existing country systems and co-ordination, yet purports to address these problems by embedding existing structures further. Both institutions should adhere to and promote 'The Three Ones', encourage unification of the NACs and the CCMs, and look to identify a lead donor in each country. Where the Fund and Bank are not working together in-country, staff members should be accountable as to why (Shakow 2006). These recommendations do not fundamentally alter existing systems of HIV/AIDS governance, but seek to embed the Bank's agenda further in clearly stipulating how the Fund can become more aligned to the Bank and the institutions established within the MAP. In emphasising the need for the Bank to engage in more horizontal interventions towards strengthening multi-sectoral health systems as a whole as opposed to vertical interventions on specific issues such as HIV/AIDS, the antecedents of the Bank's agenda for HIV/AIDS becoming its agenda for global health are established. What is particularly interesting is the acknowledgment of the Bank's leadership role within HIV/AIDS and how the Fund does not supplant this, but should become aligned to it.

The Global Fund is the new MAP in that it embeds the structures, multi-sectoral ethos and financial incentive established under the project. There is clear overlap and symmetry between the two, with the Fund falling into line with leadership principles established within the MAP. What we see therefore is a structure of HIV/AIDS governance, articulated by the Bank and embedded by the MAP, UNAIDS, the UN system and the Global Fund. These actors embed this agenda through a combination of policy and practice that has established an over-arching framework in which agenda-setting and directives within the global HIV/AIDS response are made. The only challenge to this agenda is through the US government's PEPFAR programme and the growth and financial commitments of philanthropic foundations in HIV/AIDS interventions. Although these agencies commit to the wider global agenda for HIV/AIDS articulated by the Bank, they have the financial capacity to circumvent existing structures at the state level and develop concurrent systems of delivery.

The President's Emergency Plan for AIDS Relief

Announced as part of George W. Bush's 28 January 2003 State of the Union address, PEPFAR reflects the ideological preferences of the Bush administration for bilateral over multilateral initiatives (Morrison and Summers 2003: 183). Launched just after the MAP, PEPFAR was initially a US$15 billion 5-year strategy that would integrate care, treatment and prevention programmes across the world, with a focus upon rapid disbursement and results. That is, large commitments to the provision of ART and strengthening Ministry of Health capacity. PEPFAR has since been renewed in 2008 with a pledge of US$48 billion to continue targeting HIV/AIDS, malaria and tuberculosis over 5 years. For some, the financial capacity alone has led the USA to subsequently dominate HIV/AIDS efforts at the risk of UN marginalisation. To stress its relevance, the UN must now align its interests and activities within a US-led framework (Morrison and Summers 2003: 188). Although PEPFAR may not have introduced the number and scope of new governance structures as the Bank and the MAP, its impact upon HIV/AIDS interventions is acutely felt. When conducting research in 2005–6 in East Africa, ART uptake was beginning to increase; however, a return visit in 2009 showed a significant increase in ART uptake, provision of care and treatment, and significant innovations within local healthcare centres and systems. Although this can be attributed to the many interventions and funds directed to HIV/AIDS, the clear explanatory factor for this was the arrival of PEPFAR and its focus on treatment and care of the chronically ill. In its first 5 years, PEPFAR saw care being provided for 10.1 million people infected and affected by HIV/AIDS, and counselling and testing support for 57million people. For 2008–13 the project aims to have an additional 3 million people on treatment, care for 12 million people, the prevention of 12 million new infections and the training of 140,000 new healthcare workers globally (PEPFAR 2008).[36]

PEPFAR is a highly political programme in terms of its abstinence-based prevention policies and its need to demonstrate the numbers of people it has helped, such as orphans in school, and the number of people on ART. The main contention surrounds PEPFAR's prevention conditionality – the promotion of or education about condoms is strongly discouraged 'it's either AB (abstain, be faithful) or you don't get the money … it's unfair, but …'[37] Some CSOs avoid the issue by promoting AB and only talking about C if asked.[38] Of those CSOs interviewed the majority did not speak out against condom use, but only 9 per cent in Kenya, 32 per cent in Tanzania and 24 per cent in Uganda actively stated they included condoms in their prevention training and education. The shifting focus on treatment and a scaling up of ART under PEPFAR have resulted in a shift away from holistic approaches to prevention. Many see this as problematic, as prevention is better than cure, and because of the need to have a balanced response, e.g. people may be in receipt of drugs but they cannot afford to eat or do not have access to clean water and therefore would rather not take the drugs.[39] For some CSOs, what is evident within the prevention debate is that no-one is talking about sex, sexuality or sexual feelings.[40]

CSO engagement under PEPFAR differs from the Bank, in that it funds community groups through partnerships with more established INGOs and proposals have to fit in with established priorities, 'I can't call it dialogue really, they put in a request for proposals, and people apply, and then in that proposal they outline things that need to be done.'[41] Subsequently CSOs have to change their practices to fit in with these objectives. The US government does not trust the strength of local systems and only works within such systems if they are proven to be safe.[42] As USAID Uganda representative Amy Cunningham sums up, 'as long as we can track it, we can fund it.'[43] A legal policy decision made in Washington restricts PEPFAR from using any funding channel that is not its own, hence they do not work through, or assist in the strengthening of, government systems.[44]

The lack of emphasis placed upon condoms has led to several issues with the procurement and provision of them. Previous to PEPFAR, condoms would come from a variety of sources and be distributed by the Medical Stores Department in-country with the assistance of procurement agents such as JSI or Crown Agents. Condoms were divided into family planning and HIV/AIDS condoms, but they are now managed together. Procurement becomes problematic, however, through the different processes of pre-qualification and wider donor agendas. For example, to procure condoms with Bank funds the contract has to be won through international competitive bidding, which can take up to 2 years, whereas with other organisations such as the United Nations Population Fund (UNFPA) procurement has to operate through a list of WHO pre-qualified condoms. Procurement agents therefore have to manage these systems, in partnership with the government sub-systems, while being aware of the donor's competing objectives. For example, the World Bank is willing to supply condoms as a last resort, but is slow and bureaucratic, whereas USAID is rapid and efficient, but does not want to be seen buying condoms with PEPFAR money.[45] In 2005, Uganda faced a condom shortage widely perceived as a result of USAID's position on the ABC of prevention, despite 10 million condoms existing in Uganda warehouses since May 2004 (Das 2005: 601). When conducting research in Kenya, JSI, the main procurement agent, was suffering from a shortage of condoms. The World Bank offered support under the Decentralised HIV/AIDS Response (DARE) project, which existed previous to the MAP, but the amount pledged would only sustain the country for another year without any other form of support. This is problematic as the process can take between 9 months and 2 years. Steve Kinzett of John Snow International, the main condom procurement body in East Africa, characterises the condom problem in Kenya in the following way:

> I've been stomping around this country trying to get funding for condoms for the last 9 months now. Basically saying that unless condoms were pro-cured now, because I know how long it takes to procure condoms, it takes a good 9 months, because factories have to get their production schedules and everything else. I know because I've visited condom factories in Vietnam and India. So they need time, but we need to find a donor and donors don't seem to be there for condoms, I think it's so short-sighted, I think that our distribution of condoms has contributed to the reduction in the HIV rate here in Kenya, I really do, I passionately believe in that, and erm, there's all these people whingeing on about having access to ARVs which are you know a million times more expensive than a little rubber device, it makes no sense to me whatever. Prevention is better than cure: you can't even cure AIDS.[46]

The problem with procurement highlights an additional contention with PEPFAR: its commitment to pre-existing government structures and co-ordination mechanisms such as 'The Three Ones.' PEPFAR does not demonstrate a blan-ket refusal to work with government systems as it does work in partnership with the Ministry of Health.[47] Moreover, it expresses a strong commitment to 'The Three Ones.' USAID's representatives in Uganda claim that they tried to become involved with the UAC and the wider national response, but would hear nothing from the Commission and, as a result, just identified it as a 'lost opportunity.' However, in general PEPFAR has a tendency to operate outside the NAC system or wider development partnership groups. PEPFAR has been seen to establish parallel systems of provision that undermines agents, such as the NACs and UNAIDS, by restricting their authority and questioning their legitimacy.[48] As a representative of Kenya's NACC puts it 'Americans can be difficult', or according to the Bank 'the Americans are a little bit wishy-washy about the AIDS councils.'[49] The corollary of this is that PEPFAR is seen as more efficient and less bureaucratic, demonstrating an ability to get funds to the ground rapidly. For example, when there is a funding delay or even a shortfall in condoms, it is consistently USAID that 'pick up the tab ... they always do.'[50] Similar to patterns in inter-relationships between agencies, the level of PEPFAR's involvement in wider co-ordination groups depends on the individual representative. The Kenya PEPFAR representative was regarded as 'great' by the wider donor community, as they were seen to understand the project's limits and attempt to work as effectively as possible within their wider remit.[51] The World Bank is viewed favourably by the NACs in comparison to PEPFAR, as despite any misgivings, the MAP does work within government systems and assists in strengthening these mechanisms, and, regardless of its blueprint nature, attempts to establish country-based strategies.[52] However, this would be the expected opinion of the NACs, as PEPFAR does not work with them, and the Bank through the MAP is their main source of income (specifically in the case of Kenya and Uganda) and justification. Comparatively, however, the MAP is less stringent and more flexible.

The presence of PEPFAR and its role in health system strengthening and provision of care, treatment and prevention policies sits in contention to the Bank's agenda for HIV/AIDS and assumed leadership role.[53] PEPFAR reduces the scope and influence of the Bank, as although the MAP introduces structural reform, US funding is larger and more widespread through INGO activity rather than state activity. The arrival of PEPFAR has seen an increasing shift towards a biomedical and security discourse. The rising dominance of the health agenda has in part been pushed by for-profit healthcare providers, pharmaceutical companies, trends in biotechnology and health insurance providers (Morrison and Summers 2003: 220). PEPFAR reasserts the USA's dual-track approach to international relations favoured in the aftermath of the Second World War based upon flagship bilateral projects that commit unprecedented funds to an issue for gains in security and dependency, combined with continued commitment to multilateral processes. As Chapter 2 showed with the case of the Marshall Plan and the Bank's initial mandate, the USA positions itself as a supportive member state of global institutions while establishing its pre-eminence bilaterally. In contrast to the MAP, PEPFAR establishes clear goals and the need for performance-related data. However, the multi-sectorality advocated by the MAP has become embedded within global practice and procedure and enshrined within legal covenants. Acting outside of the NAC system and only demonstrating loose adherence to 'The Three Ones' would suggest that PEPFAR challenges the HIV/AIDS agenda established by the Bank. However, PEPFAR has thus far not sought to destabilise these systems by circumventing them, and USAID does participate in the donor partnership meetings and thematic groups in which the NAC and 'The Three Ones' system remain sacrosanct. Comparatively, the Bank is seen as a more flexible and collaborative partner than USAID by both UN agencies and the NACs, and thus its leadership role continues to be supported at the global and national levels of HIV/AIDS governance. PEPFAR does signify a slight shift away from multi-sectorality back towards more biomedical approaches to HIV/AIDS; however, it does not demonstrate a clear restructuring of the governance reform agenda established under the MAP. In regard to HIV/AIDS, the Bank is able to demonstrate a degree of relative autonomy from the wider priorities of the US government through the building of alliances between states, specific types of NGO, and international organisations separate to that of PEPFAR. Far from being supplanted by PEPFAR, the Bank has adapted its role to concentrate on areas of institutional support and strengthening that do not fall under the direct remit of the US project.

Philanthropy and new forms of HIV/AIDS financing

The significant increase in HIV/AIDS financing over the last 10 years is not just the result of bilateral and multilateral commitments, but also part of efforts targeting global health, specifically infectious diseases such as HIV/AIDS, by philanthropic foundations. According to a 2004 report on AIDS financing by UNAIDS, foundation contributions towards HIV/AIDS have grown from US$7 million in 1997 to US$260 million in 2002 (UNAIDS 2004). By 2007 The Bill and Melinda Gates Foundation alone had paid out US$1.22 billion towards global health (McCoy *et al.* 2009). Foundations involved in HIV/AIDS take the form of long-established philanthropic organisations, such as the Ford Foundation, the Rockefeller Foundation and the Wellcome Trust; new foundations principally established to address issues of global public health and HIV/AIDS such as the Stephen Lewis Foundation, the Elton John AIDS Foundation and the 46664 campaign of the Nelson Mandela Foundation, and new foundations that prioritise global health as a significant part of their wider funding portfolio, such as the William J. Clinton Foundation, the Google Foundation, and the Bill and Melinda Gates Foundation. As these foundations demonstrate, they tend to have a prominent public figurehead; like any charity, are governed by a board of trustees and like any business, run by a board of directors. Priorities and initiatives of foundations vary, but in general, funding is directed to awareness raising, particularly in regard to youth programmes; community-led initiatives; improving access to treatment and care; biomedical research, with a specific focus on vaccine development; and women.

Foundations offer innovations in HIV/AIDS funding through the type of activities they fund, and their commitment to research into the epidemic. As they are non-governmental actors, mainly situated within the private sector, they are more autonomous of established structures of HIV/AIDS governance such as the in-country NAC system, and the global commitment to 'The Three Ones.' This is beneficial as it allows space for new ideas and the development of new agendas in addressing HIV/AIDS, but is somewhat problematic as it can lead to overlap, a disregard for co-ordination and sovereignty, and – crucially – a lack of transparent and accountable governance. Foundations are transparent in regard to their funding, most have excellent mechanisms of tracking where their money goes, but little can be said for their decision-making. The increased predominance of foundations within HIV/AIDS governance has been accompanied by the growth of secret meetings of the world's richest men (with the exception of Oprah Winfrey and Melinda Gates) to address global health problems through private philanthropy. An example of this is 'the good club' – a group of billionaire philanthropists such as Warren Buffet, David Rockefeller, George Soros, Bill Gates and Oprah Winfrey. This exclusive club reportedly met in 2009 and discussed the implications of the recent economic downturn upon developing countries, health and environmental crises, and government reform (Harris 2009). This sort of meeting and the lack of incentive to work inside global and national systems of governance presents a new agenda for HIV/AIDS financing that undermine the agenda and structures established by the World Bank. The perceived ability of foundations to get things done by avoiding the bureaucracy of inter-governmental donors and INGOs, who are accountable to states and their donors, is attractive to states in need of quick, efficient, healthcare financing. Foundations may seek to focus upon non-health issues, but the preponderance of organisations specifically established to fund HIV/AIDS and health issues would suggest this is unlikely. However, foundations are not a homogeneous entity, and independent of one another they do not present a considerable threat to the Bank's leadership of HIV/AIDS governance. The slight exception to this is the Bill and Melinda Gates Foundation.

The Bill and Melinda Gates Foundation was created in 2000 when the William H. Gates Foundation merged with the Gates Learning Foundation. By 2007, the Foundation had 733 employees and administrative expenses of $269 million (McCoy *et al.* 2009). The Foundation is concerned with the following issue/areas: global health, education, public libraries and support for at-risk families in Washington and Oregon. It is the Global Health Program that is of principle interest here. The money the Foundation directs towards global health has 'changed the landscape for the global-health research community' (*Lancet* 2005) in that it is the biggest source of private development assistance for health and has an annual budget more than that of the WHO (Ravishankar *et al.* 2009; McCoy *et al.* 2009). Global Health Watch (GHW 2008) describes the approach taken by the Foundation towards global health as 'venture philanthropy', wherein 'social investors' develop funding for innovative ideas and solutions. The Foundation engages in vertical health strategies as opposed to horizontal forms of health system strengthening and has made grants to a range of global health issues through multiple types of organisation. The Foundation tends to favour large INGOs such as PATH, which has received 47 grants worth $949 million; think tanks; other foundations such as the Elizabeth Glaser Paediatric AIDS Foundation; and research initiatives such as the Global Alliance for Vaccines and Immunisation (GAVI) (McCoy *et al.* 2009; *Lancet* 2005). Crucially, the Foundation also funds intergovernmental organisations such as the WHO and the World Bank, and is the biggest single donor to the WHO, giving grants towards the health metrics network, polio eradication, strengthening scale-up of maternal, neonatal and child health interventions, and scaling up procurement and production of HIV/AIDS, tuberculosis and malaria drugs (McCoy *et al.* 2009). In regard to the World Bank, the Foundation directs money to the institution in three ways: (i) grants to the IFC; (ii) grants to IBRD towards disease control and health system support; and (iii) channelling money to global health alliances through the Bank.

The scale and scope of the Bill and Melinda Gates Foundation activities lead to several concerns as regards the accountable and transparent nature of its operations. The Foundation is governed by the Gates family, with no board of trustees and no mechanisms of accountability to the WHO or to the low-income countries its grants affect (GHW 2008).[54] This is particularly problematic, as its financial commitments alone confer significant influence upon global health policy. Furthermore the foundation is said to be 'domineering', 'controlling' and that 'they monopolise agendas' (GHW 2008) through its self-appointed leadership of the 'H8' (which also includes the World Bank, WHO, GAVI Alliance, Global Fund, UNICEF, UNFPA and UNAIDS) (McCoy *et al.* 2009), and the dominance of its specific research agenda on global health (McNeil 2008; McCoy *et al.* 2009). Part of the issue of accountability is the 'venture philanthropy' nature of the Foundation's agenda for global health and its links to the private sector. The Bill and Melinda Gates Foundation is different from other foundations that have a tendency to support the arts and further education, yet is similar in that foundation money has often been acquired through tax exemption and, in some instances, avoidance. A key problem for the Gates Foundation has been the contradiction between its charitable work and that of Microsoft. Microsoft was a significant actor in pushing through the TRIPS agreement that has restricted access to medicine in developing countries, and is lobbying to strengthen intellectual property rights further (GHW 2008). In January 2007, the *LA Times* published an article that suggested the Foundation funded companies whose activities were contrary to the Foundation's charitable goals (Piller *et al.* 2007): 'these businesses include major polluters in the developing world and pharmaceutical companies who have sought to restrict access to much-needed drugs' (*Lancet* 2007). In a study conducted by Global Health Watch, it was found that despite the Foundation stating they would review their policy in light of such claims, no such change has occurred (GHW 2008).

The presence of the Bill and Melinda Gates Foundation presents the clearest challenge to the leadership of the World Bank in global health in general and its agenda for HIV/AIDS in particular. In many ways the Foundation has subsumed the Bank's role through a combination of its wealth and investments and its use of multiple implementation partners. Like the Bank, the Foundation has been strategic in bringing INGOs, the private sector and inter-governmental organisations such as the WHO on board. It has been innovative in establishing new structures such as the GAVI alliance that arguably would not have existed without the Gates money, and through identifying a leadership role within the Health 8 or 'H8.'[55] Its new form of financing presents an attractive change to those working in the field of global health who have become familiar with institutional inertia arising from bureaucracy and competition. Gates funding is seen as more straightforward as it is not channelled through the government, and thus is less susceptible to the bureaucratic delays associated with the MAP and the Global Fund.

Moreover, in concentrating on research, the Foundation is able to influence the priorities of the global health research agenda by funding specific research centres and projects. The funding the Foundation directs to the IFC and IBRD of the Bank suggests that it assists in the direction of the Bank's activities. However, despite a new 'venture philanthropy' approach to global health, the Bill and Melinda Gates Foundation's Global Health Program has not replaced the World Bank's agenda for HIV/AIDS. The principle reason for this is that it does not engage in health system strengthening, the key arena which, as argued throughout this book, is central for embedding any significant or lasting change. Like the Global Fund, the Foundation recognises the Bank's role within this and seeks to embed it further. The Bank is also canny in recognising the role of the Foundation and, as the institutional development of the Bank would suggest, bringing the Foundation in line with the idea that the Bank is the leader in health system strengthening by developing institutional partnerships through grants. Critical assessments of the Foundation and wider recognition of its dominance will eventually see minor adjustments in the Foundation's role as its partnerships and legitimacy come into question. In the field of HIV/AIDS, this has thus far not been the case for the Bank. The Bill and Melinda Gates Foundation does question the agenda for HIV/AIDS developed by the Bank through the MAP. However, in re-emphasising the role of the Bank in health system strengthening and concentrating on vertical and private as opposed to state interventions, it is yet to supplant the good multi-sectoral governance agenda articulated by the World Bank.

Retreating from HIV/AIDS?

One factor that may facilitate the decline of the multi-sectoral agenda for HIV/AIDS is the apparent withdrawal of the Bank itself from interventions into the epidemic and its governance. The Bank has not sanctioned a MAP-3, and after the end of the last MAP-2 project in sub-Saharan Africa, other than regional projects, the Bank will not have a flagship HIV/AIDS project in the sub-continent.[56] In 2009 the Bank underwent a process of taking stock of its operations in health, nutrition and population. Its report *Improving Effectiveness and Outcomes for the Poor in Health, Nutrition and Population: an evaluation of World Bank Group support since 1997* reasserts the prominence of multi-sectoral interventions into global health and the symbiotic relationship between health, poverty and development, despite the report finding that a third of the Bank's projects failed to achieve their goals (World Bank 2009; *Economist* 2009). The report recommends the Bank intensify efforts to improve performance, renew its commitment to health, nutrition and population, strengthen its support to health systems, enhance contributions from other sectors and implement a results-based agenda to improve governance within the Bank itself (World Bank 2009). Key to these recommendations is the need to enhance state capacity and reduce complexity and prioritise multi-sectoral participation. The recommendations arising from the report suggest renewed institutional directives towards health system strengthening and a shift away from vertical flagship programmes, such as the MAP, while integrating health across the Bank's other topics of development. The outcome of these recommendations is already evident in-country. In Tanzania, as part of the end of the TMAP project, the Bank is engaging in 'mopping-up' activities in ensuring the transfer of what it has developed to other organisations such as the Global Fund[57] and developing partnerships away from TACAIDS and more towards the Tanzanian Social Action Fund (TASF) and the Local Government Development Fund. The emphasis is not only on more horizontal forms of health system strengthening, but is towards mainstreaming HIV/AIDS throughout local government structures. For the Bank, the future of all community programmes on HIV/AIDS will be part of a wider package of comprehensive reform that includes education, HIV/AIDS and multi-sectoral health issues.[58] The shift towards more horizontal, health system strengthening – specifically in East Africa – does not necessarily represent a complete removal of the World Bank from HIV/AIDS. It still prioritises multi-sectoral interventions into key issues such as HIV/AIDS, and maintains its situation of the epidemic as a concern for poverty and development through wider community-based governance reform. The removal of a flagship World Bank HIV/AIDS project is mainly specific to sub-Saharan Africa. Multi-sectorality and the Bank's governance agenda for HIV/AIDS have since been extended to other parts of the world, most notably the Caribbean. The clearest example of the extension of the Bank's type of multi-sectoral agenda established in sub-Saharan Africa is the World Bank's US$155 million project, the Multi-Country HIV/AIDS Prevention and Control Adaptable Program, or in other words the Caribbean MAP. This MAP was introduced only 1 year after the first MAP lending in sub-Saharan Africa, and at time of publication was operational in nine countries.[59] Examination of the policy documents and national strategic plans of the Caribbean MAPs suggest clear alignment to the Bank's multi-sectoral agenda. HIV/AIDS is firmly seen as a development issue not a health issue, and the main co-ordinating actors in each country are the AIDS councils. For example, in the case of the Barbados Second HIV/AIDS Project, the project was housed in the National HIV/AIDS Commission of Barbados, and the responsibility for the National AIDS Program was transferred from the Ministry of Health to the Commission (World Bank 2008c). Each of the projects stresses the role of civil society, specifically the community, and the role of the Bank in institutional strengthening. The Ministry of Health is included to a greater degree in some countries than others in regard to health system capacity and the development of surveillance systems, yet it is the multi-sectoral features of civil society inclusion, AIDS council co-ordination, and HIV/AIDS as a development issue that prevail. Despite the absence of similar flagship MAP projects in other parts of the world, the Bank's involvement in health system strengthening and institutional capacity building along a multi-sectoral agenda prevails in countries of high HIV/AIDS prevalence.

Conclusion

The World Bank has set the global HIV/AIDS agenda through the widespread adoption and promotion of its own specific form of multi-sectoral interventions by other governmental and non-governmental actors both within state boundaries and at the global level of interaction. The Bank has once again shown its ability to make minor changes in response to new challenges and absorb those ideas and institutions that challenge its leadership. The global level of interaction demonstrates that the Bank's multi-sectoral agenda is not just located in sub-Saharan Africa, but has become the dominant model for HIV/AIDS interventions throughout the world. Even if the Bank was to withdraw from all HIV/AIDS and global health interventions the antecedents of multi-sectoralism are so institutionally embedded within policy and structures of decision-making that this agenda would not be reversed, and would take a substantial amount of time to develop or change. The Bank has established the antecedents of the global HIV/AIDS response through a combination of timing, financially driven incentive and positioning within the international system. The Bank's agenda for good HIV/AIDS governance is felt around the world, with little accountability or recognition as to the role of the Bank in setting it. Overlooking the role of the Bank obscures a wider recognition of the contradictions within governance reform, and how these contentions make addressing HIV/AIDS problematic not only in terms of the expression and drivers of the epidemic, but the system of governance created to respond to it. The adoption of the Bank's multi-sectoral governance agenda for HIV/AIDS reflects the type of policy convergence that Seckinelgin's work points to, but more importantly, sees an extension of post-conditionality processes identified by Harrison. HIV/AIDS interventions have seen the development of post-conditional interventions beyond that of the African state to encompass a wide range of actors within international politics, notably other private and public international organisations. Patterns of competition between actors, ownership and leadership established within the global agenda for HIV/AIDS are as inherent to the international as they are to the state. What we see therefore is an agenda for HIV/AIDS governance wrought with contradictions between liberal concepts pursued through neoliberal means, articulated by the Bank and promoted throughout the international system of states, non-state actors and intergovernmental and private philanthropic organisations. The impact of this agenda upon local communities, individuals and states within sub-Saharan Africa and their long-term ability to tackle HIV/AIDS raises questions whether such a problematic approach to HIV/AIDS is better than nothing, and why this question is reduced to the Bank's way or no way.

6 World Bank, governance and the politics of criticising HIV/AIDS

The World Bank has set and sustained the current agenda for the global HIV/AIDS response. It has done so through a combination of timing, labelling the problem of HIV/AIDS a development one and, crucially, developing specific partnerships with states, CSOs in sub-Saharan Africa and intergovernmental organisations. Yet the role of the World Bank in the field of HIV/AIDS continues to receive scant attention. This is not surprising, as the Bank has deliberately organised its agenda in such a way as to obscure its role and responsibility for it. However, it is problematic if the structures, actors and money channelled to the HIV/AIDS response are to have any progressive affect. The contradictions in the response arising from the predominance of neoliberal incentive as a means of pursuing liberal outcomes have undermined the ability and success of the global response to HIV/AIDS. These problems have become inherent to the system of HIV/AIDS governance at the individual, community, state and global level. The founding principles, ideology and structures of the response thus need to be unravelled to see where the problems of addressing HIV/AIDS lie. Hence, this chapter draws together the main findings of the book to answer the initial concern of what the Bank's agenda for HIV/AIDS looks like and how it has set it. To fully understand this agenda, the chapter revisits the governance Bank debate outlined in Chapter 1 in regards to how we can now understand the Bank's relationships with the state, civil society, the individual and global decision-making. The chapter addresses the implications of the Bank's HIV/AIDS agenda for its wider role in health, and what it begins to suggest about the relationship between East Africa and the international, before focusing upon the wider normative concern of criticising the HIV/AIDS response. It does so by unravelling the political implications of criticising the global response to the disease, why it matters and what could be done. As such, in conclusion it confronts the normative question of such an argument: is a problematic agenda for HIV/AIDS better than no agenda at all?

The World Bank's global HIV/AIDS agenda

The World Bank's global agenda for HIV/AIDS is multi-sectoral. Multi-sectoralism in theory means the involvement of all aspects of the state, public and private sector, civil society and the individual within the global response to HIV/AIDS as a means of addressing the complexity and exceptionalism of the disease. HIV/ AIDS is not an ordinary global health problem, but is a development issue; thus it needs to be addressed by actors including, and beyond, the health sector. In practice this means providing financial incentive for the state to own, direct and develop a national response to their epidemic, and facilitate and co-ordinate the work of CSOs and the private sector. Crucially, states must remove HIV/AIDS from the health sector as it is a multi-sectoral development issue, not a health issue alone. The origins of the project come from a wider shift to the more encompassing comprehensive development agenda within the Bank towards the late 1990s, and the successful model of HIV/AIDS interventions in countries such as Brazil, where the willingness of the state and civil society to address the disease was paramount. The antecedents of which have been in the Bank's mandate for state partnership and evolving commitment to change and relevance, by adapting new partnerships with CSOs and the private sector, and adopting new issues as a form of relevant expansion and leadership within international development. Central to the Bank's multi-sectoral agenda for HIV/AIDS is its commitment to good liberal governance reform that prioritises transparency, ownership, participation, civil service reform and CSO inclusion as a means of liberal democratic reform within all aspects of the sub-Saharan African state.

The Bank's multi-sectoral approach to HIV/AIDS has set the global agenda through the MAP project in sub-Saharan Africa. The MAP outlined the strategy for state response to HIV/AIDS by being the first multilateral financing project aimed at combating the disease, and reorganising structures of decision-making and responsibility for the disease using multiple new implementing and co-ordinating agencies. As such, the MAP was the first project to operationalise the multi-sectoral agenda, and remove HIV/AIDS from the Ministry of Health and into the Office of the Prime Minister/President. Furthermore, through economic incentive it facilitated the first widespread inclusion of CSOs of any multilateral HIV/AIDS programme of its kind. Key to which was the role of not the traditional partners of development and intergovernmental organisations – INGOs – but local community groups that were to be supported by new structures of local government in the form of the DACs. The combination of introducing government structures and an unprecedented amount of money to state-based HIV/ AIDS interventions, the MAP set the foundations in which all future initiatives would have to adhere to if they operated through the state system. In articulating the need for local responses, the Bank was able to use local government agencies, community groups and individuals to fully embed this agenda.

The MAP has led the response to HIV/AIDS at every level of interaction, through embedding its working practice within government structures, forming the central principles of the main international co-ordinating methods, and articulating the multi-sectoral paradigm in which every donor, government and CSO works. This is not only the result of the MAP being the first multilateral commitment to HIV/AIDS of its kind, but is part of the systematic expansion of Bank influence in development knowledge, effective management of the international system, commitment to private service delivery and maintenance of its benevolent relationship with states. The Bank has formed alliances with UN agencies, specifically UNAIDS, in which similar to states it plays a benevolent leadership role and has come to the fore in global HIV/AIDS governance at a time when the WHO is withdrawing from vertical strategies of disease intervention. In line with wider trends in its history, the Bank is adept at encompassing emerging issues into its wider development mandate, and adapting to external issues within the international system as a means of maintaining its position, relevance and influence in global politics. The MAP not only resembles the Bank's ability to do so, it entrenches the Bank's role in HIV/AIDS and subsequently as a key player in global health.

AIDS and the governance debate: post-conditionality beyond the state

The World Bank's agenda for HIV/AIDS offers several insights into existing critical governance debates on the subject. The operating structures of the MAP and their practical ramifications show a considerable alignment to the notion of post-conditional governance reform developed by Harrison. HIV/AIDS is on the agenda of the Bank because it has been framed as a development concern. The development concern is that populations with an untreated or growing HIV prevalence rate will heighten the poverty cycle in that people will be too sick to work, lacking in education, and fulfilling social functions such as child rearing and other non-remunerated activities. This will limit the economic production of a country and its position within the global knowledge economy, and as a consequence will undermine any form of economic development (Barnett and Whiteside 2002), principally market-based, neoliberal economic growth. Hence, as Harrison suggests the main priority of governance reform, and the pursuit of reform through projects such as the MAP, is economic growth. The MAP is a clear example of the implementation of the World Bank's governance reform agenda through a specific social policy that by its very nature as a multi-sectoral public health issue has wider ramifications for the state and CSOs. The MAP suggests a form of post-conditionality that goes beyond just the state to encompass civil society, the individual and the international in the form of global decision-making and agenda-setting among intergovernmental organisations. The extension of governance reform to arenas of activity beyond the state to a degree reflects Williams' more encompassing conception of good liberal governance reform that gives equal attention to the individual and civil society as it does to the state and economy. In line with Williams' conception of good governance within the Bank, civil society occupies a central role in facilitating the right kind of 'good' reform. As the MAP shows, the roles of institutions beyond the state are integral to embedding wider processes of governance reform. Intergovernmental institutions perform a specific function within this. For Seckinelgin the role of such institutions is the formation of governance regime that is governed by language and norms of behaviour based on a specific form of knowledge transfer. The Bank and MAP fit within Seckinelgin's specific depiction of the right kind of knowledge and the demarcation between perceived and lived experience in the separation of decision-making and implementation within the MAP. There is policy convergence organised around principles such as multi-sectoralism, the NAC system and 'The Three Ones' that has been articulated by the Bank through the MAP. However, contrary to Williams and Seckinelgin, the type of governance reform promoted by the MAP does not necessarily mark a wholesale shift away from neoliberalism based on liberal incentive and the use of knowledge, language and norms as its over-arching forms of influence and disciplinary adherence to multi-sectorality. The prominence of economic incentive within the MAP suggests that neoliberalism still plays an important function in the process of governance reform within HIV/AIDS interventions. This is evident when looking at the World Bank's agenda for HIV/AIDS and the outcome of the Bank's agenda for HIV/AIDS for the state, civil society, the individual and global forms of decision-making.

The state

The multi-sectoral approach to combating HIV/AIDS led by the World Bank, adopted by the international community and articulated as the global response, has had a significant impact upon the state in East Africa. The need to prioritise HIV/AIDS as an emergency and as a development project has given international organisations licence to transcend sovereign boundaries and establish agents of international organisations within the state structure. The originality and scope of the MAP as a rapid response to a development emergency combined with the acquiescence of states in need to the multi-sectoral agenda confers legitimacy onto the Bank and the types of interventions it prioritises. The Bank's approach was apolitical and ahistorical in the application of a blueprint model that ensured: (i) the establishment of the NACs while ignoring pre-existing structures within the Ministry of Health and potential tensions within the internal bureaucracies of these countries; (ii) the requirement of national and district state agencies to engage with CSOs despite longstanding mutual distrust; (iii) prioritising the role of the Ministry of Finance and private service delivery; and (iv) crucially ignoring or obfuscating the socioeconomic and historical determinants of each country's HIV/AIDS epidemic. The MAP's impact upon the state reinforces the key principles of governance reform articulated by Harrison and Williams: budget adherence, improved co-ordination, decentralisation through the DACs and civil service reform in removing responsibility for HIV/AIDS governance from the Ministry of Health to the NACs (Williams 2008: 97 and 102). Adherence to these reform principles mark states out to be 'good' reformers, both to the Bank and to other international donors that operate within its multi-sectoral agenda for HIV/AIDS, and thus in a position to receive and appropriately spend additional funds to combat the epidemic. Slight deviation from this reform agenda suggests states to be 'bad' reformers and thus not credit-worthy within the international HIV/AIDS community. Hence, reform of state-led HIV/AIDS responses has led to the construction of ownership and a willingness on the part of the government to address its epidemic through financial incentive. These factors have ultimately limited the ability of the HIV/AIDS response to fully shift the dynamic of state activity as divisions within the state, between the state and CSOs, or 'domestic squabbles' (Charnock 2006) reduce the degree to which the MAP agenda is absorbed within wider African society. Yet despite these factors it is this NAC-based system that has been adopted by multiple actors within the global HIV/AIDS response and become the legitimate operating system in which all HIV/AIDS interventions are structured.

The contentious and complex nature of the HIV/AIDS epidemic allows a considerable amount of space for the Bank to push its own brand of governance reform within the state. Where state leaders, political agencies or line ministries show a lack of good governance in regards to multi-sectoral HIV/AIDS reform, the Bank is able to hold them to ransom against the notion they are somehow in HIV/AIDS denial or unconcerned about the health of their population. A significant proportion of funds to HIV/AIDS go to support new government systems, Ministry of Health strengthening and job creation in many countries in sub-Saharan Africa. Despite emphasising its multi-sectoral nature, the Bank uses the health and illness aspect of the disease that makes it so visible in the international conscience as a means of holding the state to account for its wider failings in governance reform. One of the central functions of the application of good governance to states in sub-Saharan Africa is to promote a certain brand of governance reform through combating corruption. The field of HIV/AIDS is not exempt from this. Measures to adapt and promote safeguards form an additional layer of governance reform within the state. Safeguards against corruption within a specific state's HIV/AIDS response promote the use of private international financial auditors and the role of the local private sector in developing and maintaining monitoring and evaluation systems. These systems do not only pertain to the NAC system or the Ministry of Health, but, due to the multi-sectoral construction of the epidemic, the systems are transferred across government ministries, increasingly into the operations of CSOs and, crucially, to the Office of the President or Prime Minister. This is a vital aspect of governance reform that has become common to the HIV/AIDS response: the ability to hold presidents or prime ministers directly account for any presence of corruption in the spending of international aid earmarked for HIV/AIDS. It is integral to a state becoming a 'good' reformer. Presidents exhibit the right kind of good governance in publicly denouncing any form of corrupt practice, but are less willing to take responsibility. This highlights a familiar problem with the application of governance reform within the multi-sectoral HIV/AIDS response in the absence of any historical understanding of the political nuances of individual state systems: the will to govern or, more specifically, the will to govern in line with liberal democratic principles. Where there is an absence of will, reform operates through economic incentive as opposed to financial conditionality. Both economic conditionality and incentive rely on the transaction of funds for specific ends. They differ in that conditionalities are clearly stipulated in the form of contractual obligations between the state and the Bank, whether they are adhered to or not, they are transparent in their demands. Economic incentive is less transparent, non-contractual and more *ad hoc* in this regard. As Chapter 2 has argued, the Bank moved away from the notion of stringent conditionalities into wider forms of good governance as a means of promoting transparency and accountability. Yet when the problem of creating political will within the state occurs, the Bank refers to the type of neoliberal incentivising seen within conditionalities, yet it does so with less transparency and accountability afforded to the Bank itself.

National and international NGOs and community groups

The 'legitimate' transcendence òf state boundaries has been extended to the community level, with community groups, NGOs and INGOs becoming intertwined with the service sector aspect of state provision. Similar to states, these actors internalise and promote the logic of the Bank while assuming ownership of the project at the local level, once more under the justification of HIV/AIDS exceptionalism. It is the involvement of these national NGOs and community groups that offer the main contribution to how we can understand governance and state reform in the context of the World Bank.

The positioning of community groups and NGOs at the centre of the MAP reveals a systematic extension of governance reform on the part of the Bank. The Bank is very candid in this, freely expressing the need for the involvement of these actors to ensure mechanisms of good governance, i.e. transparency, accountability and participation in government processes and decision-making. As critical understandings of governance reform would suggest, these actors perform a central function in embedding Bank-led reforms within states. However, in the context of HIV/AIDS, in performing this function, these actors play a more crucial role in the governance agenda of the Bank. These types of CSO provide an outlet for the Bank to address any 'bad reform' within a state. Where governments fail to fully implement specific reform strategies, or are mired by internal disagreement, NGOs and community groups are targeted by the Bank to provide the following vital functions: service delivery, transmission of good reform to the community and pressure on the state for wider reform. This pressure on the state is not exerted through popular protest, campaigns and lobbying, but through competition for funds and legitimacy as good reformers. According to Williams, an integral function of good governance reform is the presence of an effective civil society that is separate from the state. Where the state fails to comply with reform measures, funds are channelled to the community or NGO sector, on the legitimate grounds of people infected or affected by HIV/AIDS needing the resources. What we see then is an extension of post-conditionality, which internalises not only governance reform practices and Bank ideology within the state and civil society, but the funding of civil society that operates as competition for who can demonstrate the most 'good' reform. CSOs are thus to a degree used as means of circumventing or addressing failures within the state to fully reform. The 'sovereign frontier' thus becomes challenged at the state and community level of governance. However, this contestation of the 'sovereign frontier' (Harrison 2004) becomes problematic in regards to the MAP. The inclusion of civil society in service delivery and competition for resources limits the capacity of CSOs to hold the state to account, as it is the state that manages and co-ordinates funds.

This argument sits in contention to wider understandings of the agency of CSOs within global politics: the role of CSOs as emancipatory, transparent advocates of social change, separate from the state and intergovernmental organisations such as the World Bank. Conceptions of civil society as occupying an autonomous Hegelian 'third sphere' of political activity between the state and the family would suggest it is CSOs holding the Bank and the state to account, and thus undermining any widespread governance reform.[1] However, engagement of CSOs is organised in such a way as to limit the influence and advocacy role of CSOs. INGOs operating at the global level of interaction do not want to engage with the Bank in regards to the MAP and most are unaware of the power it has on HIV/AIDS. National NGOs want to engage as a means of influencing and accessing governmental decision-making. Community groups want to engage so they can access funds to prevent further deaths and keep people lives. Under the rubric of '1000 flowers bloom', community groups and locally based organisations are the main partners preferred by the Bank. Such preferences are only the case in the theory of the MAP and in terms of funding alone. The majority of CSOs involved in dialogue, feedback and consultation of the community aspect of the MAP are national NGOs, network representatives of community groups and INGOs. These organisations form a select group of 'usual suspects' that tend to be based in capital cities and demonstrate close relationships with government agencies such as the NACs. Moreover, these organisations are keen to reassert their influence and knowledge on HIV/AIDS and their ability to represent community groups, thus undermining the ability of community groups to directly represent themselves. The contention between MAP theory and practice in this regard is a deliberate structure of the Bank to separate implementation from decision-making. This is a specific tool used to limit CSO influence upon decision-making within the overall structure of the MAP, and results in the separation of lived experience of people infected and affected by HIV/AIDS and their perceived experience by the Bank, as depicted by Seckinelgin.

The Bank limits influence in two distinct ways: consent as a form of legitimacy and the separation of implementation from decision-making. Dialogue is consensual rather than influential. CSOs were invited to share thoughts on the MAP during its inception after it had been created. Before the implementation of the MAP, CSOs were consulted in each of the countries to have the project; however, in the three countries examined such consultation referred more to the government alerting key CSOs to the fact money was coming in, rather than the working principles and core approach to HIV/AIDS the MAP would take. Participation at this level was marked by the 'usual suspects' familiar to the government and the Bank. Inclusion of such actors was replicated in the implementation stage of feedback and dialogue. Report-writing presented the dominant form of feedback and dialogue; however, there is no clear structure of how the findings of these reports feed back into future policy and decision-making. Participation in annual partnership meetings and the steering committees that precede them reflect the same problem. The existence of feedback structures and the introduction of the project before implementation allow the Bank to maintain the idea of community consultation within the project while limiting the impact it has upon decision-making. This gives the MAP its legitimacy and makes the Bank seem accountable to local interests and perspectives while reducing the tendency of other CSOs to confront the Bank on its activities. The Bank is in this sense absorbing external criticism as a proactive as opposed to reactive measure.

The second way in which the Bank limits influence is through the separation of implementation from decision-making. As Williams (2008: 88 and 113) argues, a central element of good governance reform is the organisation of projects that preclude certain actors from decision-making and promote those that align with the Bank's liberal values. The MAP uses a clear separation of implementation from decision-making, consent as a form of legitimacy and benevolence through state ownership and management of the project to organise and limit structures of power. The MAP is organised in such a way that the 'owners' of the project are national governments, with the Bank's role being presented as minimal. The main benefactors of MAP funds – the community groups – are often aware of the project but not aware of the Bank. All community feedback and input has to go through the DACs, then the NACs to then be fed back to the Bank. The decentralised nature of engagement is such that opinions of those involved in service delivery are not fed back to those influencing decision-making. Communities involved in implementation feel left out of decision-making but expect no different, as they are fully aware of the practical form such relations take. The problems associated with dialogue and the number of organisations managed under the MAP would suggest very little opinion is fed back to the Bank. Decision-making as to the direction and main components of the MAP are decided predominantly out of country at the global level, and specific caveats within the overall framework of the project are agreed with the government. Implementation occurs at the community level. There is thus no linkage or overlap between the two.

The structure of the MAP limits community knowledge as to the activity of the Bank, and, should such knowledge exist, community groups lack the financial capacity or leverage to target such institutions. This contradicts any emphasis placed upon community 'empowerment' and 'capacity-building' that has been prioritised within global health and highlights the political nature of these terms. This is further a specific function of limited knowledge transfer, as the type of norms and language used to enforce a specific form of governance reform identified by Seckinelgin perform an exclusionary function among different types of CSO. At the global level where advocacy groups could leverage the Bank, attention to HIV/AIDS is concentrated elsewhere. The Bank is thus able to operate within HIV/AIDS with minimal scrutiny. Moreover, it is able to influence the activities of CSOs working on HIV/AIDS with only financial reciprocal benefit to these organisations. Absorption of CSO criticism has led to a decline in transnational advocacy campaigns targeting the Bank, specifically within the remit of HIV/AIDS – and thus the Bank remains free from inertia. The result of this is that the Bank embeds its influence over developing countries, by extending its practices through state structures and CSOs to every level of society in East Africa. The legitimacy of the Bank in so doing is solidified in the widespread absorption of its approach within international organisations and donors in the response to HIV/AIDS.

Multi-sectoralism presents the image of a committed Bank that is willing to work with all actors in the response to HIV/AIDS, in line with the over-arching objectives of states. The Bank is able to maintain its benevolent role by emphasising government ownership of the projects, thus absolving itself from wider responsibility. CSOs not only work within the structure of the Bank, they assist in implementing and extending its practices to every reach of society. The Bank's role in HIV/AIDS contributes to its position within the knowledge economy and the extension of its role into global health governance, thus maintaining its influence upon the activities and decisions of governments, CSOs and organisations such as UNAIDS. Engagement is not an end in itself, but is used as a tool in which the Bank can influence wider decision-making in international arenas, extend its own brand of multi-sectoral governance reform and thus reassert its utility and claims to knowledge.

The outcome of engaging with the Bank through the MAP has led to an expansion in the number and role of various CSOs within service delivery, to the detriment of influence within decision-making. On assessment, there are no 'promises' just 'pitfalls' to engagement. The promises of engagement are that people living with HIV/AIDS are receiving the care and treatment they need, those looking after the sick are receiving funds to support their activities, and messages of prevention and empathy for those people infected are being transmitted to the wider reaches of East Africa. However, these are more promises for the HIV/AIDS response rather than the CSOs themselves. An additional promise would be the boost to local economies the MAP's injection of funds provides, and the ability of some marginal groups to seek financial support. However, the limited timing of the funding, and the small amount issued to each group, would suggest the MAP's capacity to lead to these outcomes is overstated. In stressing these potential benefits, the wider impact funding to CSOs is having upon communities is overlooked. The only promises of engagement are for those 'usual suspects' involved in discussions and decision-making structures as they are more likely to receive funds. They display close working relationships with the state, but in challenging the MAP and state structures demonstrate an ability to hold decision-makers to account.

National NGOs have come to follow the organisational procedure and working relationships between states and international donors that were previously established by INGOs. National NGOs have come to replace INGOs within such decision-making structures and present the immediate CSO partners within the MAP. Their leverage at the level of global decision-making, however, is yet to be realised. As such, they serve to promote the legitimacy of the Bank and MAP rather than the transparency and accountability of the project.

The amount of money committed to HIV/AIDS over the last 10 years, specifically to community groups, has seen an increase in organisations providing some form of service delivery in this regard. CSOs have become less mobilised by a sense of community-driven social justice or community empowerment, the need to improve participatory democracy or the will to govern, and more by money. Groups are trapped within service delivery only, with little influence upon government accountability and decision-making. Their views are fed back to decision-makers, but they still lack the ability and/or structures to enter into direct partnerships with the state and/or the Bank. The gaps between rhetoric and reality, and ownership and conditionality reduce community empowerment to frustration and distrust with donors and the introduction of a new service economy funded by the Bank. Communities do not drive development with their ideas. Instead they remain in low-cost service provision within a paradigm of HIV/AIDS response articulated in Washington, and capacity-building articulated by public health initiatives continue to be based on how to improve efficiency of delivery. These groups not only act as low-cost service deliverers, they now take the form of low-cost influencers in their role as transmitters of the Bank's multi-sectoral reform agenda for HIV/AIDS. Greater impact upon decision-making will only occur through joint collaboration, articulation of their multi-sectoral agenda and thus commitment to governance reform and a unified position towards donors. The desperate situation of HIV/AIDS, however, means that dependency on funds will continue and the fundamental problems with the response will remain unaddressed. The ethos behind community-driven development that they have a better understanding of what is happening on the ground is true, but unless this information is accessed the potential of such groups is unrealised and their purpose just a form of stop-gap short-term costly service provision.

CSO engagement within the MAP has undermined the position of INGOs as the main partners of the Bank. On initial inspection, exclusion of INGOs from funding and decision-making at every level of the MAP suggests CSO engagement has shifted from a centralised global focus to community-based activity and feedback. INGO activity has thus altered towards a supportive role in community-based activity by demonstrating their experience and utility in working with such groups. This has resulted in them occupying the position of intermediaries between the state, the Bank and the community. Their inclusion as RFAs and within development partnership groups and thematic steering committees at the national government level suggests they have become more intertwined with governments and intergovernmental organisations than ever before. The transplantation of their non-governmental status into working in partnership with such organisations has led to their wider representation as either quasi-governmental organisations or private development consultants. This status contradicts their main *modus operandi* – commitment to and close links with community empowerment – as they prevent local CSOs from participating in dialogue and partnerships directly and are often paid with funds budgeted for community groups. The emphasis placed on funding as a means of engagement has bred increased competition and mistrust between CSOs that must compete for funds to maintain their relevance and influence within decision-making. Governments are no longer circumvented by transnational advocacy networks but have become the main facilitators of Bank–CSO engagement. They are accountable for the actions of the Bank-designed MAP. They suffer from the demands of both international donors and CSOs.

In the confusion surrounding their role as implementers and co-ordinators of the MAP, government structures have come to compete with CSOs in implementation. Governments are thus involved in the delivery of Bank projects in the same way as CSOs. Under the rubric of government ownership, governments implement the policies of the Bank and as such become accountable for the problems and discrepancies, therein leaving the Bank unaccountable for its actions and policies. The Bank adopts the same approach with CSOs. In accepting funds desperately needed for the sick, CSOs become dependent upon funding to maintain operations. Should there be any problems with funding, they approach the government, not the Bank. Not only does competition for funds limit the formation of networks and collaborative mechanisms that increase a community's capacity and leverage in holding the Bank to account, it confronts the very purpose and initial role of CSOs in global politics: to confront the status quo and highlight inequalities and problems with the prevailing system. This not only undermines the positions of CSOs and governments but challenges notions of CSOs and civil society as an emancipatory concept. CSOs and governments do not challenge international decision-making. Rather, they have come to embody and implement the directives of intergovernmental organisations.

The role of NGOs and community groups in transferring 'good' reform to decentralised parts of the state not only presents a new battleground within the 'sovereign frontier' but further embeds market-oriented social policy at the community level. The funding of these CSOs through the MAP is organised in such a way as to promote the Bank's brand of accountability and legitimacy – holding the state as owners of the project to account – and limiting any emancipatory function of these groups in targeting the wider mechanisms of the MAP or the Bank itself. Civil society within this category is thus organised by funding, and market logic of competition for funds as a means of promoting efficiency and low-cost delivery. The wrong kind of advocacy, questioning the main structures of the global HIV/AIDS response suggests 'bad' reform and thus limits the direction of funds towards these 'bad' groups.

The individual

A central part of effective governance reform is the change in state behaviour to enact processes of neoliberal reform. CSO engagement within the MAP shows a clear extension of this. What is particular to HIV/AIDS governance reform is the role of the individual as a site of contestation within the sovereign frontier. For governance reform to be effective, particularly in regard to HIV/AIDS, it needs to reform individual behaviour. Individuals are seen as malleable by the Bank, and hence through the inclusion of civil society they provide an important function in governance reform (Williams 2008: 114). The Bank's agenda for the multi-sectoral HIV/AIDS response impacts upon the reform of individual behaviour in the three key ways.

First, it offers economic incentive as a means of behaviour change in regard to practicing safe sex; promoting understanding and reducing stigma towards people living with and affected by HIV/AIDS; and encouraging the use of needle exchanges and support systems for intravenous drug users. The multi-sectoral approach relies on the notion that if given the right information and education individual actors would rationally choose to protect themselves from HIV transmission. In so doing, however, it overlooks two crucial elements that create problems for effective governance reform: (i) individuals are not necessarily rational and/or subscribe to a specific form of rationality; and (ii) it presupposes individuals will conform to the 'right' knowledge or information. This reflects the ahistorical nature in which the Bank approaches governance reform at the state level, in that it operates with little awareness of the sociocultural settings it operates in developing a blueprint in which all states, communities and individuals must operate. The MAP redresses this element by funding local groups, FBOs and CSOs that work with traditional healers. However, the structures in which these groups operate remain in the over-arching framework of financial incentive for a specific form of rational behaviour change.

The second impact of the multi-sectoral agenda is the clear extension of post-conditionality to the individual in the adoption of market-based practices within individual behaviour and livelihood and ensuing social relations. Through the provision of economic incentive, individuals exhibit specific behaviour change that not only transcends safe practices associated with HIV/AIDS, but also embeds principles of good governance reform. The market created by the widespread funding or 'blooming' of CSOs in the form of local community groups has seen a shift towards individuals in East Africa adopting good governance rhetoric of ownership, participation and transparency in their interaction with one another and processes of local governance. At the centre of this adoption, is the encompassing nature of making individuals market actors. In promoting a form of CSO engagement that is based on principles of private sector service delivery, we see a reworking of social relations at the local level of communities in which individuals see HIV/AIDS as a means of income. This form of CSO engagement suggests an extension of the notion of post-conditionality, in which individuals, through their behaviour in terms of safe sex practices and means of employment, are embedding a specific form of governance reform that prioritise the principles of the market through economic incentive for behaviour change and the emergence of an HIV/AIDS market in community service delivery.

The wider embodiment of the rhetoric of good governance within individual behaviour suggests a third outcome of the Bank's multi-sectoral agenda, the promotion of liberal democracy from the individual and the community to the state. This is a key strategy of good governance reform for the Bank. A primary function of the MAP was for individuals and the community to engender good governance within the African state by holding governments to account for their activities, and thus adopting these practices in their wider social relationships. However, as this book has shown, the predominance of economic incentive has led individuals and communities adept at using the language of good governance to demonstrate their credentials as successful models to fund, yet in practice there is little substance to this. For example, in the case of female inclusion within the organisation of NGOs and community groups and their activities – an issue that is increasingly pertinent to the governance reform agenda – groups are effective at demonstrating male and female quotas and participation, but this does not mean men and women have equal status in decision-making or hierarchy.

Global agenda-setting

The extension of post-conditionality to the international in the form of global agenda-setting is complex in its involvement of multiple actors and initiatives. On the one hand, there is evidence of an extension of post-conditionality beyond the state within the Bank's global agenda for HIV/AIDS. However, on the other, this does not necessarily mean a form of post-conditionality structured by the Bank, but a general trend towards liberal convergence among global donors and inter-governmental organisations. The key here is to not see actors operating within the context of the international as a homogeneous unit. These actors can be grouped together in that they operate at the global level of interaction, either multilaterally, bilaterally or transnationally and demonstrate a widespread commitment to the principles of liberalism and good governance in state and HIV/AIDS reform. As Chapter 5 argues, many of the actors operating within the context of the HIV/AIDS response in some way align with the structures and processes established by the Bank through the MAP. However, for some this is a part of a wider inevitability of their commitment to liberal practices of good governance. For others, for example, the Global Fund and UNAIDS, this can be seen as an extension of the Bank's form of post-conditionality, in that these actors not only align with the Bank but have to enact similar characteristics, and embed and develop its structures and processes of doing business to gain greater recognition and currency within global governance. Similar to states, the Bank's recognition of these actors confers legitimacy upon them within the system of HIV/AIDS governance. The Bank can enact conditional-based change through financial support to the Global Fund and UNAIDS, yet this is relatively ineffective as these organisations can seek alternative support from multiple organisations that have considerable financial commitments to addressing the disease. Thus, the Bank is more effective in developing a form of post-conditional relationships in which actors must align with its policies to gain currency, relevance and legitimacy within the international system. This presents a different kind of post-conditionality to the state, as though it extends the notion of a blurred sovereign frontier, intergovernmental organisations are able to demonstrate significantly more autonomy from the Bank and have other means of gaining legitimacy and financial support from the UN system as a whole. Curiously, perhaps with the exception of the early years of UNAIDS under the leadership of Peter Piot, these organisations are yet to find a voice independent from that of the HIV/AIDS agenda established by the Bank. From 2008–9 both UNAIDS and the Global Fund have been undergoing periods of change, with a need to articulate their mandate and purpose in the face of new private actors and initiatives emerging in the context of global health. These institutions will have to adapt as the Bank did in its first decade of existence, and will increasingly have to align with the dominant model of HIV/AIDS governance as a means of legitimacy. As such, they will have to continue to exhibit a general commitment to the principles of multi-sectoral good governance within their wider operations.

The alignment of institutions such as the Global Fund to the Bank's agenda suggests the type of policy convergence argued by Seckinelgin towards multi-sectoralism. There is clear evidence of knowledge transfer between organisations, and the development of a common language of 'AIDS speak' around acronyms and governance norms such as ownership, participation and, crucially, multi-sectoralism. This knowledge transfer performs a key legitimating function for both new and old actors with global HIV/AIDS governance, and permeates the activities of civil society in terms of who is in, in the realm of decision-making and agenda-setting, and who can be 'legitimately' excluded. The Bank not only performs the function of transferring multi-sectoral knowledge to states, it further 'scans' other states to absorb certain policy and ideas into its wider agenda (Stiglitz 2001). This can be seen in relation to the role of Brazil and the creation of the MAP.

The relationship between the MAP and the international shows an additional dynamic to governance reform in the relationship between sub-Saharan Africa and the international. HIV/AIDS and the MAP to a certain degree reinforce the construction of the subcontinent as something separate from and influenced by the international. Much of the findings of this book and notions of governance reform and post-conditionality re-enforce such a claim: states, civil society and the individual are very much acted upon by the international in the form of intergovernmental organisations such as the Bank and wider social forces towards a convergence on good governance. The influence of the MAP in setting the global agenda for HIV/AIDS would suggest a growing ability for Africa to provide the framework for global health policy. However, as Chapter 2 outlined, if anywhere the main framework for the MAP originated in Brazil. This reveals something particular about agenda-setting and agency within the international system. Development projects increasingly follow the model of being trialled or developed in Latin American countries, and then exported and scaled up to a significant degree in sub-Saharan Africa. As with the MAP, policies such as conditional cash transfers that are now being exported by the Bank to countries in Africa have their origins or 'first generation' in high profile Latin American initiatives such as *Opportunidas* in Mexico. The transplantation of programmes from Latin America to sub-Saharan Africa suggests an element of transnational knowledge sharing between middle-income and low-income countries. This would be effective should there be a willingness to adopt such policies on the part of countries in sub-Saharan Africa, and should this knowledge sharing operate bilaterally. The Brazil STI project was such a success because the government of Brazil showed a commitment to combating HIV/AIDS; such commitment was lacking with governments in sub-Saharan Africa. Furthermore, transferral of knowledge and policy frameworks only exist to the extent that they are facilitated by the Bank and intergovernmental finance and thus the transnational nature of it is somewhat dubious. What this means for the understanding of Africa and the international is that the subcontinent remains the subject of the international for intergovernmental organisations such as the Bank, especially in the context of HIV/AIDS where the promotion of the 'right' kind of health interventions and policies is paramount.

The health Bank

The World Bank's agenda for HIV/AIDS infers that the institution has a prominent role within global health. This book has shown that the Bank has developed its role in global health over a sustained period in which it has built upon flagship projects and a holistic approach to development to articulate its role in global health governance. However, since the 1993 World Development Report *Investing in Health* (World Bank 1993), there are relatively few signs of intent from the Bank as to its future role in global health. The 2009 report *Improving Effectiveness and Outcomes for the Poor in Health, Nutrition and Population* (World Bank 2009) suggests a reaffirmation of the multi-sectoral or sector-wide approach to healthcare, but more importantly, a move away from the Bank's involvement in flagship projects such as the MAP to more horizontal forms of healthcare intervention in the form of health system strengthening. This approach is a departure from the MAP in that it does not prioritise a specific disease, but builds upon the work of governance reform within the MAP in regard to the building and restructuring of government systems and within civil society through service delivery and implementation. As Chapter 5 suggests, this renewed focus on health system strengthening can already be seen on the ground in countries in East Africa.

As well as shifting towards horizontal health system strengthening, the Bank has begun to develop its sector-wide approach to health with the introduction of new financing mechanisms. At the centre of this has been a wider commitment to social protection through conditional cash transfers. Social protection by the Bank aims to target the needs of specific groups within healthcare. Specifically, this has come to mean women and families. This approach has generated a shift in discourse within health elements of the Bank towards conditional cash transfers that direct funds straight to families as a form of comprehensive intervention for orphans and vulnerable children (OVCs). As such, the Bank is becoming more targeted in its community interventions and is showing clear recognition of the individual and, in particular, women in healthcare provision. The role of women here is of particular relevance. Social protection funds not only address the core of health provision and ensure healthy workers and consumers, but expand the market by bringing women into its logic through lending, competition and efficiency. The role of women and social protection within the Bank's position will occupy a central part of its health interventions, as the institution increasingly turns its attention towards gender-based forms of family planning such as maternal health. However, similar to the MAP, the Bank's role will remain unclear as ownership and management of its projects continue to be the responsibility of the state and implementation of civil society.

The Bank is central to understanding the governance and political economy of global health. The application of the Bank's strategy has had several implications for the political economy of global health governance. First, the state still has a role within global health. However, application of the Bank's agenda has removed health from the health sector, either taking a sector-wide approach or situating it within more centralised forms of government and the Ministry of Finance. The role of the state has not diminished, but is at the hub of the Bank's promotion of good governance. Second, the role of non-state actors is permanent within healthcare provision. However, these non-state actors are primarily community groups which have become imbued with the market logic of state interventions into healthcare. As such remuneration of healthcare at the community level is bringing women to the centre of the political economy of health. Women have played an intrinsic role within global health, but movements towards new forms of social protection by the Bank sees a new form of macro-political economy within healthcare. Third, there is a shrinking of political space for alternative approaches to global health to develop. The Bank's 'soft politics' role within global health exists in partnership with the more 'hard politics' strategies of the World Trade Organization (WTO) and the IMF. Combined, these hard and soft policy options result in a shrinking of policy space for states, international organisations and non-state actors within global health. Regardless of whether it has shifted in expression, the liberal orthodoxy promoted by the Bretton Woods institutions has been at the root of global health since the late 1970s and has become embedded within every aspect of global health strategy. Actors must align their programmes, projects and strategic plans with this orthodoxy to ensure global recognition, finance and legitimacy.

Financial crises, the emergence of new actors and institutional inertia all pose a threat to the future role of the World Bank within global health. However, its antecedents are intrinsically embedded within every level of global health policy-making to affect the future of global health for the next 20 years. The Bank will continue to make minor adjustments to its existing global health priorities and look for new health development investments as a means of maintaining its relevance and benevolent status. Furthermore, it will continue to form partnerships and alliances with states, intergovernmental organisations and new emerging actors based upon financial relationships and the articulation of the Bank's specialist expertise on health system strengthening. The basis of much of these relationships and claims to knowledge will be derived from the Bank's experience with multi-sectoralism, HIV/AIDS and the MAP. Combined, these factors maintain the Bank's position as one of the lead institutions within global health governance.

Is a World Bank agenda for HIV/AIDS better than no agenda?

The majority of the findings of this book have been critical of the MAP and the Bank's wider agenda for HIV/AIDS. This has several implications. First, it opens the debate up to the Bank for it to respond with its own evidence and counter-claims about the MAP and the successes of its wider HIV/AIDS projects. This is an important and valuable function for the promotion of transparency and accountability within the Bank itself, and for our understanding of the HIV/AIDS response. Second, the conclusions drawn from this research could be interpreted as a call to end or reduce the significant amount of funds directed to the HIV/AIDS response. This is more problematic as 2008–9 has been replete with concern from the global HIV/AIDS community that funding to combat the disease will decrease with the onset and aftermath of the global recession. This concern has arisen in tandem with speculation in the wider development and health communities that HIV/AIDS receives too much money. A decline in HIV/AIDS spending would among other things see a decline in the number of orphans and vulnerable children receiving care, support and education; a decline in the number of people living with HIV/AIDS accessing ART and condoms; and a decline in the number of people being taught about methods of HIV prevention. However, what it would not necessarily do would be to lead to a decline in the government or civil society response.

The argument therefore is not to decrease the amount of spending on HIV/AIDS, but to address the way it is spent. Significant funds continue to be channelled towards the building of infrastructure and capacity, which in practice translate to using neoliberal forms of conditional lending to incentivise collective will on the parts of government and the emergence of a private service industry in the form of CSOs. Infrastructure is important to the efficient delivery of services to people infected and affected by HIV/AIDS; however, it is a wider concern of health and development interventions more generally, yet it forms a significant part of HIV/AIDS programmes. This points to the crux of the debate of global health strategies: whether to prioritise vertical interventions into contentious issues such as HIV/AIDS over horizontal interventions into strengthening healthcare systems within a country as a whole. What the Bank's agenda for HIV/AIDS does is blur these two strategies to a complex, limited outcome. A decline in the amount of money towards government infrastructure and CSO support may undermine in the short-term some activities, but if conducted in a way as to effectively maintain successful projects and develop space for ideas that do not necessarily fit into pre-existing concepts of good governance, it could ultimately lead to more positive outcomes within the HIV/AIDS response.

Minor adjustments within the existing MAP could facilitate improved outcomes. For the Bank, funding should be more strategic in where it is allocated. The Bank should identify where it wants to work, what it wants to address and who it wants to work with based on a mapping exercise akin to a basic baseline survey. This survey should then be weighted in reference to the perceived importance of the issue to the response and the amount of funding already directed to it by other donors. The Bank should engage in direct dialogue with those organisations it funds. As such, the Bank should manage the MAP in line with the NACs' over-arching objectives instead of the NACs managing projects in line with the Bank's directives. Current methods of feedback and dialogue should be strengthened and maintained to include a clear link between CSO input and decision-making outcome within the Bank and the national strategic plan. This input needs to be fed from the country level into global decision-making within the Bank. Participation within key partnership meetings should adapt a quota of CSOs funded under the MAP, which is changed every 3 years and has a specific focus on community groups so as to avoid the dominance of the 'usual suspects'. The Bank must acknowledge its role within the success or failure of the project. For organisational changes to be realised within the MAP the Bank needs to move out of its benevolent role and identify the project as Bank designed, Bank funded and Bank organised. Crucially, the Bank should be seen.

A key function of the Bank being seen is the role of CSOs. CSOs and governments are integral to transparency within the Bank's activities as they can record and witness first hand the influence it has upon HIV/AIDS policy. However, the ability of CSOs and governments to do so is jeopardised by their reliance on Bank funds to fulfil the objectives of individual and national strategic plans. Thus CSOs funded under the MAP need to ally with those organisations, predominantly INGOs, to monitor the activities of the Bank within HIV/AIDS. Furthermore, the focus of international advocacy campaigns surrounding HIV/AIDS must begin to focus on the Bank, its impact upon governments, as well as its influence upon international decision-making within HIV/AIDS responses. CSOs are reliant upon funding and thus restricted to low-cost service provision roles only. For these organisations to have an effective impact upon decision-making, and formulation of their own policies, they require greater access to information and joint planning and collaboration. This can be strengthened by establishing networks of similar groups at the community level, support from larger organisations and their presence within the quota system established by the reorganisation of the MAP. CSOs thus need to adopt a two-track strategy in which they, first, work within the MAP-led government structures of the Bank and the NACs to attain information and secure funding, and, second, maintain networking links with a variety of CSOs to promote transparency in government and Bank activity and articulate an alternative agenda for the HIV/AIDS response.

These changes on the part of the Bank and CSOs, however, would only precipitate minor adjustments within the current system of HIV/AIDS governance. They can also only fully be realised if the problems between neoliberal incentive and liberal outcome are addressed within the broader framework of HIV/AIDS governance. This brings us to the main contention of criticising the global response to HIV/AIDS: is a problematic agenda better than no agenda at all? Many of those working within the HIV/AIDS response recognise some of the problems and dilemmas of incentivising change discussed within this book, and much discussion and consultation and many programmes have tried to address how to make the money work better. Yet the assumption is the money is working, it could just work even better. The problem with this is that despite arguments put forward by the likes of Pisani and Seckinelgin suggesting it is 'time to wake up' (Seckinelgin 2008), criticism of the global response to HIV/AIDS continues to be perceived as a direct criticism to the US$15 billion it receives annually, and a challenge to the health and well-being of those infected and affected by HIV/AIDS. However, this limits our understanding of the complexities and issues within the global response, and leads to a dependency on the current agenda being better than nothing. There needs to be a global response to HIV/AIDS; however, the current one articulated by the World Bank is flawed and undermines any long-term attempts at fully halting and reversing the spread of the disease.

Conclusion: seeing the World Bank and HIV/AIDS

HIV/AIDS represents a new frontier for the Bank in which it can extend its governance reform agenda through healthcare and gain access to the most remote aspects of society through initiatives sanctioned and promoted by the state. The Bank's role in HIV/AIDS contributes to our understanding of governance reform in unravelling the practical nuances of implementing such reform, the role of CSOs and their position within state reform, and the global reach and disciplinarity of the Bank's reform agenda. The difficulties of implementing the MAP highlight the practical blockages associated with a reform agenda that promotes a specific form of ahistorical and apolitical governance. Nationally based CSOs play a crucial role within the Bank's agenda to circumvent or address arising blockages or problems of 'bad' reform within the state. Thus in extending governance reform beyond the government-focused approach to state reform to include CSOs, individuals and the international, the Bank is not only embedding its reform agenda of competition-based free market-led interventions at every level of governance, it is confronting the 'sovereign frontier' from the bottom-up by bringing CSOs and individuals into the wider functions of the state.

The inclusion of CSOs, individuals and the international within the Bank's agenda does not indicate a shift away from neoliberal to liberal governance reform. The predominance of economic incentive as a means of creating political will on the part of the state, civil society and the individual suggests that neoliberalism remains the main driver of governance reform in sub-Saharan Africa and HIV/AIDS. The central contention for the Bank and those actors working within the global response to HIV/AIDS at every level of governance is the pursuit of liberal outcomes through neoliberal means. As the findings of this book suggest, this too is lacking. Instead neoliberal incentives create market-based outcomes within the state and civil society, and develop individuals into market actors by appealing to their economic rationality and need. The Bank's multi-sectoral agenda for HIV/AIDS thus may appear to prioritise liberal outcomes, yet in practice it is a form of neoliberal governance reform. This is unsurprising, as at the heart of the construction of HIV/AIDS as a development issue on the part of the World Bank is the need to promote economic growth through the health and subsequent productivity of populations in low-income countries.

The method in which the Bank has embedded this agenda within state, civil society and the individual enables its continued existence and influence upon HIV/AIDS beyond the MAP. The Bank's interpretation of multi-sectoralism is the operating principle in which the global response functions. The MAP already presents the model of HIV/AIDS governance in which the Global Fund and the UN agencies adhere to, yet the permeation of MAP structure to every level of community, state and global governance will ensure the maintenance and expansion of this reform agenda well after the end of the project. What we see then is a sophisticated expression of the Bank's multi-sectoral governance reform agenda that addresses the state as a stumbling block to market-led reform by appropriating state structures as a means of promoting private service delivery through civil society and the individual.

Addressing the failures of the HIV/AIDS response by looking at state agendas or lack thereof in isolation from the World Bank depoliticises any understanding of the response to the epidemic, and thus reduces the ability to tackle it and its long-wave expression. To understand the governance and global agenda for HIV/AIDS it is crucial to understand the role of political underpinnings of multi-sectoralism: at the centre of which is the World Bank. The World Bank has set and will continue to sustain the global agenda for HIV/AIDS at every level of governance through neoliberal incentive in the pursuit of neoliberal outcomes. For the war, reversal, response or agenda to combat HIV/AIDS to be won, the World Bank must be seen.

Notes

1 The complexity of HIV/AIDS governance

1 These countries are Angola, Benin, Botswana, Burkina Faso, Burundi, Cameroon, Cape Verde, Central African Republic, Chad, DR Congo, Congo Republic, Cote d'Ivoire, Eritrea, Ethiopia, The Gambia, Ghana, Guinea, Kenya, Lesotho, Madagascar, Malawi, Mali, Mauritania, Mozambique, Niger, Nigeria, Rwanda, Senegal, Sierra Leone, Sudan, Tanzania, Uganda, Zambia.

2 Pathways to multi-sectorality and HIV/AIDS

1 Keynes' and Dexter White's recommendations and vision for these institutions stemmed from what Keynes perceived to be the failings of the First World War peace conference treaty, the 1919 Treaty of Versailles, and the formation of the Atlantic Charter, 1941. It was in reaction to the agreements made within Versailles that Keynes outlined his vision for state-building and reconstruction based upon four central revisions. The first was revision of the treaty to elicit reform of reparations through the League of Nations. Germany would have to meet fixed sums in line with its capacity to pay so as to decrease friction and renew enterprise (Keynes 1924: 245–249). Second, was the settlement of inter-ally indebtedness through complete cancellation of indebtedness incurred for the purposes of War, the onus of which fell upon the US (Keynes 1924: 254–255). Inter-state indebtedness existed up to this point because of its basis in real assets and property and the minimal amount lent; this system, however, was fragile (Keynes 1924: 263). The third measure advocated was in support of the international loan; the burden of funding such resources would again fall to the US (Keynes 1924: 265). Loans to Europe would be minimal in order to renew economic organisations and benefit workers but not so much as to further national interests against a unified Europe (Keynes 1924: 267–270). Fourth, in response to the October Bolshevik Revolution of 1917, relations between Central Europe and Russia require consideration necessary to reassert Germany's place in Europe as 'a creator and organiser of wealth for her Eastern and Southern neighbours' through its policy of non-intervention (Keynes 1924: 276). Crucial to the realisation of these objectives was the need for states to move beyond self-interest in order to avoid the ill effects of a bankrupt Europe (Keynes 1924: 278).

Keynes' recommendations formed the basis of the 1941 Atlantic Charter that established a post-World War II vision for the world. Keynes and Dexter White sought to create a collaborative multilateral world order that would ensure democratic growth, security and balance of payments equilibrium (Ruggie 1982: 394–395). Abolition of exchange controls and restrictions on currency transactions would facilitate free exchange between states, while stability would be maintained through the expression of value in terms of gold (Ruggie 1982: 395). Such principles formed the basis of negotiations within the Atlantic Charter and came to underpin the wider purpose and directives of the Bank and Fund.

2 Despite being presented as non-political and above the interests of member states, the formation of the Bank was characterised by contention between the USA and British governments of the time. The central cause of disagreement was over whether the Bank and Fund were financial institutions to be directed by civil servants or institutions that had such political and economic implications they had to be closely monitored by member governments (Gardner 1956: 257). Britain viewed the Bank and IMF's role as being financial institutions independent of close member control; the USA believed their political and economic ramifications to be broad and thus thought they should be subject to close government control (Gardner 1956: 267). Britain thought the gold standard would threaten state-led expansionist policy by restricting the flow of capital and goods to global restrictions. The USA sought to use the Bank and Fund to remove restrictive state-based policies and integrate the world economy multilaterally as a means of strengthening Western Europe against Soviet power (Hogan 1987: 17). Subsequently, the US Treasury assumed the dominant role in the direction and design of the IMF and World Bank (Gardner 1956: 72). Britain agreed to the US-preferred plan as an 'unfortunate accompaniment to a badly needed loan' (Gardner 1956: 253).

3 Expressions of US influence continued to dominate the Bank in its initial selection of president. Once Eugene Meyer (June 1946 to December 1946) had been appointed as the Bank's first president, he resigned 3 months later following conflict with the US Director of the Bank, Emilio G Collado. At the time, when asked whether he would stay on and fight Meyer responded 'but I'm too old for that' (World Bank 2005).

4 *Interview* John Garrison, Senior Civil Society Specialist, World Bank 27 April 2006.

5 The Sardar Sarovar Dam on India's Narmada River was a Bank-sponsored project on a loan of US$450 million. The aim of the project was to provide river irrigation and power generation across the Narmada River; the Sardar Sarovar Dam was the biggest of all the planned dams. Controversy surrounding the dams was generated as a result of displacement of millions of indigenous community members without compensation; lack of adequate community consultation; and the long-term practical solution the dam would be to issues of power generation. The high level CSO campaign marking out the impact of the project resulted in the Bank's withdrawal after 7 years' involvement in its design. The Campaign for Sardar Sarovar and Narmada continues. For further information see: www.narmada.org; www.sardarsarovardam.org; www.irn.org

Polonoreste was the $445 million Bank sponsored Northwest Brazil Integrated Programme. The project was to pave 1,500 kilometres of rural road connecting the region of Rondonia to commercial traffic. Polonoreste resulted in the destruction of ten times more rainforest than previously estimated; the burning of forest was the single most rapid change on earth visible from space; malaria increased to infect 250,000 people; and subsequently the project was branded by the then President of the Bank, Barber Conable, a 'sobering example of an environmentally sound project gone wrong'. Subsequent to Polonoreste the World Bank launched a project in 1992 'Planafloro' to address the problems associated with Polonoreste. However, in 1996 the World Bank Inspection Panel discovered that deforestation stood at approximately 450,000 hectares a year. For further information see: www.whirledbank.org; www.forests.org

6 *Interview* David Woodward, New Economics Foundation, 17th August 2005.

7 At ex-World Bank President Paul Wolfowitz's (2005–7) first Annual Spring Meetings the Civil Society Team arranged a reception of 46 NGOs; Wolfowitz spoke for a few minutes and then 'spoke to a lot of them one on one'. It is imperative to make sure he and the Vice Presidents are talking to CSOs as much as possible. His appointment was met with disappointment by a host of INGOs such as Action Aid, Christian Aid, Greenpeace and World Development Movement; and by politicians and academics in Europe (Richburg and Frankel 2005) and the US (Bretton Woods Project 2005). Despite

initial concerns, Wolfowitz provoked a positive reaction by CSOs such as CIVICUS, with its then President, Aruna Roo praising him for his dialogue (Bond 2007).

8 *Interview* John Garrison, Senior Civil Society Specialist, World Bank 27 April 2006.
9 *Interview* Yasmin Tayyab, Civil Society Team, World Bank, 25 April 2006.
10 *Interview* Juraj Mesik, Senior Community Foundations Specialist, World Bank, 24 April 2006.
11 *Interview* Eleanor Fink, Foundations Co-ordinator, World Bank 20 April 2006; *Interview* Katherine Marshall, Development Dialogue on Values and Ethics, World Bank, 21 April 2006.
12 *Interview* Jeff Thindwa, Senior Civil Society Specialist, World Bank, 1 May 2006.
13 *Interview* Eleanor Fink, Foundations Co-ordinator, World Bank 20 April 2006.
14 *Interview* Nadeem Mohammed, Senior Operations Officer, ACT Africa, World Bank, 24 April 2006.
15 *Interview* John Garrison, Senior Civil Society Specialist, World Bank 27 April 2006.
16 *Interview* Debrework Zewdie, Director Global HIV/AIDS Program, World Bank, 3 May 2006.
17 *Interview* Jacomina de Regt, Senior Lead Specialist for Social Development Africa, World Bank 20 April 2006.
18 *Interview* Debrework Zewdie, Director Global HIV/AIDS Program, World Bank, 3 May 2006.

3   Owning HIV/AIDS: the state

1 *Interview* Albertus Voetberg, Senior Health Specialist/TTL World Bank, Kenya 7 April 2005.
2 *Interview* Adam Lagerstedt, Senior Health Specialist, World Bank, Kenya, 16 November 2005.
3 *Interview* Adam Lagerstedt, Senior Health Specialist, World Bank, Kenya, 16 November 2005.
4 *Interview* Peter Okwero, Senior Health Specialist/TTL World Bank, Kenya 1 November 2005.
5 *Interview* Julius Byenka, Uganda AIDS Commission, 11 October 2005.
6 *Interview* Julius Byenka, Uganda AIDS Commission, 11 October 2005.
7 *Interview* Asha Abdullah, Zanzibar HIV/AIDS Commission, 31 January 2006.
8 *Interview* Hashim Kalinga, TACAIDS, 14 February 2006.
9 *Interview* Paul Stannard, Crown Agents, 10 January 2006.
10 *Interview* Nick Southern, CARE International, Tanzania, 9 January 2006.
11 *Interview* Joseph Temba, TACAIDS, Tanzania 9 January 2006.
12 *Interview* Ursula Bahati, National AIDS Control Council (NACC), Kenya, 14 November 2005; *Interview* Hashim Kalinga, TACAIDS, 14 February 2006; *Interview* Joseph Temba, TACAIDS, 10 February 2006; *Interview* Rustica Tembele, TACAIDS, 6 January 2006; *Interview* Julius Byenka, Uganda AIDS Commission, 11 October 2005.
13 *Interview* Edna Baguma, World Vision, Uganda, 20 October 2005; *Interview* Emmanuel Malangalila, Senior Health Specialist/TTL, World Bank Tanzania, 20 January 2006; *Interview* Adam Lagerstedt, Senior Health Specialist, World Bank, Kenya, 16 November 2005.
14 *Interview* Hashim Kalinga, TACAIDS, 14 February 2006.
15 *Interview* Ursula Bahati, National AIDS Control Council (NACC), Kenya, 14 November 2005.
16 *Interview* Robert Okumu, Tororo District AIDS Committee, Uganda, 14 October 2005; *Interview* Mr Lavanda, Mbeya Municipal Council, Tanzania 6 February 2006.
17 *Interview* Mina Nakawuka, Kampala District HIV/AIDS Council, Uganda, 28 October 2005.

18 *Interview* Mr. Lavanda, Mbeya Municipal Council, Tanzania, 6 February 2006; *Interview* Boniface Ntalo, Jinga District AIDS Council, Uganda, 13 October 2005.

19 *Interview* Hashim Kalinga, TACAIDS, 14 February 2006; *Interview* Boniface Ntalo, Jinga District AIDS Council, Uganda 13 October 2005; *Interview* Wilson Behwera, Masaka District HIV/AIDS Council, Uganda, 26 October 2005; *Interview* Robert Okumu, Tororo District AIDS Committee, Uganda, 14 October 2005.

20 *Interview* Wilson Behwera, Masaka District HIV/AIDS Council, Uganda, 26 October 2005; *Interview* Deo Mtasiwa, District Medical Officer, Tanzania, 16 February 2006; *Interview* Mina Nakawuka, Kampala District HIV/AIDS Council, Uganda, 28 October 2005; *Interview* Boniface Ntalo, Jinga District AIDS Council, Uganda, 13 October 2005; *Interview* Robert Okumu, Tororo District AIDS Committee, Uganda, 14 October 2005; *Interview* Evodis Pangani, Ilala Municipal Council, Tanzania, 16 February 2006; *Interview* Suzan Wandera Mukono District HIV/AIDS Council, Uganda, 20 October 2005; *Questionnaire* Benson Tatala Mpanguleka, Handeni District HIV/AIDS Council, Tanzania, 17 May 2006; *Questionnaire* Elisabeth Naegele, RFA Moshi, Tanzania, 13 May 2006.

21 *Interview* Mr. Lavanda, Mbeya Municipal Council, Tanzania, 6 February 2006.

22 *Interview* Joseph Temba, TACAIDS, 10 February 2006; *Interview* Rustica Tembele, TACAIDS, 6 January 2006.

23 *Interview* Julius Byenka, Uganda AIDS Commission, 11 October 2005; *Interview* Morris Lekule, TACAIDS, 4 January 2006.

24 *Interview* Emmanuel Malangalila, Senior Health Specialist/TTL, World Bank, Tanzania, 20 January 2006; *Interview* Ursula Bahati, National AIDS Control Council (NACC), Kenya, 14 November 2005; *Interview* Adam Lagerstedt, Senior Health Specialist, World Bank, Kenya, 16 November 2005.

25 *Interview* Julius Byenka, Uganda AIDS Commission, 11 October 2005; *Interview* Morris Lekule, TACAIDS, 4 January 2006.

26 *Interview* Albertus Voetberg, Senior Health Specialist, World Bank, Kenya 15 November 2005; *Int.* Malangalila, 20 January 2006; *Interview* Adam Lagerstedt, Senior Health Specialist, World Bank, Kenya, 16th November 2005.

27 *Interview* Annalise Trama, UNAIDS, Kenya, 21 December 2005; *Interview* Steve Kinzett, John Snow Inc (JSI) Kenya, 23 November 2005; *Interview* Emmanuel Malangalila, Senior Health Specialist/TTL, World Bank, Tanzania, 20 January 2006.

28 *Interview* Tim Rosche, John Snow Inc (JSI), Tanzania, 18 January 2006.

29 *Interview* Joseph Temba, TACAIDS, 10 February 2006.

30 *Interview* Annalise Trama, UNAIDS, Kenya, 21 December 2005.

31 *Interview* Awene Gavyole, WHO, Tanzania, 13 February 2006.

32 *Interview* Adam Lagerstedt, Senior Health Specialist, World Bank, Kenya, 16 November 2005.

33 *Interview* Tim Rosche, John Snow Inc (JSI), Tanzania, 18 January 2006.

34 *Interview* Julius Byenka, Uganda AIDS Commission, 11 October 2005.

35 These findings are based on extensive visits to the NACC: in one instance the NACC was open to my participation in the JAPR and was extremely accommodating and helpful in this respect; the corollary of this was when I attempted to access information on the District Technical Committees and I was told that the information, i.e. names and addresses, were classified without a letter of introduction from the British High Commission, British Council or whoever they then chose. In a separate incident when attending the NACC for information on the NGOs nationally funded under the KHADREP I was left waiting for 6 hours after being told the person I needed was in a meeting, and then eventually that that person had gone home.

36 *Interview* Nick Southern, CARE International, 9 January 2006.

37 *Interview* Barabona Mubondo, WAMATA (People in the fight against HIV/AIDS in Tanzania) Tanzania, 20 January 2006; *Interview* George Tembo, UNAIDS, Geneva, 25 May 2006.

38 *Interview* Kathleen Okatcha, KORDP (Kenya Orphans Rural Development Programme) Kenya, 16 November 2005.
39 *Interview* Claudia Hunger, GTZ, Tanzania, 6 February 2006; *Interview* Samuel Nyantahe, Utegi Technical Enterprises – RFA Dar es Salaam, Mara, Shinyanga, Tanzania, 9 January 2006; *Interview* Idi Saadat, Zanzibar HIV/AIDS Commission, 31 January 2006.
40 *Interview* Bob Duolf, CARE International, Tanzania, 4 January 2006.
41 *Interview* Morris Lekule, TACAIDS, 4 January 2006.
42 *Interview* Wilson Behwera, Masaka District HIV/AIDS Council, Uganda 26 October 2005.
43 In 2005 Sir Edward Clay, the then UK High Commissioner to Kenya, made a speech documenting the levels of corruption within the Kenya government, accusing the government of bribery, accounting for 8 per cent of Kenya's Gross Domestic Product (GDP), that is undermining Kenya's economic growth and donor aid commitments. Such an accusation made international headlines because of the comment 'they can hardly expect us not to care when their gluttony causes them to vomit all over our shoes' (BBC News, 2004). Clay's comments were in response to a longstanding problem of corruption within the Kenya government that culminated in the Anglo Leasing and Finance Company Ltd affair under the leadership of the 'anti-corruption' Presidency of Mwai Kibaki. The crisis of corruption within Kenya is effectively addressed in Michela Wrong's (2009) book on whistleblower John Githongo *Its Our Turn To Eat: The Story of a Kenyan Whistleblower*. This problem was also expressed in an interview with Steve Kinzett, John Snow Inc (JSI), Kenya, 23 November 2005.
44 *Interview* Rowlands Lenya, TAPWAK (The Association of People With AIDS in Kenya), Kenya, 10 November 2005.
45 *Interview* Albertus Voetberg, Senior Health Specialist, World Bank, Kenya 7 April 2005.
46 *Interview* Claudia Hunger, GTZ, Tanzania, 6 February 2006.
47 *Interview* Hashim Kalinga, TACAIDS, 14 February 2006.
48 *Interview* Claudia Hunger, GTZ, Tanzania, 6 February 2006; *Interview* Hashim Kalinga, TACAIDS, 14 February 2006; *Interview* Emmanuel Malangalila, Senior Health Specialist/TTL, World Bank, Tanzania, 20 January 2006; *Interview* Robert Mukama, RFA Iringa and Ruvuma, Tanzania, 8 February 2006; *Interview* Joseph Temba, TACAIDS, 10 January 2006.
49 *Interview* Claudia Hunger, GTZ Tanzania, 6 February 2006; *Interview* Kenneth Simbaya, SPW (Student Partnerships Worldwide), Tanzania, 7 February 2006; *Interview* Amanda Childress, Africare/USAID, 14 February 2006.
50 *Interview* Awene Gavyolea, WHO, Tanzania, 13 February 2006.
51 *Interview* Joseph Temba, TACAIDS, 10 February 2006; *Interview* Pfiriael Kiwia, Kimara Peer Educators, Tanzania, 15 February 2006; *Interview* Ursula Bahati, National AIDS Control Council (NACC), Kenya, 14 November 2005; *Interview* Robert Mukama, RFA Iringa and Ruvuma, Tanzania, 8 February 2006.
52 *Interview* Rubaramira Ruranga, NGEN+ (National Guidance and Empowerment Network of People Living with HIV/AIDS), Uganda, 31 October 2005.
53 *Interview* Claudia Hunger, GTZ, Tanzania, 6 February 2006; *Interview* Margrethe Juncker, Reach Out, Uganda, 11 October 2005; *Interview* Mr. Lusewa, WAVUMO, Tanzania, 17 January 2006; *Interview* Wilberforce Mayanja, Philly Lutaaya Initiative/ AIDS Information Centre, Uganda, 8 October 2005; *Interview* Eve Mwai, St Johns Ambulance, Kenya, 29 November 2005; *Interview* Stigmata Tenga, ST Associates, Tanzania 13 January 2006.
54 *Interview* Patrick Ogen, Youth Alive, Uganda, 19 October 2005; *Interview* Dorothy Kaloli, Dogodogo Centre, Tanzania, 4 January 2006; *Interview* Kenneth Simbaya, SPW (Students Partnership Worldwide), Tanzania, 7 February 2006; *Interview* Barabona Mubondo, WAMATA (People in the fight against HIV/AIDS in Tanzania), Tanzania,

20 January 2006; *Interview* Duncan Hervey, Save the Children, Zanzibar, 27 January 2006; *Interview* Hashim Kalinga, TACAIDS, 14 February 2006; *Interview* Victor Mulimila, Faraja Trust Fund, Tanzania, 19 January 2006.

55 *Interview* Aisling Quiery, Merlin, Kenya, 31 December 2005; *Interview* Bob Duolf, CARE International, 4 January 2006; *Interview* Duncan Hervey, Save the Children, Zanzibar, 27 January 2006.

56 *Interview* George Tembo, UNAIDS, Geneva, 25 May 2006.

57 *Interview* Awene Gayole, World Health Organisation (WHO), Tanzania, 13 February 2006; *Interview* Samuel Nyantahe, Utegi Technical Enterprises – RFA Dar es Salaam, Mara, Shinyanga – Tanzania, 9 January 2006.

58 *Interview* Aisling Quiery, Merlin, Kenya, 21 December 2005; *Interview* Carole Kariuki, Kenya Private Sector Alliance, Kenya, 16 December 2005; *Interview* Deus Kihamba, TGNP (Tanzania Gender Networking Programme), Tanzania, 20 January 2006.

59 *Interview* Morris Lekule, TACAIDS, 4 January 2006; *Interview* Stella Chale, NACP (National AIDS Control Programme) 10 January 2006; *Interview* Emmanuel Malangalila, Senior Health Specialist/TTL World Bank, Tanzania, 20 January 2006.

60 *Interview* Rustica Tembele, TACAIDS, 6 January 2006.

61 *Interview* Dorcus Kameta, National AIDS/STD Control Programme (NASCOP), Kenya, 11 November 2005; *Interview* Joseph Temba, TACAIDS, 10 February 2006; *Interview* Idi Saadat, Zanzibar HIV/AIDS Commission, 31 January 2006.

62 *Interview* Emmanuel Malangalila, Senior Health Specialist/TTL, World Bank, Tanzania, 20 January 2006; *Interview* Anne Austen, Futures Group, Kenya, 18 November 2005; *Interview* George Tembo, UNAIDS, Geneva, 25 May 2006.

63 *Interview* Ursula Bahati, National AIDS Control Council (NACC), Kenya, 14 December 2005; *Interview* Morris Lekule, TACAIDS, 4 January 2006.

64 *Interview* Nadeem Mohammed, Senior Operations Officer, ACT Africa, World Bank, 24 April, 2006; *Interview* Jacomina de Regt, Senior Lead Specialist for Social Development Africa, World Bank 20 April 2006.

65 *Interview* Victor Mulimila, Faraja Trust Fund, Tanzania, 19 January 2006.

66 *Interview* Robert Okumu, Tororo District AIDS Committee, Uganda, 14 October 2005; *Interview* Boniface Ntalo, 13 October 2005.

67 *Interview* Albertus Voetberg, Senior Health Specialist, World Bank, Kenya 15 November 2005; *Interview* Peter Okwero, Senior Health Specialist/TTL World Bank, Uganda 1 November 2005.

68 *Interview* Jacomina de Regt, Senior Lead Specialist for Social Development Africa, World Bank 20 April 2006.

69 *Interview* Julius Byenka, Uganda AIDS Commission, 11 October 2005; *Interview* Morris Lekule, TACAIDS, 4 January 2006.

70 *Interview* Debrework Zewdie, Director Global HIV/AIDS Program, World Bank, 3 May 2006.

71 *Interview* Emmanuel Malangalila, Senior Health Specialist/TTL, World Bank, Tanzania, 20 January 2006; *Interview* Debrework Zewdie, Director Global HIV/AIDS Program, World Bank, 3 May 2006.

72 *Interview* Debrework Zewdie, Director Global HIV/AIDS Program, World Bank, 3 May 2006.

73 *Interview* Nadeem Mohammed, Senior Operations Officer, ACT Africa, World Bank, 24 April, 2006.

74 *Interview* Nadeem Mohammed, Senior Operations Officer, ACT Africa, World Bank, 24 April, 2006.

75 *Interview* Peter Okwero, Senior Health Specialist/TTL, World Bank, Uganda, 1 November 2005.

76 *Interview* Adam Lagerstedt, Senior Health Specialist, World Bank, Kenya, 16 November 2005.

77 Adam Lagerstedt, Senior Health Specialist, World Bank, Kenya, 16 November 2005.

78 *Interview* Peter Okwero, Senior Health Specialist/TTL, World Bank, Uganda, 1 November 2005; *Interview* Adam Lagerstedt, Senior Health Specialist, World Bank, Kenya, 16 November 2005.
79 The constituents of the JICC are Government – Office of the President, Ministry of Health, Ministry of Finance, Ministry of Education, Science and Technology and the NACC; Private Sector – Kenya Association of Manufacturers; Kenya HIV/AIDS Business Coalition; Development Partners – WHO, World Bank, UNAIDS, UNICEF, UNFPA, USAID, CDC, German Development Co-operation (GDC), Japan International Co-operation Agency (JICA), Swedish International Co-operation Agency (SIDA); Civil Society (including FBOs and Research Institutions) – Kenya Catholic Secretariat, Christian Health Association of Kenya (CHAT), Supreme Council of Kenya Muslims, African Medical and Research Foundation (AMREF), Kenya AIDS NGOs Consortium (KANCO), Care International, Sanaar Art Promotions, People Living with HIV/AIDS, Organisation of Kenya Network of Women living with HIV/AIDS (KENWA), Network of people living with HIV/AIDS in Kenya (NEPHAK), Nyumbani Children's Home, Kenya Medical Association, University of Nairobi Medical School, Kenya Medical Research Institute.
80 *Interview* Annalise Trama, UNAIDS, Kenya, 21 December 2005; *Interview* Ursula Bahati, National AIDS Control Council (NACC), Kenya, 14 November 2005; *Interview* Adam Lagerstedt, Senior Health Specialist, World Bank, Kenya, 16 November 2005.
81 *Interview* Idi Juma, KANCO (Kenya AIDS NGOs Consortium), Kenya, 8 November 2005; *Interview* Albertus Voetberg, Senior Health Specialist, World Bank, Kenya 15 November 2005; *Interview* Annalise Trama, UNAIDS, Kenya, 21 December 2005.
82 *Interview* Rustica Tembele, TACAIDS, 6 January 2006; *Interview* Nicodemus Mwaduma, RFA Lindi and Mtwara, Tanzania, 6 January 2006; *Interview* Hashim Kalinga, TACAIDS, 14 February 2006.
83 *Interview* Hashim Kalinga, TACAIDS, 14 February 2006.
84 The organisations appointed RFAs are as follows: SACHITA Associates - Iringa/Ruvuma; GTZ International – Mbeya/Rukwa; GFA Medica – Tanga/Kilimanjaro; Action Aid – Dodoma/Singida/Morogoro/Coast; DAC Consultants – Lindi/Mtwara; KOSHIKA/ Utegi Technical Enterprises – Dar es Salaam/Mara/Shinyaga; TANESA – Mwanza/ Kagera; ST Associates – Arusha/Manyara; Care International – Tabora/Kigoma.
85 *Interview* Joseph Temba, TACAIDS, 10 February 2006.
86 *Interview* Hashim Kalinga, TACAIDS, 14 February 2006; *Interview* Emmanuel Malangalila, Senior Health Specialist/TTL World Bank, Tanzania, 20 January 2006; *Interview* Samuel Nyantahe, Utegi Technical Enterprises - RFA Dar es Salaam, Mara Shinyanga – Tanzania, 9 January 2006.
87 *Interview* Hashim Kalinga, TACAIDS, 14 February 2006; *Interview* Emmanuel Malangalila, Senior Health Specialist/TTL World Bank, Tanzania, 20 January 2006; *Interview* Joseph Temba, TACAIDS, 10 February 2006.
88 *Interview* Stigmata Tenga, ST Associates – RFA Arusha, Manyara – Tanzania, 13 January 2006.
89 *Interview* Emmanuel Malangalila, Senior Health Specialist/TTL World Bank, Tanzania, 20 January 2006.
90 *Interview* Stigmata Tenga, ST Associates – RFA Arusha, Manyara – Tanzania, 13 January 2006; *Interview* Robert Mukama, RFA Iringa and Ruvuma, Tanzania, 8 February 2006; *Interview* Rose Mushi, Action Aid – RFA Morogoro, Coast, Singida, Dodoma – Tanzania, 9 January 2006; *Interview* Samuel Nyantahe, Utegi Technical Enterprises – RFA Dar es Salaam, Mara, Shinyanga – Tanzania, 9 January 2006; *Interview* Nicodemus Mwaduma, RFA Lindi and Mtwara, Tanzania, 5 January 2006.
91 *Interview* Hashim Kalinga, TACAIDS, 14 February 2006.
92 *Interview* Robert Mukama, RFA Iringa and Ruvuma, Tanzania, 8 February 2006; *Interview* Claudia Hunger, GTZ – RFA Mbeya, Rukwa - Tanzania, 6 February 2006.

93 *Interview* Nicodemus Mwaduma, RFA Lindi and Mtwara, Tanzania, 5 January 2006; *Interview* Robert Mukama, RFA Iringa and Ruvuma, Tanzania, 8 February 2006; *Interview* Hashim Kalinga, TACAIDS, 14 February 2006.

94 *Interview* Claudia Hunger, GTZ – RFA Mbeya, Rukwa - Tanzania, 6 February 2006.

95 *Interview* Stigmata Tenga, ST Associates – RFA Arusha, Manyara – Tanzania, 13 January 2006.

96 *Interview* Stigmata Tenga, ST Associates – RFA Arusha, Manyara – Tanzania, 13 January 2006; *Interview* Claudia Hunger, GTZ – RFA Mbeya, Rukwa – Tanzania, 6 February 2006.

97 *Interview* Mr Lavanda, Mbeya Municipal Council, Tanzania, 6 February 2006.

98 *Interview* Claudia Hunger, GTZ – RFA Mbeya, Rukwa – Tanzania, 6 February 2006; *Interview* Stigmata Tenga, ST Associates – RFA Arusha, Manyara – Tanzania, 13 January 2006.

99 *Interview* Samuel Nyantahe, Utegi Technical Enterprises – RFA Dar es Salaam, Mara, Shinyanga – Tanzania, 9 January 2006.

100 *Interview* Edina Hauli, SHDEPHA+ (Service Health and Development for people living with HIV/AIDS), Tanzania, 8 February 2006; *Interview* Nelson Chusio, IDYDC (Iringa Development of Youth, Disabled and Children Care), Tanzania, 8 February 2006.

101 *Interview* Pfiriael Kiwia, Kimara Peer Educators, Tanzania, 15 February 2006; *Interview* Victor Mulimila, Faraja Trust Fund, Tanzania, 17 January 2006.

102 *Interview* Claudia Hunger, GTZ – RFA Mbeya, Rukwa – Tanzania, 6 February 2006; *Interview* Robert Mukama, RFA Iringa and Ruvuma, Tanzania, 8 February 2006; *Interview* Nicodemus Mwaduma, RFA Lindi and Mtwara, Tanzania, 6 January 2006; *Interview* Nyantahe, Utegi Technical Enterprises – RFA Dar es Salaam, Mara, Shinyanga – Tanzania, 9 January 2006.

103 *Interview* Agnes Msokaa, SWAAT (Society for Women and AIDS in Africa), Tanzania, 15 January 2006.

104 *Interview* Alex Pius Margery, TANEPHA (Tanzania National Network of People with HIV/AIDS) Tanzania, 6 January 2006.

105 *Interview* Joseph Temba, TACAIDS, 10 February 2006.

106 *Interview* Asha Abdullah, Zanzibar HIV/AIDS Commission, 31 January 2006.

4 Constructing multi-sectoralism: the community

1 *Interview* Kathleen Okatcha, KORDP (Kenya Orphans Rural Development Programme), Kenya, 16 November 2005; *Interview* Samson Ndege, Pathfinder, Kenya, 16 November 2005.

2 *Interview* Emmanuel Malangalila, Senior Health Specialist/Task Team Leader, World Bank, Tanzania, 20 January 2006; *Interview* Peter Okwero, Senior Health Specialist/ Task Team Leader, World Bank, Uganda, 1 November 2005; *Interview* Albertus Voetberg, Senior Health Specialist/TTL World Bank, Kenya, 7 April 2006; *Interview* Joseph Mwamaja, UMATI Eastern (Society of Family Planning), Tanzania, 17 January 2006; *Interview* Mr. Lusewa, WAVUMO Community organisation, Tanzania, 17 January 2006.

3 *Interview* Bernadette, Population Services International (PSI), Uganda, 6 October 2005; *Interview* Kenneth Simbaya, SPW (Student Partnerships Worldwide), Tanzania, 7 February 2006; *Interview* Idi Saadat, Zanzibar AIDS Commission, Zanzibar, 31 January 2006.

4 *Interview* Paschal Wambiya, ILO (International Labour Organisation), Kenya, 19 December 2005; *Interview* Suzan Ngugi, KENWA (Kenya Network of Women with HIV/ AIDS), Kenya, 24 November 2005; *Interview* Joyce Mkongo, SHDEPHA+ (Service Health and Development for People living with HIV/AIDS), Tanzania, 6 February 2006; *Interview* Herbert Mugumya, Save the Children, Uganda, 1 November 2005; *Interview* Joezif Jaxon, Foundation for Civil Society, Tanzania, 10 February 2006.

5 *Interview* Stephen Kiirya, Uganda AIDS Commission, 11 April 2005.
6 *Interview* Angella Nakiyimba, CIPA, Uganda, 27 October 2005; *Interview* Victor Mulimila, Faraja Trust Fund, 19 January 2006; *Interview* Julius Byenka, Uganda AIDS Commission, 11 October 2005; *Interview* Benon Kasigazi, UGANET, Uganda, 31 October 2005; *Interview* Immam Kasozi, Uganda Muslim Youth Association, 24 October 2005.
7 *Interview* Adam Lagerstedt, Senior Health Specialist, World Bank, Kenya, 16 November 2005.
8 *Interview* Hashim Kalinga, TACAIDS, Tanzania, 14 February 2006; *Interview* Nadeem Mohammed, Senior Operations Officer, ACT Africa, World Bank, 24 April 2006.
9 *Interview* Ursula Bahati, National AIDS Control Council (NACC), Kenya, 14 November 2005.
10 Examples of FBOs funded under the MAP: Kenya – Jehovah Jiveh Christian Homes, Kagumo Catholic Parish Life Giving Care Centre, Nairobi Yearly Meeting of Friends Church, Supreme Council of Kenya Muslims; Tanzania – The Anglican Church of Tanzania, Good Samaritan Mission, Youth Alive Club; and Uganda – Uganda Muslim Youth Association, Uganda Catholic Secretariat, Youth Alive.
11 *Interview* Katherine Marshall, Development Dialogue on Values and Ethics, World Bank, 21 April 2006.
12 *Interview* Elitha Chusi, Alpha Dancing Group, Tanzania, 8 February 2006; *Interview* Pfiriael Kiwia, Kimara Peer Educators, Tanzania, 15 February 2006; *Interview* Victor Mulimila, Faraja Trust Fund, Tanzania, 17 January 2006; *Interview* Lilian Gitau, St John's Ambulance, Kisumu, Kenya, 14 December 2005; *Interview* Dorothy Kalioli, Dogodogo Centre, Tanzania, 4 January 2006; *Interview* Mr. Lusewa, WAVUMO, Tanzania, 17 January 2006; *Interview* Jenipher Nakiyimba, Hunger Free World, 27 October 2005; *Interview* Zachary Ngare, HOYWIK, Kenya, 18 November 2005; *Interview* Wilberforce Mayanja, Philly Lutaaya Initiative/AIDS Information Centre Volunteer, Uganda, 5 October 2005.
13 *Interview* Aisling Quiery, Merlin, Kenya, 21 December 2005; *Interview* Christine Jamet, Medicins Sans Frontieres, Kenya, 10 November 2005; *Interview* Samson Ndege, Pathfinder, Kenya, 16 December 2005; *Interview* Daniel, Federation of Women's Groups, Kenya, 10 November; *Interview* Isabella Karanja, National Council of Women, Kenya, 24 November 2005; *Interview* Edina Hauli, SHDEPHA+, Tanzania, 14 February 2006; *Interview* Kenneth Simbaya, SPW, Tanzania, 7 February 2006; *Interview* Lucy Mphuru, Engender Health, Tanzania, 5 January 2006; *Interview* Sam Mwakapeje, TASO Jinga, Uganda, 12 October 2005; *Participatn Observation.* Wakisi AIDS Programme, 25 October 2006.
14 *Interview* Zachary Ngare, HOYWIK, Kenya, 15 November 2005.
15 *Interview* Lilian Gitau, St John's Ambulance, Kisumu, Kenya, 14 December 2005; *Interview* Wilberforce Mayanja, Philly Lutaaya Initiative/AIDS Support Organisation volunteer, 5 October 2005; *Interview* Angella Nakiyimba, CIPA, Uganda, 27 October 2005; *Interview* Zachary Ngare, HOYWIK, Kenya, 15 November 2005.
16 *Interview* Nelson Chusio, IDYDC, Tanzania, 8 February 2006; *Interview* Dorcus Kameta, National AIDS/STD Control Programme, Kenya, 11 November 2005.
17 Albertus Voetberg, Senior Health Specialist, World Bank, Kenya 15 November 2005; *Interview* Suzan Ngugi, KENWA, Kenya, 24 November 2005.
18 Peer educators are trained by CSOs to visit local communities, youth groups, schools and social clubs and educate people on means of prevention, care, treatment and psychosocial support for HIV/AIDS. Peers educators normally come from the communities they talk to, and are seen by donors and governments alike as an effective means of communicating prevention messages.
19 *Interview* Ursula Bahati, National AIDS Control Council (NACC), Kenya, 14 November 2005; *Interview* Annalise Trama, UNAIDS, Kenya, 21 December 2005.
20 *Interview* Adam Lagerstedt, Senior Health Specialist, World Bank, Kenya, 16 November 2005.

21 The reputation of Ngugi is such that she was featured in Newsweek's Special Issue on 'AIDS 25 Years On' as a friend of Peter Piot, Director of UNAIDS (Cowley 2006).

22 *Interview* Justin Lugoi, Tanzania Red Cross, 5 January 2006.

23 *Interview (telephone)* Bruce MacKay, Futures Group, UK, 8 July 2005.

24 *Interview* Dickson Mbugua, Matatu Welfare Association, Kenya, 23 November 2005; *Interview* Rowlands Lenya, TAPWAK, Kenya, 10 November 2005; *Interview* Benon Kasigazi, UGANET, Uganda, 31 October 2005; *Interview* Boniface Ntalo, Jinga District AIDS Council, Uganda, 13 October 2005; *Interview* Kennedy Otundo, Family Planning Association of Uganda, 28 October 2005; *Interview* Immam Kasozi, Uganda Muslim Youth Association, Uganda, 24 October 2005; *Interview* Wyclef Ojuru, Uganda Scouts Association, 1 November 2005; *Interview* Flora Kajela, World Vision, 12 February 2006; *Interview* Idi Saadat, Zanzibar HIV/AIDS Commission, 31 January 2006.

25 *Interview* Vincent Kalimire, Foundation for African Development, Uganda, 17 October 2005.

26 *Interview* Marren Akatsa-Bukachi, EASSI, Uganda, 5 October 2005; *Interview* Peace Kyameruku, NAWOU, Uganda, 7 October 2005.

27 *Interview* Albertus Voetberg, Senior Health Specialist, World Bank, Kenya, 7 April 2005

28 Positive mothers are able to transfer HIV to their newborns through breastfeeding. Part of PMTCT is to educate women about the risks of breast-feeding when HIV positive. There is evidence from groups working on PMTCT that men become suspicious of women not wanting to do so, hence the need to include them in PMTCT education.

29 *Interview* Isabella Karanja, National Council of Women in Kenya, 24 November 2005.

30 *Interview* Wilson Behwera, Masaka District HIV/AIDS Council, Uganda, 26 October 2005; *Interview* Hashim Kalinga, TACAIDS, Tanzania, 14 February 2006; *Interview* Justin Lugoi, Tanzania Red Cross, 5 January 2006; *Interview* Lucy Mphuru, EngenderHealth, Tanzania, 5 January 2006.

31 *Interview* Adam Lagerstedt, Senior Health Specialist, World Bank, Kenya, 16 November 2005.

32 *Interview* Barabona Mubondo, WAMATA, Tanzania, 20 January 2006; *Interview* Joseph Temba, TACAIDS, Tanzania, 10 February 2006; *Interview* Nelson Chusio, IDYDC, Tanzania, 8 February 2006; *Interview* Chudi Okafor, World Bank, Washington DC, 27 April 2006; *Interview* Boniface Ntalo, Jinga District AIDS Council, Uganda, 13 October 2005; *Interview* Evodis Pangani, Ilala Municipal Council, 16 February 2006; *Interview* Patricia Chale, PSI, Tanzania, 16 January 2006.

33 *Interview* Joseph Temba, TACAIDS, Tanzania, 10 February 2006; *Interview* Annalise Trama, UNAIDS, 21 December 2005; *Interview* Ursula Bahati, National AIDS Control Council (NACC), Kenya, 14 November 2005.

34 *Interview* Ursula Bahati, National AIDS Control Council (NACC), Kenya, 14 November 2005; *Interview* Samson Ndege, Pathfinder, Kenya, 16 December 2005; *Interview* Joseph Temba, TACAIDS, Tanzania, 10 February 2006; *Interview* Morris Lekule, TACAIDS, Tanzania, 4 January 2006; *Interview* Robert Mukama, RFA Iringa and Ruvuma, Tanzania, 8 February 2006; *Interview* Emmanuel Malangalila, Senior Health Specialist/TTL, World Bank, Tanzania, 20 January 2006.

35 *Interview* Idi Juma, KANCO, Kenya, 19 October 2005; *Interview* Herbert Mugumya, Save the Children, Uganda, 1 November 2005.

36 *Interview* Wilson Behwera, Masaka District AIDS Council, Uganda, 26 October 2005; *Interview* Sylvan Kaboha, AIM, Uganda, 14 October 2005; *Interview* Pfiriael Kiwia, Kimara Peer Educators, Tanzania, 15 February 2006; *Interview* Elitha Chusi, Alpha Dancing Group, Tanzania, 8 February 2006.

37 *Interview* Nadeem Mohammed, Senior Operations Officer, ACT Africa, World Bank, 24 April 2006.

38 *Interview* Nadeem Mohammed, Senior Operations Officer, ACT Africa, World Bank, 24 April 2006.
39 *Interview* Emmanuel Malangalila, Senior Health Specialist/TTL, World Bank, Tanzania, 20 January 2006; *Interview* Debrework Zewdie, Director Global HIV/AIDS Program, World Bank, 3 May 2006.
40 *Interview* Edna Baguma, World Vision, Uganda, 20 October 2005; *Interview* Agnes Msokaa, SWAAT, Tanzania, 15 January 2006.
41 *Interview* Nelson Chusio, IDYDC, Tanzania, 8 February 2006; *Interview* Victor Mulimila, Faraja Trust Fund, Tanzania, 17 January 2006; *Interview* Sylvan Kaboha, AIM, Uganda, 14 October 2005; *Interview* Angella Nakiyimba, CIPA, Uganda, 27 October 2005; *Interview* Joyce Mkongo, SHDEPHA+, Tanzania, 6 February 2006; *Interview* Kenneth Simbaya, SPW, Tanzania, 7 February 2006.
42 *Interview* Annalise Trama, UNAIDS, Kenya, 21 December 2005.
43 *Interview* Suzan Ngugi, KENWA, Kenya, 24 November 2005.
44 *Interview* Samson Ndege, Pathfinder, Kenya, 16 December 2005; *Interview* Ursula Bahati, National AIDS Control Council (NACC), Kenya, 14 November 2005; *Interview* Harriet Kivumbi, OXFAM, Uganda, 19 October 2005; *Interview* Hashim Kalinga, TACAIDS, Tanzania, 14 February 2006.
45 *Interview* Jacomina de Regt, Senior Lead Specialist for Social Development Africa, World Bank 20 April 2006; *Interview* Albertus Voetberg, Senior Health Specialist, World Bank, Kenya 15 November 2005; *Interview* Debrework Zewdie, Director Global HIV/AIDS Program, World Bank, 3 May 2006.
46 *Interview* Raphael Maligo, AMREF, Tanzania, 5 January 2006; *Interview* Idi Saadat, Zanzibar HIV/AIDS Commission, 31 January 2006.
47 *Interview* Harrier Kivumbi, OXFAM, Uganda, 19 October 2005.
48 *Interview* Paul Zeitz, Global AIDS Alliance, Washington DC, 26 April 2006.
49 *Interview* Yasmin Tayyab, World Bank, Washington DC, 25 April 2006; *Interview* Debrework Zewdie, Director Global HIV/AIDS Program, World Bank, 3 May 2006.
50 *Interview* Amanda Childress, Africare/USAID, Tanzania, 14 February 2006; *Interview* Hanningtone Kataka, KUSCCO, Kenya, 23 November 2005; *Interview* Awene Gavyole, WHO, Tanzania, 13 February 2006.
51 *Interview* Julius Byenka, Uganda AIDS Commission, 11 October 2005.
52 *Interview* Joseph Temba, TACAIDS, Tanzania, 10 February 2006; *Interview* Amina Kassim, ABCT, Tanzania, 9 January 2006; *Interview* Evodis Pangani, Ilala Municipal Council, 16 February 2006; *Interview* Hashim Kalinga, TACAIDS, Tanzania, 14 February 2006.
53 *Interview* Anne, K-VWORC, Kenya, 25 November 2005; *Interview* Eve Mwai, St John's Ambulance, Kenya, 29 November 2005; *Interview* Deus Kibamba, TGNP, Tanzania, 20 January 2006; *Interview* Godfrey Magumba, UPHOLD, Kenya, 11 November 2005; *Interview* Joseph Temba, TACAIDS, Tanzania, 10 February 2006.
54 *Interview* Sylvan Kaboha, AIM, Uganda, 14 October 2005; *Interview* Wilson Behwera, Masaka District HIV/AIDS Council, Uganda, 26 October 2005.
55 *Interview* Anne, K-VWORC, Kenya, 25 November 2005; *Interview* Wilberforce Mayanja, Philly Lutaaya Initiative/AIDS Information Centre volunteer, 5 October 2005.
56 *Interview* Angella Nakiyimba, CIPA, Uganda, 27 October 2005.
57 *Interview* Isabella Karanja, National Council of Women of Kenya, 24 November 2005.
58 Quote: anonymous, St Stephen's Church Widow's Group, Kisumu, Kenya, 13 December 2005.
59 *Interview* Eve Mwai, St John's Ambulance, Kenya, 29 November 2005; *Interview* Rowlands Lenya, TAPWAK, Kenya, 10 November 2005; *Interview* Julius Byenka, Uganda AIDS Commission, 11 October 2005; *Interview* Dennis Bemwenzaki, PASADA, Tanzania, 14 February 2006; *Interview* Joezif Jaxon, Foundation for Civil

Society, Tanzania, 10 February 2006; *Interview* Barabona Mubondo, WAMATA, Tanzania, 20 January 2006.

60 *Interview* Pfiriael Kiwia, Kimara Peer Educators, Tanzania, 15 February 2006; *Participant Observation* Wakisi AIDS Programme, Uganda, 25 October 2005.

61 *Interview* Emmanuel Malangalila, Senior Health Specialist/TTL, World Bank, Tanzania, 20 January 2006.

62 *Interview* Rowlands Lenya, TAPWAK, Kenya, 10 November 2005; *Interview* Isabella Karanja, National Council of Women, Kenya, 24 November 2005; *Interview* Kellen Karokora, Keera Community Services, Uganda, 31 October 2005; *Interview* Salvator Hakororo, CARE International, Tanzania, 4 January 2006; *Interview* Steve Kinzett, John Snow Inc (JSI), Kenya, 23 November 2005.

63 *Interview* Nelson Chusio, IDYDC, Tanzania, 8 February 2006; *Interview* Patience Talugende, ISESWU, Uganda, 19 October 2005; *Interview* Deus Kibamba, TGNP, Tanzania, 20 January 2006.

64 *Interview* Benon Kasigazi, UGANET, Uganda, 31 October 2005; *Interview* Victor Mulimila, Faraja Trust Fund, Tanzania, 19 January 2006.

65 *Interview* Alex Pius Margery, TANEPHA, Tanzania, 6 January 2006; *Interview* Dickson Mbugua, Matatu Welfare Association, Kenya, 23 November 2005; *Interview* Immam Kasozi, Uganda Muslim Youth Association, Uganda, 24 October 2005.

66 *Participant Observation* St Stephen's Church Widow's Group, Kenya, 13 December 2005.

67 *Interview* Nicodemus B. Mwaduma, RFA Lindi and Mtwara, Tanzania, 5 January 2006; *Interview* Boniface Ntalo, Jinga District AIDS Council, Tanzania, 13 October 2005; *Interview* Sheila Coutinho, UNICEF, Kenya, 4 November 2005.

68 *Interview* Adam Lagerstedt, Senior Health Specialist, World Bank, Kenya, 16 November 2005; *Interview* Emmanuel Malangalila, Senior Health Specialist/TTL, World Bank, Tanzania, 20 January 2006; *Interview* Albertus Voetberg, Senior Health Specialist, World Bank, Kenya 15 November 2005.

69 *Interview* Benson Owenga Anjere, Kenya Programme of Disabled Persons (KPDP), Kenya, 28 November 2005; *Interview* Elitha Chusi, Alpha Dancing Group, Tanzania, 8 February 2006; *Interview* Kellen Karokora, Keera Community Services, Uganda, 31 October 2006; *Interview* Immam Kasozi, Uganda Muslim Youth Association, Uganda, 24 October 2005; *Interview* Rowlands Lenya, TAPWAK, Kenya, 10 November 2005; *Interview* Henry Mpungu, Kampala AIDS Fighters Association, Uganda, 6 October 2005; *Interview* Victor Mulimila, Faraja Trust Fund, Tanzania, 17 January 2006; *Interview* Hilda Angola Orimba, WOWESOK, Kenya, 9 November 2005; *Interview* Rubaramira Ruranga, NGEN+, Uganda, 31 October 2005; *Interview* Patience Talugende, ISESWU, 19 October 2005.

70 *Interview* Samson Ndege, Pathfinder, Kenya, 16 December 2005; *Interview* Margaret Mwaniki, Girl Guides Kenya, 22 December 2005.

71 *Interview* Patrick Ogen, Youth Alive, Uganda, 19 October 2005.

72 *Interview* Eve Mwai, St John's Ambulance, Kenya, 19 November 2005; *Interview* Dickson Mbugua, Matatu Welfare Association, Kenya, 23 November 2005; *Interview* Joseph Olita, Gallamoro, Kenya, 17 November 2005; *Interview* Leonora Obara, WOFAK, Kenya, 23 November 2005; *Interview* Suzan Ngugi, KENWA, Kenya, 24 November 2005; *Interview* Allan Kiwanuka, THETA, Uganda, 19 October 2005; *Interview* Harriet Kivumbi, OXFAM, Uganda, 19 October 2005; *Interview* Kellen Karokora, Keera Community Services, Uganda, 31 October 2005; *Interview* Patrick Ogen, Youth Alive, Uganda, 19 October 2005; *Interview* Patience Talugende, ISESWU, Uganda, 19 October 2005; *Interview* Amina Kassim, ABCT, Tanzania, 9 January 2006; *Interview* Duncan Hervey, Save the Children, Zanzibar, 27 January 2006; *Interview* Joseph Mwamaja, UMATI Eastern, Tanzania, 17 January 2006; *Interview* Justin Lugoi, Tanzania Red Cross, 5 January 2006; *Interview* Raphael Maligo, AMREF, Tanzania, 5 January 2006; *Interview* Benon Kasigazi, UGANET, Uganda, 31 October 2005.

73 *Interview* Peace Kyamureku, NAWOU, Uganda, 7 October 2005.
74 *Interview* Margrethe Juncker, Reach Out Mbuya, Uganda, 11 October 2005; *Interview* Peter Masika, TAYOA, Tanzania, 9 January 2006; *Interview* Henry Mpungu, Kampala AIDS Fighters Association, Uganda, 6t October 2005; *Interview* Angella Nakiyembe, CIPA, Uganda, 11 October 2005; *Participant Observation* Kawempe Positive Women Union, Uganda, 17 October 2005; *Participant Observation* Positive Women's Vision in Action, Uganda, 17 October 2005; *Participant Observation* St Stephen's Church Widows Group, Kenya, 13 December 2005; *Participant Observation* TAYOA, Tanzania, 9 January 2006; *Participant Observation* Wakisi AIDS Programme, Uganda, 25 October 2005.
75 *Interview* Angella Nakiyimba, CIPA, Uganda, 27 October 2005; *Interview* Boniface Ntalo, Jinga District HIV/AIDS Council, Uganda, 13 October 2005.
76 *Participant Observation,* St Stephen's Church Widows Group, Kenya, 13 December 2005.
77 *Interview* Kathleen Okatcha, KORDP, Kenya, 16 November 2005.
78 *Interview* P firiael Kiwia, Kimara Peer Educators, Tanzania, 15 February 2006.
79 *Interview* Emmanuel Malangalila, Senior Health Specialist/TTL, World Bank, Tanzania, 20 January 2006; *Interview* Nadeem Mohammed, Senior Operations Officer, ACT Africa, World Bank, 24 April 2006; *Interview* Peter Okwero, Senior Health Specialist/ TTL World Bank, Uganda 1 November 2005.
80 *Interview* Emmanuel Malangalila, Senior Health Specialist/TTL, World Bank, Tanzania, 20 January 2006.
81 *Participant Observation* Joint AIDS Programme Review (JAPR), Kenya, 30 November 2005
82 *Interview* Samson Ndege, Pathfinder, Kenya, 16 December 2005.
83 *Participant Observation* Joint AIDS Programme Review (JAPR), Kenya, 30 November 2005.
84 Throughout the interview process in Kenya, Ngugi's name was often mentioned, specifically by Bank representatives. Her role within the JAPR and wider relations with UNAIDS' country representatives and World Bank TTLs was evident throughout the research process in Kenya.
85 *Interview* Paschal Wambiya, ILO, Kenya, 19 December 2005; *Interview* Patience Talugende, ISESWU, Uganda, 19 October 2005; *Interview* Kennedy Otundo, Family Planning Association of Uganda, 28 October 2005; *Interview* Mary Namatou, CAWODISA, Uganda, 20 October 2005.
86 *Interview* Patience Talugende, ISESWU, Uganda, 19 October 2005.
87 *Interview* Annalise Trama, UNAIDS, Kenya, 21 December 2005.
88 *Interview* Benon Kasigazi, UGANET, Uganda, 31 October 2005; *Interview* Lucy Shilling, TASO, Uganda, 12 October 2005; *Interview* Vincent Kalimire, Foundation for African Development, Uganda, 17 October 2005; *Interview* Flora Kajela, World Vision, Tanzania, 13 February 2006; *Interview* Joseph Mwamaja, UMATI, Tanzania, 17 January 2006; *Interview* Nelson Chusio, IDYDC, Tanzania, 8 February 2006; *Interview* Isabella Karanja, National Council of Women of Kenya, 24 November 2005.
89 *Interview* Jacqueline Nakiwala, Uganda Catholic Secretariat, 28 October 2005; *Interview* Justin Lugoi, Tanzania Red Cross, 5 January 2006; *Interview* Stephen Chale, Plan, Tanzania, 16th January 2006; *Interview* Victor Mulimila, Faraja Trust Fund, Tanzania, 19 January 2006.
90 *Interview* Wilberforce Mayanja, Philly Lutaaya Initiative/AIDS Information Centre, Uganda, 5 October 2005.
91 *Interview* Barabona Mubondo, WAMATA, Tanzania, 20 January 2006.
92 Kalinga, Hashim. 14 February 2006. TACAIDS (Tanzania Commission for AIDS) – Tanzania.
93 *Interview* Emmanuel Malangalila, Senior Health Specialist/TTL, World Bank, Tanzania, 20 January 2006.

94 *Interview* Maria Tungaraza, Futures Group, Tanzania, 18 January 2006; *Interview* Peter Masika, TAYOA, Tanzania, 9 January 2006.

95 *Interview* George Tembo, UNAIDS, Geneva, 25 May 2006.

96 *Participant Observation* WOFAK Annual General Meeting, Kenya, 17 December 2005.

97 *Interview* Hilda Agola Orimba, WOWESOK, Kenya, 9 November 2005; *Interview* Marren Akatsa-Bukachi, EASSI, Uganda, 5 October 2005.

98 *Interview* Benson Owenga Anjere, Kenya Programme of Disabled Persons (KPDP), 28 November 2005

99 *Interview* Harriet Kivumbi, OXFAM, Uganda, 19 October 2005; *Interview* Kennedy Otundo, Family Planning Association of Uganda, 28 October 2005; *Interview* Peace Kyamureku, NAMOU, Uganda, 7 October 2005; *Interview* Duncan Hervey, Save the Children, Zanzibar, 27 January 2006; *Interview* Erena Casas, Medicos du Mondo, Zanzibar, 27 January 2006.

100 *Interview* Natalie Conesta, Catholic Relief Services, Uganda, 18 October 2005; *Interview* Herbert Mugumya, Save the Children, Uganda, 1 November.

101 *Interview* Natalie Conesta, Catholic Relief Services, Uganda, 18 October 2005; *Interview* Bec Shaw-Crompton, PANOS, London, 19 August 2005; *Interview* (telephone) Rachel Baggaley, Christian Aid, UK, 15 August 2005.

102 *Interview* Bec Shaw-Crompton, PANOS, London, 19 August 2005.

103 *Interview* Nick Southern, CARE International, Tanzania, 9 January 2006.

104 *Interview* Natalie Conesta, Catholic Relief Services, Uganda, 18 October 2005; *Interview* Christine Jamet, Medecins Sans Frontieres, Kenya, 10 November 2005.

105 *Interview* Anne Austen, Futures Group, Kenya, 18 November 2005; *Interview* Jacomina de Regt, Senior Lead Specialist for Social Development Africa, World Bank 20 April 2006.

106 *Participant Observation* St Stephen's Church Widows Group, Kenya, 13 December 2005; *Interview* Alex Pius Margery, TANEPHA, Tanzania, 6 January 2006.

107 *Interview* Lucy Keough, World Bank, Washington DC, 24 April 2006; *Interview* John Garrison, Senior Civil Society Specialist, World Bank 27 April 2006; *Interview* Yasmin Tayyab, Civil Society Team, World Bank, 25 April 2006; *Interview* Juraj Mesik, Senior Community Foundations Specialist, World Bank, 24 April 2006; *Interview* Eleanor Fink, Foundations Co-ordinator, World Bank 20 April 2006; *Interview* Katherine Marshall, Development Dialogue on Values and Ethics, World Bank, 21 April 2006.

5   Setting a global agenda

1 One interviewee alleged that the debate between the WHO and pharmaceutical companies resulted in many heated debates within the Global Health Assembly, to the extent that certain WHO staff members who spoke out against the companies received death threats. *Interview* Anonymous; *Interview* David Woodward, New Economics Foundation, 17 August 2005.

2 *Interview* Nazneen Damji, Programme Specialist on HIV and AIDS, UNIFEM, New York, 10 May 2006

3 The 2006 meeting stressed the need to reiterate financial commitment, which had so far been working to the detriment of the Global Fund, to the response through mechanisms such as the Fund; a commitment to 'The Three Ones' principles; affordable treatment for all; and a need to push the agenda forward. Preceding these meetings, CSOs were actively campaigning UN agencies and influential governments to place certain issues on the agenda. However, despite such campaigns due to political contention and complexity, the document to be agreed upon remained short and concise. UNGASS 2001, is 52 pages long, with 103 action points, whereas UNGASS 2006, Res. 60/262 is eight pages long, with 53 action points.

4 *Interview* George Tembo, UNAIDS, Geneva, 25 May 2006.
5 'The Global Response to HIV/AIDS: Making the Money Work' was a high level meeting held in London 9 March 2005. The meeting was attended by donor and developing country governments, civil society, UN agencies, and multilateral and international institutions. The focus of the meeting was on how much money would be needed over the following 3 years to tackle the epidemic at a global level; what the international community needs to do to ensure the money reaches those most in need; and who will do what – the international division of labour. A central outcome of this meeting was the formation of the UNAIDS-based Global Task Team.
6 *Interview* George Tembo, UNAIDS, Geneva, 25 May 2006; *Interview* Annalise Trama, UNAIDS, Kenya, 21 December 2005; *Interview* Kristan Schoultz, UNAIDS, Kenya, 5 April 2005.
7 *Interview* Elise Ayers, USAID, Uganda, 25 October 2005; *Interview* Purnima Kashyap, World Food Programme (WFP), Uganda, 7 October 2005; *Interview* Amanda Childress, Africare/USAID, Tanzania, 14 February 2006; *Interview* Awene Gavyole, WHO, Tanzania, 13 February 2006.
8 *Interview* Annalise Trama, UNAIDS, Kenya, 21 December 2005; *Interview* Kristan Schoultz, UNAIDS, Kenya, 5 April 2005.
9 *Interview* Lene Olsen, World Food Programme, Kenya, 28 November 2006; *Interview* Jacomina de Regt, Senior Lead Specialist for Social Development Africa, World Bank 20 April 2006.
10 *Interview* Kristan Schoultz, Country Director, UNAIDS, Kenya, 5 April 2005.
11 *Interview* Purnima Kashyap, World Food Programme (WFP), Uganda, 7 October 2005; *Interview* Assumpta Rwenchungura, World Food Programme (WFP) Tanzania, 9 January 2006.
12 *Interview* Julius Byenka, Uganda HIV/AIDS Commission, 11 October 2005; *Interview* Rustica Tembele, TACAIDS, Tanzania, 9 January 2006; *Interview* Ursula Bahati, National AIDS Control Council (NACC), Kenya, 14 November 2005; *Interview* Stephen Wiktor, CDC (Centers for Disease Control), Tanzania, 3 February 2006.
13 *Interview* Julius Byenka, Uganda HIV/AIDS Commission, 11 October 2005.
14 *Interview* Booker Odenyo, Crown Agents, Kenya, 9 November 2005.
15 *Interview* Rustica Tembele, TACAIDS, Tanzania, 9 January 2006.
16 Co-ordination within healthcare policies has become increasingly problematic with the increase in a multiplicity of actors. Kent Buse and Gill Walt (1997: 450–453) argue that this increase in actors has been the result of a growth of players, increase in external resources, competition for these resources, rapid succession of donors, increased volume and importance of aid, project proliferation and shifts, policy conditionality, heightened scrutiny and debate over UN mandates. Buse and Walt suggest co-ordination could be improved by recipient management of external resources, capacity-building for such management, planning, round table conferences, donor-driven co-ordination mechanisms, geographical zoning, sector aid, lead agency sub-sector specialisation, donor consortia, harmonisation of aid procedure, reforms with donor agencies to facilitate co-ordination, inter-agency intelligence gathering (Buse and Walt, 1997: 454–460). However, most of these recommendations have been integrated within HIV/ AIDS policy, yet remain problematic.
17 *Interview* Sam Ibanda, UNDP, Tanzania, 26 October 2005.
18 *Interview* Lene Olsen, WFP, Kenya, 28 November 2005.
19 *Interview* Purnima Kashyap, WFP, Uganda, 7 October 2005.
20 *Interview* Peter Okwero, Senior Health Specialist/Task Team Leader, World Bank, Uganda, 1 November 2005.
21 *Interview* Peter Piot, Executive Director UNAIDS (1995–2008), Director Institute for Global Health, Imperial College, London, 6 July 2009.
22 *Interview* Peter Piot, Executive Director UNAIDS (1995–2008), Director Institute for Global Health, Imperial College, London, 6 July 2009.

23 *Interview* Ntombekhaya Matsha, Global Fund, Geneva, 25 May 2006.
24 *Interview* Christine Jamet, Medicins Sans Frontieres, Kenya, 10 November 2005.
25 *Interview* Joseph Temba, TACAIDS, Tanzania, 10 February 2006.
26 *Interview* Harriet Kivumbi, OXFAM, Uganda, 19 October 2005.
27 *Interview* Steve Kinzett, John Snow Inc (JSI), Kenya, 23 November 2005.
28 *Interview* Suzan Ngugi, KENWA (Kenya Network of Women with HIV/AIDS), Kenya, 24 November 2005.
29 *Interview* Rowlands Lenya, TAPWAK (The Association of People with AIDS in Kenya), Kenya, 10 November 2005; *Interview* Benson Owenga Anjere, Kenya Programme of Disabled Persons (KPDP), Kenya, 28 November 2005.
30 *Interview* Julius Byenka, Uganda HIV/AIDS Commission (UAC), Uganda, 11 October 2005.
31 *Interview* Nick Southern, CARE International, Tanzania, 9 January 2006.
32 *Interview* Jacomina de Regt, Senior Lead Specialist for Social Development Africa, World Bank 20 April 2006; *Interview* Holly Wong, IAVI (International AIDS Vaccine Initiative), New York, 10 May 2006.
33 *Interview* Jacomina de Regt, Senior Lead Specialist for Social Development Africa, World Bank 20 April 2006.
34 *Interview* Ntombekhaya Matsha, Global Fund, Geneva, 25 May 2006.
35 *Interview* Ntombekhaya Matsha, Global Fund, Geneva, 25 May 2006.
36 PEPFAR has projects in the following countries: Botswana, Cambodia, Cote d'Ivoire, Ethiopia, Guyana, Haiti, India, Kenya, Malawi, Mozambique, Namibia, Nigeria, Russia, Rwanda, South Africa, Tanzania, Uganda, Vietnam, Zambia, Zimbabwe.
37 *Interview* Wyclef Ojuru, Uganda Scouts Association, Uganda, 1 November 2005; *Interview* Justin Lugoi, Tanzania Red Cross, Tanzania, 5 January 2006.
38 *Interview* Justin Lugoi, Tanzania Red Cross, Tanzania, 5 January 2006; *Interview* Nelson Chusio, IDYDC (Iringa Development of Youth, Disabled and Children Care), Tanzania, 8 February 2006.
39 *Interview* Patrick Ogen, Youth Alive, Uganda, 19 October 2005; *Interview* Julius Byenka, Uganda HIV/AIDS Commission (UAC), Uganda, 11 October 2005; *Interview* Purnima Kashyap, WFP, Uganda, 7 October 2005; *Interview* Alex Pius Margery, TANEPHA (Tanzania National Network of People with HIV/AIDS), Tanzania, 6 January 2006.
40 *Interview* Rubaramira Ruranga, NGEN+ (National Guidance and Empowerment Network for People Living with HIV/AIDS), Uganda, 31 October 2005.
41 *Interview* Samson Ndege, Pathfinder, Kenya, 16 December 2005; *Interview* Lucy Mphuru, EngenderHealth, Tanzania, 5 January 2006; *Interview* Allan Kiwanuka, THETA (Traditional and modern Health practitioners Together against AIDS and other diseases), Uganda, 19 October 2005.
42 *Interview* Peter Okwero, Senior Health Specialist/Task Team Leader, World Bank, Uganda, 1 November 2005; *Interview* Adam Lagerstedt, Senior Health Specialist, World Bank, Kenya, 16 November 2005.
43 *Interview* Amy Cunningham, USAID, Uganda, 25 October 2005.
44 *Interview* Adam Lagerstedt, Senior Health Specialist, World Bank, Kenya, 16 November 2005.
45 *Interview* Tim Rosche, John Snow Inc (JSI), Tanzania, 18 January 2006; *Interview* Herbert Mugumya, Save the Children, Uganda, 1 November 2005.
46 *Interview* Steve Kinzett, JSI, Kenya, 23 November 2005.
47 *Interview* Amanda Childress, Africare/USAID, Tanzania, 14 February 2006; *Interview* Amy Cunningham, USAID, Uganda, 25 October 2005; *Interview* Bob Duolf, CARE International, Tanzania, 4 January 2006; *Interview* Dorcus Kameta, National AIDS/STD Control Programme (NASCOP), Kenya, 11 November 2005; *Interview* Stephen Wiktor, CDC (Centers for Disease Control and Prevention), Tanzania, 3 February 2006.

48 *Interview* Annalise Trama, UNAIDS, Kenya, 21 December 2005; *Interview* Ursula
    Bahati, National AIDS Control Council (NACC), Kenya, 14 November 2005.
49 *Interview* Albertus Voetberg, Senior Health Specialist/TTL World Bank, Kenya, 15
    November 2005
50 *Interview* Tim Rosche, John Snow Inc (JSI), Tanzania, 18 January 2006.
51 *Interview* Annalise Trama, UNAIDS, Kenya, 21 December 2005.
52 *Interview* Julius Byenka, Uganda HIV/AIDS Commission (UAC), Uganda, 11 October,
    2005; *Interview* Ursula Bahati, National AIDS Control Council, Kenya, 14 November
    2005).
53 PEPFAR was very much George W. Bush's project. He was careful to authorise the
    extension of the project for another 5 years before he left office. How the programme
    will change under the leadership of Barack Obama is thus far unclear. Eric Goosby was
    sworn in as the new US Global AIDS Co-ordinator in September 2009. Goosby has
    extensive experience in clinical medicine and HIV/AIDS treatment programmes. How
    his and Obama's leadership will impact upon the policies of PEPFAR were unclear at
    the time of press.
54 On the 4 June 2009, I attended 'A conversation between Bill Gates Sr. and Howard
    Davies' at the LSE. During the question part of the conversation I asked how the
    Foundation was accountable to the states it affects, Gates' reply was that it was not an
    issue and that the Foundation did not need to be accountable in this way. The emphasis
    was on the Foundation doing good work, and was non-governmental, hence structures
    of accountability and transparency were not relevant.
55 The members of the Health 8 are WHO, UNICEF, UNFPA, UNAIDS, Global Fund,
    World Bank, GAVI, and the Bill and Melinda Gates Foundation.
56 *Interview* Jacomina de Regt, Senior Lead Specialist for Social Development Africa,
    World Bank 20 April 2006.
57 *Interview* Emmanuel Malangalila, Senior Health Specialist/Task Team Leader, World
    Bank, Tanzania, 6 May 2009.
58 *Interview* Emmanuel Malangalila, Senior Health Specialist/Task Team Leader, World
    Bank, Tanzania, 6 May 2009.
59 The countries with Caribbean MAP funding are: Barbados, Dominican Republic,
    Jamaica, Grenada, St Kitts and Nevis, Trinidad and Tobago, Guyana, St Lucia, St
    Vincent and the Grenadines. The Caribbean MAP also funds the regional Pan Caribbean
    Partnership Against HIV/AIDS.

6   World Bank, governance and the politics of criticising HIV/AIDS

 1 The 'third sphere' refers to the Hegelian notion of civil society occupying the space
    between the public and private sectors. This approach to a 'global civil society' has
    been adopted by the likes of Scholte, Schechter, Baker and Chandler. Such theorists
    are keen to emphasise the diverse, competing and wide-ranging aspect of global civil
    society, indicating that the concept makes preconceived notions of international poli-
    tics and global governance or the state and institutions 'fuzzy' at the edges (Baker and
    Chandler 2005: 2–3; Schechter 1999: 64 and 67; Smouts 1999: 296). What is central to
    this understanding is the idea that the global civil society emergent in the early 1990s
    occupies the space between the public state apparatus and the private household realm
    (Schechter 1999: 66). As Scholte (2000a: 174–175; 2000b: 146) argues, civil society is
    not the state, not the market and non-governmental.
       The most prolific literature on the relationship between international financial insti-
    tutions (IFIs) and CSOs has been generated by Jan Aart Scholte and research into the
    'third sphere' realm of CSO activity. Scholte conceives of engagement between IFIs
    and CSOs as occurring through the global trend towards privatisation and challenges
    to human security, social justice and democracy. CSOs in this regard refer to those
    operating across countries and not necessarily those working in specific communities.

These two factors have led to a 'lateral shift' in which CSOs have been motivated to take action against perceived social injustice. IFIs use such motivation as a means to include CSOs in specific project interventions (Scholte 2002: 14). Scholte understands civil society as existing through voluntary associations (Scholte 2000a: 177; 2000b: 148). These voluntary associations encompass 'civic activity' that addresses transworld issues; promote cross-border communication; have a global organization; maintain supraterritorial solidarity (Scholte 2000a: 180); and demonstrate an ability to engage with 'transplanetary governance institutions' such as UN agencies, the World Bank, IMF and WTO (Scholte 2005: 219). In occupying such space, CSOs are attributed transformatory value in their ability to alter the prevailing global economic order (Schechter 1999: 64) and the importance placed upon capacity to 'shape contemporary global governance' (Scholte 2000b: 152). Scholte argues that civil society has a significant role in global finance through the increased reliance on CSOs such as NGOs in the provision of service delivery (Scholte 2002a). Value is tempered with a wider understanding of both the positive and negative effects of engagement as reflected in his work on the IMF and WTO (Scholte 1998: 191–196; 2004: 217–218 and 223–230).

Bibliography

Abbasi, K. (1999a) 'The World Bank and world health: changing sides' *British Medical Journal* 318: 865–869.

Abbasi, K. (1999b) 'The World Bank and world health: under fire' *British Medical Journal* 318: 1003–1006.

Abbasi, K. (1999) 'The World Bank and world health: interview with Richard Feachem' *British Medical Journal* 318: 1206–1208.

Ahmad, K. (2005) 'Lawsuit against HIV/AIDS funding policy' *Lancet: Infectious Diseases* 5: 675.

Ankrah, E.M. (1989) 'AIDS: methodological problems in studying its prevention and spread' *Social Science and Medicine* 29(3): 265–276.

Ankrah, E.M. (1991) 'AIDS and the social state of health' *Social Science and Medicine* 32: 967–980.

Baker, G. and Chandler, D. (2005) 'Introduction: global civil society and the future of world politics' in G. Baker and D. Chandler (eds) *Global Civil Society: Contested Futures.* London: Routledge 1–14.

Barnett, T., Whiteside, A. and Desmond, C. (2001) 'The social and economic. impact of HIV/AIDS in poor countries: a review of studies and lessons' *Progress in Development* 1(2): 151–170.

Barnett, T. and Whiteside, A. (2002) *AIDS in the Twenty-first Century: Disease and Globalization.* London: Palgrave.

BBC (2004) 'UK Envoys Speech on Kenya Corruption' *BBC News* 14 July 2004. http://news.bbc.co.uk/1/hi/world/africa/3893625.stm (accessed February 2010).

BBC (2006) 'Kenyan first lady in Aids storm' *BBC News* 19 May 2006. http://news.bbc.co.uk/1/hi/world/africa/4997336.stm (accessed February 2010).

Becker, C.M. (1990) 'The Demo-Economic Impact of the AIDS Pandemic in Sub-Saharan Africa' *World Development* 18: 1599–1619.

Bedford, K. (2008) 'Governing intimacy in the World Bank' in S.M. Rai and G. Waylen *Global Governance: Feminist Perspectives.* Basingstoke: Palgrave.

Berridge, V. (1996) *AIDS in the UK: the Making of Policy, 1981–1994.* Oxford: Oxford University Press.

Berridge, V. (2002) *AIDS in the UK: the Making of Policy, 1981–1994,* 2nd edition. Oxford: Oxford University Press.

Beyen, J.W. (1948) 'The International Bank for Reconstruction and Development' *International Affairs* 24: 534–542.

Blough, R. (1968) 'The World Bank Group' *International Organization* 22(1): 152–181.

Bond, P. (2007) 'Civil society and Wolfowitz's World Bank: reform or rejection revisited' in D. Moore (ed.) *The World Bank: Poverty, Development and Hegemony.* Pietermaritzburg: University of KwaZulu-Natal Press, pp. 479–506.

Bortolotti, B. and Perotti, E. (2007) 'From Government to Regulatory Governance: Privatization and the Residual Role of the State' *World Bank Research Observer* 22: 53–66.

Boserup, E. (1986) *Women's Role in Economic Development.* Aldershot: Gower.

Bretton Woods Project (2005) 'Opposition Swells to appointment of Wolfowitz to head of World Bank' *Bretton Woods Project* 17 March 2005. www.brettonwoodsproject.org/article.shtml?cmd%5B126%5D=x-126-155498 (accessed February 2010).

Broad, R. (2006) 'Research, knowledge, and the art of 'paradigm maintenance': the World Bank's Development Economics Vice-Presidency (DEC)' *Review of International Political Economy* 13(3): 387–419.

Brockerhoff, M. and Biddlecom, A.E. (1999) 'Migration, sexual behaviour and the risk of HIV in Kenya' *International Migration Review* 33: 833–856.

Brown, G.W. (2009) 'Multisectoralism, Participation and Stakeholder Effectiveness: Increasing the Role of Non-State Actors in The Global Fund to Fight AIDS, Tuberculosis and Malaria' *Global Governance* 15(2): 169–177.

Brown, G.W. (2010) 'Safeguarding Deliberative Global Governance: The Case of the Global Fund to Fight AIDS, Tuberculosis and Malaria' *Review of International Studies*, Special Issue: Deliberation and Global Governance (forthcoming).

Buse, K. (1994) 'Spotlight on international organisations: the World Bank' *Health Policy and Planning* 9(1): 95–99.

Buse, K. and Gwin, C. (1998) 'The World Bank and global co-operation in health: the case of Bangladesh' *Lancet* 351: 665–669.

Buse, K. and Walt, G. (1997). 'An unruly melange? Co-ordinating existing resources to the health sector: a review' *Social Science and Medicine* 45(3): 449–463.

Caldwell, J.C., Orubuloye, I.O., and Caldwell, P. (1992) 'Under-reaction to AIDS in sub-Saharan Africa' *Social Science and Medicine* 34: 1169–1182.

Cassels, A. (1996) 'Aid instruments and health systems development: an analysis of current practice' *Health Policy and Planning* 11(4): 354–368.

Charnock, G. (2006) 'Improving the mechanisms of global governance? The Ideational Impact of the World Bank on the National Reform Agenda in Mexico' *New Political Economy* 11(1): 73–98.

Cheru, F. (2002) 'Debt, adjustment and the politics of effective response to HIV/AIDS in Africa' *Third World Quarterly* 23(2): 299–312.

Chirambo, K. (2007) 'AIDS and Democracy in Africa' in N. Poku, A. Whiteside, and B. Sandkjaer (eds) *AIDS and Governance.* Aldershot: Ashgate, pp. 67–91.

Cowley, G. (2006) 'AIDS at 25' *Newsweek* 7 May 2006.

Das, P. (2008) 'Condom crisis in Uganda' *Lancet: Infectious Diseases* 5: 601–602.

de Bruyn, M. (1992) 'Women and AIDS in developing countries' *Social Science and Medicine* 34(3): 249–262.

deWaal, A. (2003) 'How will HIV/AIDS transform African governance?' *African Affairs* 102(406): 1–23.

Doyle, C. and Patel, P. (2008) 'Civil society organisations and global health initiatives: problems of legitimacy' *Social Science and Medicine* 66: 1928–1938.

Economist (editorial) (2009) 'Promising to try harder' *Economist* 2 May 2009.

Elbe, S. (2005) 'AIDS, Security and Biopolitics' *International Relations* 19(4): 403–419.

Elbe, S. (2008). 'Risking lives: AIDS, security and three concepts of risk' *Security Dialogue* 39: 177–198.

Epstein, H. (2007). *Invisible Cure: Africa, the West, and the Fight Against AIDS*. London: Penguin.

Feinberg, R.E. (1988) 'The changing relationship between the World Bank and the International Monetary Fund' *International Organization* 42: 545–560.

Feinberg, R.E. (1997). 'The changing relationship between the World Bank and the International Monetary Fund' in P. Diehl (eds) *Global Governance: International Organisations in an Interdependent World*. London: Lynne Reiner, pp. 217–232.

FHI/USAID (2002) 'Behaviour change communication for HIV/AIDS: a strategic frame-work'. www2.unescobkk.org/hivaids/FullTextDB/aspUploadFiles/bccstrategy.pdf (accessed February 2010).

Fisher, A.G.B. (1947) 'The future of International Economic Institutions: lessons of the. Inter War period' *The Year Book of World Affairs* 27(1): 178–201.

Fiszbein, A. and Schady, N. (2009) *Conditional Cash Transfers: Reducing Present and Future Poverty*. Washington, DC: World Bank.

Fried, E.R. and Owen, H.D. (eds) (1982) *The Future Role of the World Bank*. Washington, DC: The Brookings Institutions.

Gardner, R.N. (1956) *Sterling Dollar Diplomacy*. Oxford: Clarendon Press.

Gilson, L. and Mills, A. (1995) 'Health sector reforms in sub-Saharan Africa: lessons of the last ten years' *Health Policy and Planning* 32: 215–243.

Global AIDS Alliance (2007) 'President Museveni's Visit Protested by HIV/AIDS Experts' www.globalaidsalliance.org/index.php/746/ (accessed February 2010).

Global Fund. (2007) *Press Release: The Global Fund welcomes Ugandan Corruption Inquiry*. www.theglobalfund.org/en/pressreleases/?pr=pr_060602b (accessed February 2010).

Global Fund. (2007) 'The country coordinating mechanisms' www.theglobalfund.org/en/ccm/?lang=en (accessed February 2010).

GHW (2008) *Global Health Watch 2*. London: Zed Books.

Goldman, M. (2005) *Imperial Nature: the World Bank and Struggles for Social Justice in the Age of Globalization*. London: Yale University Press.

Griffin, P. (2006) 'The World Bank' *New Political Economy* 11(4): 571–581.

Harman, S. (2007) 'The World Bank: Failing the Multi-Country AIDS Program: Failing HIV/AIDS' *Global Governance* 13: 485–492.

Harman, S. (2009) 'The causes, contours and consequences of multi-sectoral response to HIV/AIDS' in S. Harman and F. Lisk (eds) *Governance of HIV/AIDS: Making Participation and Accountability Count*. London: Routledge, pp. 165–179.

Harman, S. (2009) 'The World Bank and health' in A. Kay and O.D. Williams (eds) *Global Health Governance: Crisis, Institutions and Political Economy*. Basingstoke: Palgrave Macmillan.

Harman, S. (2009) 'Bottlenecks and benevolence: how the World Bank is helping communities 'cope' with HIV/AIDS' *Journal of Health Management* 11(2): 279–313.

Harman, S. (2009) 'Fighting HIV/AIDS: Reconfiguring the state?' *Review of African Political Economy* 36(121): 353–367.

Harman, S. and Lisk, F. (eds) (2009) *Governance of HIV/AIDS: Making Participation and Accountability Count*. London: Routledge.

Harris, P. (2009) 'They're called the good club–and they want to save the world' *Observer* www.guardian.co.uk/world/2009/may/31/new-york-billionaire-philanthropists (accessed February 2010).

Harrison, G. (2002) *Issues in the Contemporary Politics of Sub-Saharan Africa: The Dynamics of Struggle and Resistance.* Basingstoke: Palgrave MacMillan.

Harrison, G. (2004a) *The World Bank and Africa: the Construction of Governance States.* London: Routledge.

Harrison, G. (2004b) 'HIPC and the Architecture of Governance' *Review of African Political Economy* 31(99): 125–164.

Hayes, S. (2009) 'The home-based care alliance in Kenya: improving governance and transforming communities in the context of HIV/AIDS' in S. Harman and F. Lisk (eds) *Governance of HIV/AIDS: Making Participation and Accountability Count.* London: Routledge pp. 79–97.

Hogan, M.J. (1987) *The Marshall Plan: America, Britain and the Reconstruction of Western Europe, 1947–1952.* Cambridge: Cambridge University Press.

Human Rights Watch (2005). 'The less they know the better' www.hrw.org/en/node/11803/section/7 (accessed February 2010).

Keck, M.E. and Sikkink, K. (1998) *Activists Beyond Borders.* New York: Cornell University Press.

Keynes, J.M. (1924) *Economic Consequences of Peace,* 2nd edition. London: St Martin's Street.

Kindelberger, C.P. (1951) 'Bretton Woods Revisited' *International Organization* 5(1): 32–47.

Knorr, K. (1948) 'The Bretton Woods Institutions in Transition' *International Organization* 2(1): 19–38.

Labonte, R. and Laverack, G. (2001) 'Capacity-building in health promotion, Part 2: For whom? And for what purpose?' *Critical Public Health* 11(2): 129–138.

Lancet (editorial) (2005) 'Bill Gates: a 21st century Robin Hood?' *Lancet* 365: 911–912.

Lancet (editorial) (2007) 'Governance questions at the Gates Foundation' *Lancet* 369: 163.

Laverack, G. and Labonte, R. (2000) 'A planning framework for community empowerment goals within health promotion' *Health Policy and Planning* 15(3): 255–262.

Lawson, A. (1999) 'Women and AIDS in Africa: sociocultural dimensions of the HIV/AIDS epidemic' *International Social Science Journal* 51: 391–400.

Lee, K. and Goodman, H. (2002) 'Global policy networks: the propagation of health care financing reform since the 1980s' in Kelley Lee, Kent Buse, and Suzanne Fustukian (eds) *Health in a Globalising World.* Cambridge: Cambridge University Press pp. 97–119.

Lisk, F. (2009) *Global Institutions and HIV/AIDS Epidemic.* London: Routledge.

Loewenson, R. (1995) 'Structural adjustment and health policy in Africa' *Radical Journal of Health* 1: 49–61.

Maclean, S. (2008) 'Microbes, madcows, and militaries: exploring the links between health and security' *Security Dialogue* 29: 475–494.

Mallaby, S. (2004) *The World's Banker: A Story of Failed States, Financial Crises, and the Wealth and Poverty of Nations.* London: Yale University Press.

Maman, S., Campbell, J., Sweat, M.D. and Gielen, A.C. (2000) 'The intersections of HIV and violence: directions for future research and interventions' *Social Science and Medicine* 50: 459–478.

McCoy, D., Kembhavi, G., Patel, J., and Luintel, A. (2009). 'The Bill and Melinda Gates Foundation's grant-making programme for global health' *Lancet* 373: 1645–1653.

McInnes, C. (2007) 'HIV/AIDS and National Security' in N. Poku, A. Whiteside and B. Sandkjaer (eds) *AIDS and Governance.* Aldershot: Ashgate, pp. 93–111.

McNeil, D.G. (2008) 'Gates Foundation's Influence Criticized' *The New York Times* www.nytimes.com/2008/02/16/science/16malaria.html (accessed February 2010).

Mikesell, R.F. (1972) 'The emergence of the World Bank as a development. institution,' in A.L. Keith Acheson, John F. Chant, Martin F.J. Frachowny (eds) *Bretton Woods Revisited.* Basingstoke: MacMillan pp. 70–84.

Morrison, J.S. and Summers, T. (2003) 'United to fight HIV/AIDS?' *Washington Quarterly* 26(4): 177–193.

Mosley, P., Harrigan, J. and Toye, J. (1991) *Aid and Power: The World Bank and Policy-based Lending,* 2nd edition. London: Routledge.

Mwamunyange, J. (2007) 'Kikwete's HIV test boosts Tanzania's war on AIDS' *The East African* 27 July 2007.

National AIDS Control Council (NACC) (2005) *Joint AIDS Programme Review 2005: JAPR Programme.* Nairobi: NACC.

Nelson, P. (2002) 'New agendas and new patterns of international NGO political action' *Voluntas* 13(4): 377–392.

O'Brien, R., Goetz, A.-M., Scholte, J.A. and Williams, M. (2000) *Contesting Global Governance: Multilateral Economic Institutions and Global Social Movements.* Cambridge: Cambridge University Press.

Owoh, K. (1996) 'Fragmenting Health Care: The World Bank Prescription for Africa' *Alternatives* 21(2): 211–235.

Packard, R. M. and Epstein, P. (1991) 'Epidemiologists, social scientists, and the structure of medical research on AIDS in Africa' *Social Science and Medicine* 33(7): 771–794.

Peet, R. (2003) *Unholy Trinity: The IMF, World Bank and WTO.* London: Zed Books.

PEPFAR. (2008) *Human Resources for Health.* www.pepfar.gov/strategy/ghi/134855.htm (accessed February 2010).

Piller, C., Sanders, E. and Dixon, R. (2007) 'Dark cloud over good works of Gates Foundation' *Los Angeles Times* 7 January 2007 www.latimes.com/news/nationworld/nation/la-na-gatesx07jan07,0,6827615.story (accessed February 2010).

Pisani, E. (2008) *The Wisdom of Whores.* London: Granta Books.

Poku, N.K. (2001) 'Africa's AIDS crisis in context: "how the poor are dying"' *Third World Quarterly* 22(2): 191–204.

Poku, N.K. (2002) 'Poverty, debt, and Africa's HIV/AIDS crisis' *International Affairs* 78(3): 531–546.

Poku, N.K. and Sandkjaer, B. (2007). 'HIV/AIDS and the African State' in N. Poku, A. Whiteside and B. Sandkjaer (eds) *AIDS Governance.* Aldershot: Ashgate pp. 9–28.

Rabiu, R. (2009) 'Nigeria: World Bank threatens to withhold HIV/Aids Funds' *Daily Trust* 20 July 2009 http://allafrica.com/stories/printable/200907201425.html (accessed July 2009).

Rau, B. (2007). 'The politics of civil society in confronting HIV/AIDS' in N. Poku, A. Whiteside and B. Sandkjaer (eds) *AIDS and Governance* Aldershot: Ashgate, pp. 165–175.

Ravishankar, N., Gubbins, P., Cooley, R.J., Leach-Kemon, K., Michaud, C.M., Jamison, D.T. and Murray, C.J.L. (2009). 'Financing of global health: tracking development assistance for health from 1990 to 2007' *Lancet* 373: 2113–2124.

Rich, B. (2002) 'The World Bank under James Wolfensohn' in Jonathan R Pincus.and Jeffrey A Winters (eds) *Reinventing the World Bank.* London: Cornell University Press 26–53.

Richburg, K.B. and Frankel, G. (2005) 'Nomination shocks, worries Europeans' *The Washington Post* 17 March 2005 www.washingtonpost.com/wp-dyn/articles/A41350-2005Mar16.html (accessed February 2010).

Rifkin, S.B. (1986) 'Lessons from community participation in health programmes' *Health Policy and Planning* 1(3): 240–249.

Ruggie, J.G. (1982) 'Transactions and change: embedded liberalism in the post-war economic order' *International Organization* 39(2): 379–415.

Sanders, D. and Sambo, A. (1991) 'AIDS in Africa: the implications of economic recession and structural adjustment' *Health Policy and Planning* 6(2): 157–165.

Schechter, M.G. (1999) 'Globalization and civil society' in M.G. Schechter (ed.) *The Revival of Civil Society: Global and Comparative Perspectives.* London: MacMillan pp. 61–101.

Scholte, J.A. (1998) 'IMF meets civil society' *Finance and Development* 35(3): 42–45.

Scholte, J.A. (2000) 'Global Civil Society' in N. Woods (ed.) *The Political Economy of Globalisation.* London: MacMillan pp. 173–202.

Scholte, J.A. (2000b) 'Civil society and governance in the global polity' in M. Ougaard and R. Higgott (eds) *Towards a Global Polity.* London: Routledge, pp. 146–159.

Scholte, J.A. (2002a) 'Civil Society and democracy in global governance' *Global Governance* 8(3): 281–304.

Scholte, J.A. (2002b) 'Civil society and the governance of global finance' in J.A. Scholte and A. Schnabel (eds) *Civil Society and Global Finance.* London: Routledge, pp. 11–32.

Scholte, J.A. (2004) 'Civil society and democratically accountable global governance' *Government and Opposition* 39(2): 211–233.

Scholte, J.A. (2005) *Globalization: A Critical Introduction,* 2nd edition. London: Palgrave MacMillan.

Scholte, J.A., O'Brien, R. and Williams, M. (1999) 'The WTO and civil society' *Journal of World Trade* 33(1): 107–123.

Scholte, J.A. and Schnabel, A. (2002a) *Civil Society and Global Finance.* London: Routledge.

Scholte, J.A. and Schnabel, A. (2002b) 'Introduction' in J.A. Scholte and A. Schnabel (eds) *Civil Society and Global Finance.* London: Routledge, pp. 1–8.

Seckinelgin, H. (2005) 'A global disease and its governance: HIV/AIDS in sub-Saharan Africa and the agency of NGOs' *Global Governance* 11(3): 351–368.

Seckinelgin, H. (2008) *International Politics of HIV/AIDS: Global Disease–Local Pain.* Oxon: Routledge.

Sender, J. (2002) 'Reassessing the role of the World Bank in sub-Saharan Africa' in J.R Pincus and J.A. Winters (eds) *Reinventing the World Bank* London: Cornell University Press 185–202.

Shakow, A. (2006). *Global Fund-World Bank HIV/AIDS Programs: Comparative Advantage Study* Washington, DC: World Bank.

Shilts, R. (1988) *And the Band Played On.* New York: St Martin's Griffin.

Singer, P.W. (2002). 'AIDS and International Security' *Survival* 44(1): 145–158.

Siringi, S. (2004) 'Kenya AIDS council controversy' *Lancet: Infectious Diseases* 4:193.

Smouts, M.C. (1999) 'Multilateralism From Below: a prerequisite for Global Governance' in M. Schechter (ed.) *Future Multilateralism: The Political and Social Framework.* London: MacMillan, pp. 293–308.

Stiglitz, J. (2001) 'Scan globally, reinvent locally: knowledge infrastructure and the. localization of knowledge,' in H.J Chang (ed.) *Joseph Stiglitz and the World Bank: the Rebel Within.* London: Anthem Press, pp. 194–219.

Stiglitz, J. (2003) 'Democratizing the IMF and the World Bank: Governance and Accountability,' *Governance* 16(1): 111–139.

Stillwaggon, E. (2003) 'Racial metaphors: interpreting sex and AIDS in Africa' *Development and Change* 34: 809–832.

Strand, P. (2007) 'Comparing AIDS governance: a research agenda on responses to the AIDS epidemic' in N. Poku, A. Whiteside and B. Sandkjaer (eds) *AIDS and Governance.* Aldershot: Ashgate, pp. 217–236.

TACAIDS and GTZ (2005). *Facilitation Notes for the CSO Mapping and Capacity Assessment Tool.* Dar es Salaam: TACAIDS.

Tuozzo, M.F. (2004) 'World Bank, governance reforms, and democracy in Argentina' *Bulletin of Latin American Research* 23(1): 100–118.

Ugalde, A. and Jackson, J.T. (1995) 'The World Bank and international health policy: a critical review' *Journal of International Development* 7: 525–541.

Ulin, P.R. (1992) 'African women and AIDS: negotiating behavioural change' *Social Science and Medicine* 34(1): 63–73.

UNAIDS (2004) *Financing the Expanded Response to AIDS* www.unaids.org/bangkok2004/docs/Financing2response.pdf (accessed February 2010).

UNAIDS (2005a) *The 'Three Ones' in Action: Where We Are and Where We Go From Here* Geneva: UNAIDS.

UNAIDS (2005b) *Global Task Team: on Improving AIDS Co-ordination Among Multilateral Institutions and International Donors.* Geneva: UNAIDS.

UNAIDS (2009). 'Men who have sex with men' www.unaids.org/en/PolicyAndPractice/KeyPopulations/MenSexMen/ (accessed February 2010).

UNGASS UN General Assembly (2001) *UN General Assembly Special Session on HIV/AIDS (UNGASS): Declaration of Commitment on HIV/AIDS.* New York: UN.

United Nations Security Council Resolution 1308 (SCRes 1308) (17 July 2000) http://daccess-dds-ny.un.org/doc/UNDOC/GEN/N00/536/02/PDF/N0053602.pdf?OpenElement (accessed February 2010).

Wade, R. (1996) 'Japan, the World Bank, and the Art of Paradigm Maintenance: The East Asian Miracle in Political Perspective' *New Left Review* 3–38.

Wade, R. (2002) 'US hegemony and the World Bank: the fight over people and ideas' *Review of International Political Economy* 9(2): 215–243.

Whiteside, A. (2002) 'Poverty and HIV/AIDS in Africa' *Third World Quarterly* 23(2): 313–332.

Williams, D. (1999) 'Constructing the economic space: the World Bank and the making of Homo Oeconomicus' *Millennium* 28(1): 79–99.

Williams, D. (2008) *World Bank and social transformation in world politics.* London: Routledge.

Wolfensohn, J. (2000) 'Impact of AIDS on peace and security in Africa' speech delivered to UN Security Council January 2000, excerpts also available http://web.worldbank.org/WBSITE/EXTERNAL/NEWS/0,,contentMDK:20020328~menuPK:34457~pagePK:34370~piPK:34424~theSitePK:4607,00.html (accessed February 2010).

Woods, N. (2006) *The Globalizers: The IMF, the World Bank and their Borrowers.* London: Cornell University Press.

Wrong, M. (2009) *It's Our Turn to Eat: the Story of a Kenyan Whistle Blower.* London: Fourth Estate.

World Bank (Akin, J.S., Birdsall, N., and De Ferranti, D.M.) (1987) *Financing Health Services in Developing Countries: an Agenda for Reform.* Washington, DC: World Bank.

World Bank (1989) *Sub-Saharan Africa: From Crisis to Sustainable Growth.* Washington, DC: World Bank.

World Bank (1992) *Effective implementation: Key to development impact. Report of the Portfolio Management Task Force.* Washington, DC: World Bank.

World Bank (1993) *World Development Report: Investing in Health.* Washington, DC: World Bank.

World Bank (1994) *Governance: The World Bank's Experience.* Washington, DC: World Bank.

World Bank (2000a) 'Uganda–HIV/AIDS Control Project: Project Appraisal Document' www.wds.worldbank.org/servlet/WDSContentServer/WDSP/IB/2001/01/26/00009494 6_01010505342442/Rendered/PDF/multi_page.pdf (accessed February 2010).

World Bank (2000b) 'Kenya–Decentralised Reproductive Health and HIV/AIDS: Project Appraisal Document' www.wds.worldbank.org/servlet/WDSContentServer/WDSP/I B/2000/12/20/000094946_00112305412221/Rendered/PDF/multi_page.pdf (accessed February 2010).

World Bank (2000c) 'Kenya–Decentralised Reproductive Health and HIV/AIDS: Project Information Document' www.wds.worldbank.org/servlet/WDSContentServer/WDSP/I B/2000/06/15/000094946_00061505322832/Rendered/PDF/multi0page.pdf (accessed February 2007).

World Bank (2000d) 'Kenya–HIV/AIDS Disaster Response Project: Project Information Document' www.wds.worldbank.org/servlet/WDSContentServer/WDSP/IB/2000/07/08/ 000094946_00070706145866/Rendered/PDF/multi0page.pdf (accessed February 2010).

World Bank (2000e) 'Kenya–HIV/AIDS Disaster Response Project: Project Appraisal. Document' www.wds.worldbank.org/servlet/WDSContentServer/WDSP/IB/2000/10/2 1/000094946_00082605465154/Rendered/PDF/multi_page.pdf (accessed July 2007).

World Bank (2003a) 'Tanzania–Multi Sectoral AIDS project: Updated Project. Information Document' www.wds.worldbank.org/servlet/WDSContentServer/WDSP/IB/2003/07/08/ 000094946_03062104112344/Rendered/PDF/multi0page.pdf (accessed February 2010).

World Bank (2003b) 'Tanzania–Multi Sectoral AIDS project: Project Appraisal Document' www.wds.worldbank.org/servlet/WDSContentServer/WDSP/IB/2003/06/23/00001200 9_20030623113128/Rendered/PDF/25761.pdf (accessed February 2010).

World Bank (2003c) 'Tanzania–Multi Sectoral AIDS project: Environmental Assessment'. www.wds.worldbank.org/servlet/WDSContentServer/WDSP/IB/2003/05/23/00009494 6_03051404055513/Rendered/PDF/multi0page.pdf (accessed February 2010).

World Bank (2003d) 'Tanzania–Multi Sectoral AIDS project: Integrated Safeguards Data Sheet' www.wds.worldbank.org/servlet/WDSContentServer/WDSP/IB/2001/11/28/000 094946_01112104010494/Rendered/PDF/multi0page.pdf (accessed February 2010).

World Bank (2004a) *Brazil AIDS and STD Control Project: Implementation Completion and Results Report.* Washington, DC: World Bank http://web.worldbank.org/external/ projects/main?pagePK=64283627&piPK=73230&theSitePK=841609&menuPK=8416 56&Projectid=P006546 (accessed February 2010).

World Bank (2004b) *Brazil AIDS and STD Control Project II: Implementation Completion and Results Report.* Washington, DC: World Bank. http://web.worldbank.org/external/ projects/main?pagePK=64283627&piPK=73230&theSitePK=841609&menuPK=8416 56&Projectid=P054120 (accessed February 2010).

World Bank (2005) 'Chronology' http://siteresources.worldbank.org/EXTARCHIVES/ Resources/WB_Historical_Chronology_1944_2005.pdf (February 2010).

World Bank (2007a) *The Africa Multi-Country AIDS Program 2000–2006.* Washington, DC: World Bank.

World Bank (2007b) *IDA proposed umbrella restructuring and amendment of the financial agreements for the projects under Multi-Country HIV/AIDS Program for Africa (MAP).* Washington, DC: World Bank www.wds.worldbank.org/external/default/ WDSContentServer/WDSP/IB/2007/06/18/000020439_20070618105330/Rendered/ PDF/Pages0from0399060IDA1R2007001880AFR.pdf (accessed February 2010).

World Bank (2007c) 'Comprehensive Development Framework (CDF)' http://web. worldbank.org/WBSITE/EXTERNAL/PROJECTS/0,,contentMDK:20120725~menuPK:4 1393~pagePK:41367~piPK:51533~theSitePK:40941,00.html (accessed February 2010).

World Bank (2007d) 'Poverty Reduction Strategy Papers (PRSPs)' http://web.worldbank. org/WBSITE/EXTERNAL/TOPICS/EXTPOVERTY/EXTPRS/0,,menuPK:384207~pa gePK:149018~piPK:149093~theSitePK:384201,00.html (accessed February 2010).

World Bank (2007e) 'Community Driven Development' http://web.worldbank.org/WBSITE/ EXTERNAL/TOPICS/EXTSOCIALDEVELOPMENT/EXTCDD/0,,menuPK:430167 ~pagePK:149018~piPK:149093~theSitePK:430161,00.html (accessed February 2010).

World Bank (2007f) 'Private sector and HIV/AIDS: multi-sectoral response' http:// web.worldbank.org/WBSITE/EXTERNAL/COUNTRIES/AFRICAEXT/ EXTAFRHEANUTPOP/EXTAFRREGTOPHIVAIDS/0,,contentMDK:21646264~page PK:34004173~piPK:34003707~theSitePK:717148,00.html (accessed February 2010).

World Bank (2007g) Healthy Development: The World Bank Strategy for Health, Nutrition and Population Results Washington, DC: World Bank. http://sitere-sources.worldbank.org/HEALTHNUTRITIONANDPOPULATION/Resources/ 281627-1154048816360/HNPStrategyFinalTextAnnexes.pdf>http://siteresources. worldbank.org/HEALTHNUTRITIONANDPOPULATION/Resources/ 281627-1154048816360/HNPStrategyFinalTextAnnexes.pdf (accessed February 2010).

World Bank (2008a) 'World Bank Group Historical Chronology' http://siteresources. worldbank.org/EXTARCHIVES/Resources/WB_Historical_Chronology_1944_2005. pdf (accessed February 2010).

World Bank (2008b) *Brazil AIDS and STD Control Project III: Implementation Completion and Results Report.* Washington DC: World Bank http://web.worldbank.org/external/ projects/main?pagePK=64283627&piPK=73230&theSitePK=841609&menuPK=8416 56&Projectid=P080400 (accessed February 2010).

World Bank (2008c) *Barbados Second HIV/AIDS Project* http://web.worldbank.org/external/ projects/main?pagePK=64283627&piPK=73230&theSitePK=841609&menuPK=8416 56&Projectid=P106623 (accessed February 2010).

World Bank (2009) *Improving Effectiveness and Outcomes for the Poor in Health, Nutrition and Population: an evaluation of World Bank Group support since 1997.* http://sit-eresources.worldbank.org/EXTWBASSHEANUTPOP/Resources/hnp_full_eval.pdf (accessed February 2010).

World Health Organization (2009) 'About 3 by 5 initiative' www.who.int/3by5/about/en/ (accessed February 2010).

Youde, J. (2007) *AIDS, South Africa, and the Politics of Knowledge.* Aldershot: Ashgate.

Zaidi, S.A. (1994) 'Planning the health sector: for whom, by whom?' *Social Science and Medicine* 39: 1385–1393.

Interviews

Abdullah, Asha. 31 January 2006. Zanzibar HIV/AIDS Commission – Zanzibar.

Akatsa-Bukachi, Marren. 5 October 2005. East African Sub-regional Support Initiative (EASSI) – Uganda.

Anjere, Benson Owenga. 28 November 2005. Kenya Programme of Disabled Persons (KPDP) – Kenya.

Anne. 25 November 2005. K-VWORC (Kenya Voluntary Women's Rehabilitation Centre) – Kenya.

Austen, Anne. 18 November 2005. Futures Group – Kenya.

Avalle, Oscar. 4 May 2006. World Bank – New York City, USA.

Ayers, Elise. 25 October 2005. USAID – Uganda.

Baggaley, Rachel. 15 August 2005. Christian Aid UK (by telephone).

Baguma, Edna. 20 October 2005. World Vision – Uganda.

Bahati, Ursula. 14 November 2005. National AIDS Control Council – Kenya.

Behwera, Wilson. 26 October 2005. Masaka District HIV/AIDS Council – Uganda.

Bemwenzaki, Dennis. 14 February 2006. PASADA (Pastoral Activities and Services for people with AIDS) – Tanzania.

Bernadette. 6 October 2005. PSI (Population Services International) – Uganda.

Bonici, Francois. 22 May 2006. World Economic Forum – Geneva, Switzerland.

Byenka, Julius. 11 October 2005. Uganda HIV/AIDS Commission – Uganda.

Casas, Erena. 27 January 2006. Medicos du Mondo – Zanzibar.

Cashion, Joe. 4 May 2006. The Clinton Foundation – New York City, USA.

Chale, Patricia. 13 February 2006. PSI (Population Services International) – Tanzania.

Chale, Stella. 10 January 2006. NACP (National AIDS Control Programme) – Tanzania.

Chale, Stephen. 16 January 2006. Plan – Tanzania.

Childress, Amanda. 14 February 2006. Africare/USAID – Tanzania.

Chusi, Elitha. 8 February 2006. Alpha Dancing Group – Tanzania.

Chusio, Nelson. 8 February 2006. IDYDC (Iringa Development of Youth, Disabled and Children Care) – Tanzania.

Conesta, Natalie. 18 October 2005. Catholic Relief Services – Uganda.

Coutinho, Sheila Marunga. 4 November 2005. UNICEF (United Nations Children's Fund) – Uganda.

Cunningham, Amy. 25 October 2005. USAID – Uganda.

Curioni, Gaspard. 4 May 2006. World Bank – New York City, USA.

Damji, Nazneen. 10 May 2006. UNIFEM (United Nations Development Fund for Women) – New York City, USA.

Daniel. 10 November 2005. Federation of Women's Groups – Kenya.

Duolf, Bob. 4 January 2006. Care International – Tanzania.

Fink, Eleanor. 20 April 2006. World Bank – Washington DC, USA.

Garrison, John. 27 April 2006. World Bank – Washington DC, USA.

Gavyole, Awene. 13 February 2006. WHO (World Health Organization) – Tanzania.

Gitau, Lilian. 14 December 2005. St John's Ambulance, Kisumu – Kenya.

Gladel, Christian. 5 May 2006. IAVI (International AIDS Vaccine Initiative) – New York City, USA.

Hakororo, Salvator. 4 January 2006. Care International – Tanzania.

Hauli, Edina. 8 February 2006. SHDEPHA+ (Service Health and Development for People living with HIV/AIDS), Iringa – Tanzania.

Hervey, Duncan. 27 January 2006. Save the Children – Zanzibar.

Hunger, Claudia. 6 February 2006. GTZ (Deutsche Gesellschaft fur Technische Zusammenarbeit – German Society for Technical Co-operation) – Tanzania.

Ibanda, Sam. 26 October 2005. UNDP – Tanzania.

Jamet, Christine. 10 November 2005. Medicins Sans Frontieres – Kenya.

Jaxon, Joezif. 10 February 2006. Foundation for Civil Society – Tanzania.

Juma, Nabembezi. 19 October 2005. AMREF (African Medical and Research Foundation) – Uganda.

Juma, Idi. 8 November 2005. KANCO (Kenya AIDS NGOs Consortium) – Kenya.

Juncker, Margrethe. 11 October 2005. Reach Out – Uganda.

Kaboha, Sylvan. 14 October 2005. AIM (The Uganda AIDS/HIV Integrated Model District Programme), Tororo Branch – Uganda.

Kajela, Flora. 13 February 2006. World Vision – Tanzania.

Kalimire, Vincent. 17 October 2005. Foundation for African Development – Uganda.

Kalinga, Hashim. 14 February 2006. TACAIDS (Tanzania Commission for AIDS) – Tanzania.

Kalioli, Dorothy. 4 January 2006. Dogodogo Centre – Tanzania.

Kameta, Dorcus. 11 November 2005. National AIDS/STD Control Programme (NASCOP) – Kenya.

Karanja, Isabella. 24 November 2005. National Council of Women of Kenya – Kenya.

Kariuki, Carole. 16 December 2005. Kenya Private Sector Alliance – Kenya.

Karokora, Kellen. 31 October 2005. Keera Community Services – Uganda.

Kashyap, Purnima. 7 October 2005. World Food Programme – Uganda.

Kasigazi, Benon. 31 October 2005. UGANET (Uganda Network on Law, Ethics and HIV/ AIDS) – Uganda.

Kasozi, Immam. 24 October 2005. Uganda Muslim Youth Association – Uganda.

Kassim, Amina. 9 January 2006. ABCT (AIDS Business Coalition Tanzania) – Tanzania.

Kataka, Hanningtone. 23 November 2005. KUSCCO (Kenya Union of Savings and Credit Co-operatives) – Kenya.

Kenindo, Edward. 9 November 2005. WOWESOK (Women and Orphans Welfare Society of Kenya) – Kenya.

Keough, Lucy. 25 April 2006. World Bank – Washington DC, USA.

Kibamba, Deus. 20 January 2006. TGNP (Tanzania Gender Networking Programme) – Tanzania.

Kiirya, Stephen. 11 April 2005. Uganda HIV/AIDS Commission – Uganda.

Kinzett, Steve. 23 November 2005. JSI (John Snow Inc) – Kenya.

Kisage, Irene. 6 October 2005. ACET (AIDS, Care, Education and Training) – Uganda.

Kivumbi, Harriet. 19 October 2995. OXFAM – Uganda.

Kiwanuka, Allan. 19 October 2005. THETA (Traditional and modern Health practitioners Together against AIDS and other diseases) – Uganda.

Kiwia, Pfiriael. 15 February 2006. Kimara Peer Educators – Tanzania.

Knaul, Felicia. 16 November 2005. Child Welfare Society of Kenya – Kenya.

Kyamureku, Peace. 7 October 2005. NAWOU (National Association of Women's Organisations in Uganda) – Uganda.

Lagerstedt, Adam. 16 November 2005. World Bank – Kenya.

Lavanda, Mr. 6 February 2006. Mbeya Municipal Council – Tanzania.

Lekule, Morris. 4 January 2006. TACAIDS – Tanzania.

Lenya, Rowlands. 10 November 2005. TAPWAK (The Association of People with AIDS in Kenya) – Kenya.

Lucy. 15 November 2005. PSI – Kenya.

Lugoi, Justin. 5 January 2006. Tanzania Red Cross – Tanzania.

Lusewa, Mr. 17 January 2006. WAVUMO – Tanzania.

Mackay, Bruce. 8 July 2005. Futures Group – Telephone, UK.

Magumba, Godfrey. 11 October 2005. UPHOLD (Uganda Program for Human and Holistic Development) – Uganda.

Malangalila, Emmanuel. 20 January 2006. World Bank – Tanzania.

Malangalila, Emmanuel. 6 May 2009. World Bank – Tanzania.

Maligo, Raphael. 5 January 2006. AMREF – Tanzania.

Margery, Alex Pius. 6 January 2006. TANEPHA (Tanzania National Network of People with HIV/AIDS) – Tanzania.

Marshall, Katherine. 21 April 2006. World Bank – Washington DC, USA.

Masika, Peter. 13 January 2006. TAYOA (Tanzania Youth Aware Trust Fund) – Tanzania.

Matsha, Ntombekhaya. 25 May 2006. The Global Fund to Fight AIDS, Tuberculosis and Malaria – Geneva, Switzerland.

Mayanja, Wilberforce. 5 October 2005. Philly Lutaaya Initiative/AIDS Information Centre Volunteer – Uganda.

Mbugua, Dickson. 23 November 2005. Matatu Welfare Association – Kenya.

Mbonigaba, William. 19 October 2995. UWESO (Uganda Women's Effort to Save Orphans) – Uganda.

Menezes, Alex. 10 May 2006. IAVI (International AIDS Vaccine Initiative) – New York City, USA.

Mesik, Juraj. 24 April 2006. World Bank – Washington DC, USA.

Mkongo, Joyce. 6 February 2006. SHDEPHA+ (Service Health and Development for People living with HIV/AIDS) – Tanzania.

Mohammed, Nadeem. 24 April 2006. World Bank – Washington DC, USA.

Mphuru, Lucy. 5 January 2006. EngenderHealth – Tanzania.

Mpungu, Henry. 6 October 2005. Kampala AIDS Fighters Association – Uganda.

Msokaa, Agnes. 15 January 2006. SWAAT (Society for Women and AIDS in Africa Tanzania) – Tanzania.

Mtasiwa, Deo. 16 February 2006. District Medical Officer, Dar es Salaam – Tanzania.

Mubondo, Barabona. 20 January 2006. WAMATA (Walio Katika Mapambano Na AIDS Tanzania – People in the fight against AIDS in Tanzania) – Tanzania.

Mugumya, Herbert. 1 November 2005. Save the Children – Uganda.

Mukama, Robert. 8 February 2006. Regional Facilitating Agent (RFA) Iringa and Ruvuma – Tanzania.

Mulimila, Victor. 17 January 2006. Faraja Trust Fund – Tanzania.

Mulongo, David. 3rd February 2006. UMATI (Chama Cha Uzazi na Malezi Bora Tanzania – Society of Family Planning, Tanzania) – Tanzania.

Mushi, Rose. 9 January 2006. Action Aid–Regional Facilitating Agent (RFA) Morogoro, Coast, Singida and Dodoma – Tanzania.

Mwaduma, Nicodemus B. 6 January 2006. Regional Facilitating Agent (RFA) Lindi and Mtwara – Tanzania.

Mwai, Eve. 29 November 2005. St John's Ambulance – Kenya.

Mwakapeje, Sam. 12 October 2005. TASO (The AIDS Support Organisation), Jinga – Uganda.

Mwamaja, Joseph. 17 January 2006. UMATI, Eastern (Chama Cha Uzazi na Malezi Bora Tanzania – Society of Family Planning, Tanzania) – Tanzania.

Mwaniki, Margaret. 22 December 2005. Girl Guides Kenya – Kenya.

Nakiwala, Jacqueline. 28 October 2005. Uganda Catholic Secretariat – Uganda.

Nakawuka, Mina. 28 October 2005. Kampala District HIV/AIDS Council – Uganda.

Nakiyembe, Jenipher. 11 October 2005. Hunger Free World – Uganda.

Nakiyimba, Angella. 27 October 2005. CIPA (Community Initiative for the Prevention of HIV/AIDS/STIs) – Uganda.

Namatou, Mary. 20 October 2005. CAWODISA (Children and Wives of Disabled Soldiers Association) – Uganda.

Ndege, Samson. 16 December 2005. Pathfinder – Kenya.

Ndyetanbura, Elly. 10 January 2006. UNDP (United Nations Development Programme) – Tanzania.

Ngare, Zachary. 15 November 2005. HOYWIK (Humanity for Orphans, Youths and Widows Initiatives Kenya) – Kenya.

Ngugi, Suzan. 24 November 2005. KENWA (Kenya Network of Women with HIV/AIDS) – Kenya.

Ntalo, Boniface. 13 October 2005. Jinga District AIDS Council - Uganda.

Ntege, Vincent F. 1 November 2005. Uganda National Farmer's Federation – Uganda.

Nyantahe, Samuel. 9 January 2006. Utegi Technical Enterprises – RFA Dar es Salaam, Mara, Shinyanga – Tanzania.

Obara, Leonora. 23 November 2005. WOFAK (Women Fighting AIDS in Kenya) – Kenya.

Odenyo, Booker. 9 November 2005. Crown Agents – Kenya.

Ofoso-Amaah, Waafus. 28 April 2006. World Bank – Washington DC, USA.

Ogen, Patrick. 19 October 2005. Youth Alive – Uganda.

Ojuru, Wyclef. 1 November 2005. Uganda Scouts Association – Uganda.

Okafor, Chudi. 27 April 2006. World Bank – Washington DC, USA.

Okatcha, Kathleen. 16 November 2005. KORDP (Kenya Orphans Rural Development Programme) – Kenya.

Okumu, Robert. 14 October 2005. Tororo District AIDS Committee – Uganda.

Okwero, Peter. 1 November 2005. World Bank – Uganda.

Olita, Joseph. 17 November 2005. Gallamoro – Kenya.

Olsen, Lene. 28 November 2005. World Food Programme – Kenya.

Orimba, Hilda Agola. 9 November 2005. WOWESOK (Women and Orphans Welfare Society of Kenya) – Kenya.

Otundo, Kennedy. 28 October 2005. Family Planning Association of Uganda – Uganda.

Pangani, Evodis. 16 February 2006. Ilala Municipal Council – Tanzania.

Piot, Peter. 6 July 2009. Director, Institute of Global Health, Imperial College London, ex-Executive Director of UNAIDS (1995–2008).

Quiery, Aisling. 21 December 2005. Merlin – Uganda.

deRegt, Jacomina. 20 April 2006. World Bank – Washington DC, USA.

Rosche, Tim. 18 January 2006. JSI (John Snow Inc) – Tanzania.

Ruranga, Rubaramira. 31 October 2005. NGEN+ (National Guidance and Empowerment Network of People Living with HIV/AIDS) – Uganda.

Rwenchungura, Assumpta. 9 January 2006. World Food Programme – Tanzania.

Saadat, Idi. 31 January 2006. Zanzibar HIV/AIDS Commission – Zanzibar.

Schoultz, Kristan. 5 April 2005. UNAIDS – Kenya.

Shaw-Crompton, Bec. 19 August 2005. Panos – London, UK.

Shilling, Lucy. 12 October 2005. TASO (The AIDS Support Organisation) – Uganda.

Simbaya, Kenneth. 7 February 2006. SPW (Students Partnerships Worldwide) – Tanzania.

Southern, Nick. 9 January 2006. Care International – Tanzania.

Stannard, Paul. 10 January 2006. Crown Agents – Tanzania.

Talugende, Patience. 19 October 2005. ISESWU (Integrated Services for the Empowerment of Soldier's Wives Network in the Uganda People's Defence Forces) – Uganda.

Tayyab, Yasmin. 24 April 2006. World Bank – Washington DC, USA.

Temba, Joseph. 10 February 2006. TACAIDS – Tanzania.

Tembele, Rustica. 6 January 2006. TACAIDS – Tanzania.

Tembo, George. 25 May 2006. UNAIDS – Geneva, Switzerland.

Tenga, Stigmata. 13 January 2006. ST Associates – Tanzania.

Thindwa, Jeff. 1 May 2006. World Bank – Washington DC, USA.

Trama, Annalise. 21 December 2005. UNAIDS – Kenya.

Tungaraza, Maria. 18 January 2006. Futures Group – Tanzania.

Voetberg, Albertus. 7 April 2005. World Bank – Kenya.

Voetberg, Albertus. 15 November 2005. World Bank – Kenya.
Wambiya, Paschal. 19 December 2005. ILO (International Labour Organisation) – Kenya.
Wandera, Suzan. 20 October 2005. Mukono District HIV/AIDS Council – Uganda.
Warimu, Mary. 17 November 2005. Pledge Action International – Kenya.
Wiktor, Stephen. 3rd February 2006. CDC (Centers for Disease Control and Prevention) – Tanzania.
Williams, Glenn. 12 August 2005. Strategies for Hope – Telephone, UK.
Woodward, David. 17 August 2005. New Economics Foundation – London, UK.
Wong, Holly. 10 May 2006. IAVI – New York, USA.
Zeitz, Paul. 26 April 2006. Global AIDS Alliance – Washington DC, USA.
Zewdie, Debrework. 3 May 2006. World Bank – Washington DC, USA.

Participant observation

AIDS Information Centre – Kampala. 5 October 2005; 13 October 2005. Uganda.
AIDS Information Centre – Jinga. 12 October 2005. Uganda.
Alpha Dancing Group – 8 February 2006. Tanzania.
Joint Annual HIV/AIDS Forum (JAPR). 30 November 2005. Kenya.
Kawempe Positive Women Union. 17 October 2005. Uganda.
KENWA Drop In Centre. 29 November 2005. Kenya.
Philly Lutaaya Initiative. 17 October 2005. Uganda.
Positive Lives Exhibition. 24 October 2005. Uganda.
Positive Women's Vision in Action. 17 October 2005. Uganda.
St John's Ambulance, Kisumu – Kadibo & Mamboleo Youth Support Group. 14. December 2005. Kenya.
St Stephen's Church Widow's Group. 13 December 2005. Kenya.
TAYOPA (Tanzania Young People living with HIV/AIDS). 9 January 2005. Tanzania.
Wakisi AIDS Programme. 25 October 2005. Uganda.
WOFAK Annual General Meeting. 17 December 2005. Kenya.

Questionnaires

Mpanguleka, Benson Tatala. 17 May 2006. Handeni District HIV/AIDS Council – Tanzania.
Naegele, Elisabeth. 13 May 2006. RFA Moshi – Tanzania.

Index